Oxford University Press

Oxford   New York

Athens   Auckland   Bangkok   Bogota   Bombay   Buenos Aires
Calcutta   Cape Town   Dar es Salaam   Delhi   Florence   Hong Kong
Istanbul   Karachi   Kuala Lumpur   Madras   Madrid   Melbourne
Mexico City   Nairobi   Paris   Singapore   Taipei   Tokyo   Toronto

and associated companies in
Berlin   Ibadan

Published by Oxford University Press, Inc.,
198 Madison Avenue, New York, New York 10016

Oxford is a registered trademark of Oxford University Press

Library of Congress Cataloging-in-Publication Data

Patterson, Anita Haya.
From Emerson to King : democracy, race, and the politics of
protest / by Anita Haya Patterson.
p.   cm.—(W. E. B. Dubois Institute)
Includes bibliographical references and index.
ISBN-0-19-510915-5
1. Afro-Americans—Intellectual life.   2. Emerson, Ralph Waldo,
1803–1882—Influence.   3. Emerson, Ralph Waldo, 1803–1882—Political
and social views.   4. United States—Race relations.   5. Democracy—
United States.   6. Afro-Americans—Civil rights.   I. Title.
II. Series: W. E. B. Debois Institute (Series)
E185.86P29   1997
305.8'00973—dc21
96-38150
CIP

1 2 3 4 5 6 7 8 9

Printed in the United States of America
on acid-free paper

From
Emerson
to King

Democracy,

Race, and

the Politics

of Protest

Anita Haya Patterson

New York   Oxford • Oxford University Press   1997

From

Emerson

to King

W. E. B. DU BOIS INSTITUTE
Henry Louis Gates, Jr., Series Editor

The Open Sore of a Continent
A Personal Narrative of the Nigerian Crisis
Wole Soyinka

From Emerson to King
Democracy, Race, and the Politics of Protest
Anita Haya Patterson

For Orlando

Thus was a world sought for and found,
Out of the Unknown sought for and found.
—E. M. Roach, "Discovery"

Acknowledgments

A number of people have been important in the writing of this book. I am indebted to Sacvan Bercovitch, Elaine Scarry, Stanley Cavell, Barbara Johnson, Werner Sollors, and Larry Buell for their constructive criticism of the Ph.D. dissertation on which the book is based. Preston Williams, Bob Gooding-Williams, and Henry Louis Gates generously offered comments that helped me to improve the work.

Time for research and writing was made possible in part by a Charlotte W. Newcombe fellowship from the Woodrow Wilson Foundation, as well as a year at the Institute for the Humanities at the University of Illinois at Chicago. Earlier versions of sections in the introduction and in chapters 7 and 8 appeared in *The Massachusetts Review* and *Salmagundi*.

I am grateful to my parents, Arthur and Tomiko, for being there for me over the years. Finally, for his love and guidance in the art of living, I thank my husband Orlando.

Contents

SIX
The Claims of Double-Consciousness:
Race, Nationalism, and the Problem of

PART III   PROTEST

SEVEN
W. E. B. Du Bois and the Critique of Liberal

EIGHT
Martin Luther King Jr.: Publicity, Disobedience,
and the Revitalization of American

From

Emerson

to King

Reconciling Race and Rights

The experience in Montgomery did more to clarify my thinking on the question of nonviolence than all the books that I had read.... Many issues I had not cleared up intellectually concerning nonviolence were now solved in the sphere of practical action.

—Martin Luther King, Jr.,
"Pilgrimage to Nonviolence"

Is a democracy, such as we know it, the last improvement possible in government? Is it not possible to take a step further towards recognizing and organizing the rights of man?

—Henry David Thoreau,
"Resistance to Civil Government"

Rights are markers of citizenship that allow us to exist in legally protected, formal relations to one another. As Patricia Williams has argued, "[R]ights imply a respect that places one in the referential range of self and others . . . the attainment of rights signifies the respectful behavior, the collective responsibility, properly owed by a society to one of its own."[1] This strong regard for the autonomy of individual citizens—the vision of the self as an abstract bearer of rights—reflects a particular definition of privacy and property that is the legacy of John Locke, an intellectual legacy that is central to liberal theories of "the nation."[2] In the tradition of liberal nationalism, rights have been defined as entailing obligations that bind individuals together as a political community, a community that is—in theory, but often not in practice—infinitely permeable and expansive because any person who meets the qualifications for citizenship can join.[3]

In contrast to the regard for equality implicit in the democratic vocabulary of rights, the term "race," in the sense I am using it here, represented a complex of ideas and associations that was generally used during the nineteenth century to categorize and differentiate between large groups of individ-

3

uals. In America, race was popularly defined as shared biological descent, and the widespread doctrine of racial inequality associated with this biological concept asserted the superiority of the Anglo-Saxon race above all others.[4]

More recently, race has emerged as a guiding concept in theoretical discussions of individual and national identity. Various meanings have been assigned to the term "race" in contemporary analyses, each of which implies a particular set of social commitments.[5] The seeming intractability of debates over the relative importance of race as a category of self-representation; the pervasive tendency on the part of policy makers and the media to present the issue of social divisiveness in purely racial terms; and the waning efficacy of appeals *either* to rights *or* race as the fundamental basis for thinking about identity have underscored the challenge of defining America as a diverse, but nonetheless unified, political community. A great deal is thus at stake in the attempt to arrive at a clearer understanding of the historical relationship between democratic values and racial attitudes in the development of American nationalist rhetorics, literature, and culture.[6]

I began writing this book because I was drawn to thinking about the constraints and possibilities of Emerson's political thought. I was interested in his contribution to what has amounted to a national obsession with the meaning of democracy and the way his work has provoked American artists and intellectuals to discover, harness, and direct the creative energies of this obsession toward writing novels, philosophical essays, sermons, speeches, poems, and so on. During the course of my researches, I discovered that nineteenth-century America produced a literature fraught with contradiction. For example, Emerson insists on equal access to rights as barriers to injustice, but in the same breath he contradicts democratic principles by expressing his belief that natural, racial inequalities are fundamental to any account of American identity.

What I have found to be most compelling and bewildering about Emerson's writing—what has made it hardest for me to know how to think about him—is that his defense of rights and his racism are intimately and deliberately connected. Although Emerson recognizes the necessity of rights, he also reminds us again and again that the economic ties and contractual obligations that bind individuals together in accordance with a rights-based, democratic framework are insufficient to represent the self and political community. For Emerson, the Lockean, liberal model of civil society as a community of autonomous, self-owning citizens who have been brought into association with one another by acts of voluntary consent to a social contract is not, by any stretch of the imagination, intimate or cohesive enough to represent his vision of America. As a result of this dissatisfaction with liberal contractarianism and rights rhetoric, Emerson also embraces a "scientific," Anglo-Saxonist, racialist rhetoric that affirms the existence of the intimate ties of race as shared descent, ties representing obligations that are not at all assumed by volitional acts of consent, but rather are born into or found as already existing.[7] Discovering the falseness of my wishful assumption that Emerson's defense of rights should have nothing to do with his racism, I arrived instead at a disturbing, contradictory logic: namely, that the fervent, critical recuperation of American democracy undertaken by Emerson was shaped and indeed made conceptually coherent only through his recourse to racialist language and ideology.[8]

The first broad objective in this book, then, is to show that, read in their entirety, Emerson's writings exhibit a consistent pattern of contradiction that is fundamental to his critical reassessment of democratic values. Emerson has been described by critics either as antinomian or as an ideologue—as subversive of all institutional controls or as an apologist for capitalism. Parts I and II demonstrate that neither of these approaches does justice to the complexity of his outlook.[9] Forever poised between the poles of contradiction, he simultaneously opposes *and* promotes mainstream American ideals such as the right to private ownership and self-ownership, individual autonomy, and the notion that legitimate government and community are created by voluntary acts of consent to social contract.[10] In particular, I argue that this political critique is expressed precisely by means of Emerson's recourse to racialist language and values.[11]

Chapter 1 discusses Emerson's self-contradictory account of citizenship in *Representative Men*—how his notion of the "representative" self works simultaneously to bar and to facilitate access to the public realm of politics. Chapter 2 explores Emerson's critique of ownership: his contradictory claim that "we own and disown our relation to [nature] by turns."[12] The literary and religious contexts of this critique are illuminated in chapter 3, in which it is shown that Protestant emblem poetry contributed to his radical embrace of contradiction in thinking about personhood and community.[13] In chapter 4, I consider the ethical consequences of Emerson's critique of ownership, especially his reconceptualization of the "obligations" or loyalties that inspire acts of social reform. We examine a fundamental shift in Emerson's thinking on the issue of obligation in chapter 5—Emerson's abandonment of his early interest in the utopian possibilities of *friendship* as the basis for political obligation and social cohesion in favor of a scientific concept of *race*.[14]

My second major objective is to show that Emerson's balancing act between the poles of contradiction is reconceived in the late essay "Fate" as "double-consciousness." In chapter 6, I argue that although democracy and racialism imply opposing views of the self and national identity, the two are not at cross purposes in Emerson's thought. Instead, they are dialectically reconfigured, at once supplementing and critically correcting each other, in the process generating a new notion of identity: "double-consciousness." Emerson's incessant elaboration upon the condition of double-consciousness leads him, in my view, to embrace a vision of American national identity that is both myopic and innovative. Viewed historically, it is myopic to the degree that he accepted the violent, racist policy of westward expansion that prevailed in nineteenth-century America. Nonetheless, viewed philosophically and conceptually, the idea of double-consciousness was to prove extremely productive for later thinkers—such as W. E. B. Du Bois—who were concerned with the task of reconciling racial and national identity in America.

What is the nature of Emerson's legacy? How have his insights fared in succeeding generations? Part III of this book suggests in general, preliminary terms the significance of Emerson's legacy for work undertaken by four African-American intellectuals: Booker T. Washington, W. E. B. Du Bois, Martin Luther King, Jr., and most recently Cornel West. Each of these writers develops a rhetoric and style that shows a unique confrontation with and inheritance of Emerson's interpretation of "America." Chapter 7 examines the ways in which Booker T. Washington and W. E. B. Du Bois expanded the scope of double-consciousness in developing models of African-American identity that underscore obligations associated with both blackness and American citizenship.

The concluding chapter focuses on Emerson's contribution to King's political philosophy and the revitalization of American democratic culture during the 1960s.[15] It includes a discussion of West's work that illuminates both the meaning of "the public" in Emerson and the relationship of African-American philosophy to public action. I end by discussing one major consequence of King's critical engagement with the Emersonian tradition: namely, the development of an innovative poetics of protest in works by contemporary African-American authors writing in the wake of 1960s activism. By documenting Emerson's importance for subsequent developments in African-American protest writing, I offer a corrective to Shamoon Zamir's recent dismissal of Emerson's thought as having "failed" Du Bois in the last two decades of the nineteenth century.[16]

In deliberately calling on Emerson to underwrite their critical reassessment of democratic values, these African-American philosophers are rhetorically entering, as it were, the American mainstream in their effort to reform society and build a political consensus. By showing this, my study opens inviting prospects for provocative new readings that document the transformation of mainstream rhetoric and values in the development of other ethnic American literatures in the United States.[17]

It has not been my primary intent to add yet another "political" reading of Emerson. Rather, I have sought to explain how the contradiction that is fundamental to his thinking about American identity has given rise to such a diverse array of political readings; how it is that Emerson can be read as promoting the most impenetrable complacency or willful blindness to existing social conditions while at the same time opening the possibility for critique and the development of politically effective adversarial rhetorics. In claiming that contradiction is central to Emerson's concept of the self, I do not mean to suggest that Emerson is unwittingly ambivalent about or unequivocally indebted to democracy and the marketplace, as some new Americanist critics have argued.[18] Nor do I find Emerson's writings to be antidemocratic. Rather, contradiction is a deliberate rhetorical gesture that underscores both the limits and the necessity of these cherished cultural values to represent American identity. The creative energies of resistance that motivate Emerson's critique of liberalism, as well as his peculiar strategy of contradiction, developed during the Jacksonian era, a period of extraordinary conflict and social change.[19] My efforts to explore Emerson's political critique in all its aspects—its sociohistorical necessity and political logic, as well as its rhetorical, poetic, and literary historical significances—distinguish my approach from that of critics who pay close scrutiny to Emerson's language but for the most part avoid questions of social and political context.[20]

From all that has been said, it should be clear that I am not interested in presenting yet another "revisionary" reading of Emerson which amounts to nothing more than a politically correct charge of racism—something that has become all too familiar in current critical discussions of racism and the American literary tradition.[21] These interpretations are popular insofar as they invite a communal sense of moral outrage, and the inherent weakness of this mode of argumentation does not matter, if all we are doing is preaching to the converted. But contrary to the best of intentions, the danger of such generalizations is that they have convinced many scholars that, in fact, racism is not something that can be usefully talked about, or, at any rate, that it would be better left well enough alone.

In my attempt to develop an interpretative framework that effectively addresses this complicated matter of racism in the American literary tradition—what Toni Morrison has suggestively referred to as "the work writers do to unhobble the imagination from the demands of [racialist] language"[22]—I have tried to say much more about race in the work of Emerson's imagination than simply to point out the fact of its existence. I want to trace the *uses* of race in Emerson's writings: to learn *how* racism contributes to the compelling beauty and seductiveness of his nationalist vision, and *why* it mobilizes such powers of luminous description.[23]

Rather than dismissing Emerson as a racist, this study is deliberately designed to *prevent* uninformed interpretations that obscure his importance for contemporary social thought. It shows that in his contradictory engagement with notions of rights and race, Emerson generates a critique of American democracy that remains of enormous value, a utopian double vision of nationhood and citizenship that sharply questions the adequacy of market relations as the sole basis for political obligation and community. The inheritance of Emerson undertaken by African-American philosophers requires a systematic acknowledgment of the uses and dangers of American racial and nationalist rhetoric. My own reading of Emerson and his legacy makes the precise terms of their critique comprehensible to a wider audience.

PART I

Ownership

ONE

Defining the Public

Representative Men

The emphasis raised at the outset and sustained throughout this book on the significance of race and rights as being constitutive of Emerson's concept of American identity immediately calls our attention to a related subject: his inquiry into the exact nature of the public realm in which civil rights may be properly exercised or violated and in which racial identities are constituted. In recent years, there has been a growing interest in characterizing and critiquing the liberal public sphere as a category of bourgeois society.[1] For many political theorists, this critique has hinged upon claims regarding the conditions for participation in rational-critical debate over public issues, and the unacknowledged gender-, class-, and race-based exclusions that have historically impeded the full realization of an ideally democratic process.[2]

Although the topic of "the public" may seem new in these recent formulations, these debates have been commonplace for some time. The problem of publicity is, and traditionally has been regarded by liberal theorists as, central to the matter of political representation. This connection is one Emerson explicitly develops in *Representative Men*, published in 1850, a work in which he puts forward the underlying principles of political representation that are fundamental to his task of literary representation. Literary critics have been quick to point out the connection between literary and political representation, and few would deny that political power entails the power of representation and self-representation. At the end of this book, we should be in a position to state whether, and how, Emerson's idea of "the representative" contributes to Martin Luther King Jr.'s public performance of American philosophy and attempt to facilitate black Americans' access to political representation during the 1960s. For the moment, given a clearer understanding of how the concept of political representation provides structure and justification for Emerson's art, we may be better able to appreciate his imaginative work, and the nature of literary representation itself.

Political philosophers have begun to recognize the seriousness and value of Emerson's writings as a conceptual resource for contemporary debates regarding "the public" and political representation. As Hannah Pitkin has observed, Emerson's writings cast light on the meaning of representation because "we learn what representation is, not merely from the history of representative government, but also from knowing about representational art."[3] The interests and exclusions built into Emerson's vision of the public, which is cast as a public of Representative Men—Plato, Swedenborg, Montaigne, Shakespeare, Napoleon, and Goethe—should be immediately obvious to anyone who has even glanced at the book's title and table of contents. The real difficulty lies in getting beyond such politically correct truisms, however true they may be. In this chapter, I propose to explore the meaning of "the public" in *Representative Men*, and to demonstrate how it fits with Emerson's theory of "the representative," a theory that simultaneously registers and repudiates liberal habits of belief about the nature of political representation. I will argue three primary points that are crucial to understanding the larger question of the public as it pertains to the problem of representation in *Representative Men*. First, Emerson's concept of "the representative" expresses a contradictory picture of the self as being both privately self-owning (or bounded) and boundless, a self that is both confined to the private and given over to a larger public commonwealth. Second, Emerson's description of "representativeness" in *Representative Men* requires that he simultaneously repudiate and enlist both nineteenth-century democratic and racialist discourses to describe the varied and conflicting relationships of obligation and difference that attach the representative to the public. I will conclude by showing that this rhetoric of contradiction—a contradiction between, on the one hand, Emerson's democratic universalism or commitment to what Judith Shklar has identified as his "democratic ethos"[4] and, on the other hand, the racialism that circumscribes his notion of the representative self—works simultaneously to bar and facilitate access, to install and remove exclusions to the public realm of representation.

The familiar rallying cry of the American Revolution that "taxation without representation is tyranny"—the claim that political representation is what distinguishes just government from tyranny—reveals the extent to which this concept of representation is linked to the liberal ideal of self-government. In the *Federalist Papers*, James Madison defined representation as "a substitute for a meeting of citizens in person" and argued that it established an essential, common interest between the people and the government, securing prospects for liberty by ensuring the government's "immediate dependence on, and an intimate sympathy with, the people."[5] Viewed in Madison's terms, the primary significance of political representation lies in the fact that it defines and establishes the right of suffrage, so fundamental to functioning of representative or "republican" government, in the Constitution.[6] Following Madison, many liberal theorists still regard the act of voting or choosing one's representative as an act of rational, voluntary consent to the bonds of civil society, an act through which an individual marks his rightful place in the public realm of politics.[7]

The public, political realm constructed in the Constitution was made possible only insofar as large groups of individuals were excluded from representation in it. Ironically, the liberation of the framers themselves from striving for the necessities of life—what Hannah Arendt regards as the precondition for the enjoyment of freedom and equality in the polis—came about precisely as a result of the daily labors of these politically invisible persons.[8] The formula for representation arrived at during the course of constitutional debates was one that encoded a particular definition of the public realm, allowing for the exclusion of blacks from an apparently universal consensus of "all men," and thus afforded a rhetorical means of sanctioning slavery even in a document that purported to secure the blessings of liberty. As William Paterson of New Jersey made abundantly clear, the question under consideration was never one of whether the slaves would be represented in the legislature but, rather, whether a slave owner would gain any increment in representation for each slave he owned. He asked, "If Negroes are not represented in the States to which they belong, why should they be represented in the General Government? What is the true principle of Representation? It is an expedient by which an assembly of certain individuals chosen by the people is substituted in place of the inconvenient meeting of the people themselves. If such a meeting of the people was actually to take place, would the slaves vote? They would not. Why then should they be represented."[9] The slavery issue divided the delegates along sectional lines in the debate over representation. Madison himself pointed out that "having or not having slaves" was more fundamental to the apportionment of the lower house of the national legislature than state size, and thus that "the institution of slavery and its consequences formed the line of discrimination" between the Northern and the Southern states (*Records*, II, 10).

Records of the debate over representation that took place during the Constitutional Convention show the strong influence of a popular tradition in Lockean liberalism and the significance of Locke's notion of "property rights" for the constitution-making process. In the *Second Treatise of Government*, Locke defines the individual as proprietor of his own person and rightful owner of his body. For Locke, property is an important construct not only in his model of the self; it is also essential to his description of the origin and development of political relations. Property renders consent to society meaningful because without property there is no major cause for protection and admission into the public realm. This idea that government exists in order to ensure the protection of property rights was repeatedly invoked by convention delegates: Governor Morris of Pennsylvania insisted that "property ought to be taken into the estimate as well as the number of inhabitants" and that "an accurate view of the matter would nevertheless prove that property was the main object of Society."

> The savage State was more favorable to liberty than the Civilized; and sufficiently so to life. It was preferred by all men who had not acquired a taste for property; it was only renounced for the sake of property which could only be secured by the restraints of regular Government. These ideas might appear to some new, but they were nevertheless just. If property then was the main object of Government certainly it ought to be one measure of the influence due to those who were affected by the Government. (*Records*, I, 533)

Two South Carolinians present at the Convention concurred with Morris's view and thus protected their sectional interests: John Rutledge remarked that "the gentleman last up [i.e., Morris] had spoken some of his sentiments precisely. Property was certainly the principal object of Society" (*Records*, I, 534). Pierce Butler pursued the matter by contending "strenuously that property was the only just measure of representation. This was the great object of Government: the great cause of war, the great means of carrying it on" (*Records*, I, 541–542).

Habitual appeals to the sacrosanct and Lockean notion of property rights allowed the framers of the Constitution to uphold liberal ideals while at the same time accommodating the political reality of slavery. South Carolinians such as Butler wanted to tie representation directly to "wealth," a common euphemism for slaves.[10] Insisting that the labor of a slave in South Carolina was as productive and valuable as that of a freeman in Massachusetts, Butler went on to claim that "as wealth was the great means of defense and utility to the Nation they are equally valuable to it with freemen; and that consequently an equal representation ought to be allowed for them in a Government which was instituted principally for the protection of property, and was itself to be supported by property" (*Records*, I, 580–581). Another Southerner, Charles Cotesworth Pinkney, stated that "the rule of wealth should be ascertained and not left to the pleasure of the Legislature; and that property in slaves should not be exposed to danger under a Government instituted for the protection of property" (*Records*, I, 593–594). And Edmund Randolph of Virginia "urged strenuously that express security ought to be provided for including slaves in the ratio of Representation. He lamented that such a species of property existed. But as it did exist the holders of it would require this security" (*Records*, I, 594).

The formula for political representation inscribed in the Constitution the contradictory and dual character of the slave's legal status as "chattels personal."[11] Although the original Virginia Plan proposed a proportional representation based on the number of free inhabitants in each state, on June 13 this ratio was modified to include three-fifths of "other persons."[12] The contradictory status of slaves as being both of persons and property that emerged out of the debate over political representation was the source of endless controversy. James Wilson of Pennsylvania observed that he "did not well see on what principle the admission of blacks in proportion of three fifths could be explained. Are they admitted as Citizens? Then why are they not admitted on an equality with White Citizens? Are they admitted as property? Then why is not other property admitted into the computation?" (*Records*, I, 587). Responding to Randolph's motion to strike out the word "wealth" as a description for slaves, Governor Morris pointed out the "incoherence" of the formula:

> If Negroes were to be viewed as inhabitants they ought to be added in their entire number, and not in the proportion of 3/5. If as property, the word wealth was right, and striking it out should produce the very inconsistency which it was meant to get rid of.—The train of business and the late turn which it had taken, had led him he said, into a deep meditation on it, and he would candidly state the result. . . . Either this distinction is fictitious or real: If it be real, instead of attempting to blend incompatible things, let us at once take a friendly leave of each other. (*Records*, I, 604)

In the *Federalist Papers*, in his account of a Southerner's position in the debate concerning the three-fifths clause of the Constitution, Madison was careful to consider representation in light of the "mixed character" of the slave's legal status as being both of property and of persons.

> Representation relates more immediately to persons, and taxation more immediately to property, and we join in the application of this distinction in the case of our slaves. But we must deny the fact that slaves are considered merely as property, and in no respect whatever as persons. The true state of the case is that they partake of both of these qualities: being considered by our laws in some respects as persons, and in other respects as property. . . . The federal Constitution, therefore, decides with great propriety in the case of our slaves, when it views them in the mixed character of persons and of property. . . . Let the case of the slaves be considered, as it is in truth a peculiar one. Let the compromising expedient of the Constitution be mutually adopted which regards them as inhabitants, but as debased by servitude below the equal level of free inhabitants; which regards the *slave* as divested of two fifths of the *man*. (Nos. 54, 337, 339)

The practice of expedient compromise as the source of mutual agreement was thought to be central and necessary to the creation of the Constitution.[13] That the act of creation was perceived as inventive and the framers of the Constitution as committed to the practical manufacture of a legal instrument marked by the process of political compromise is visible throughout the *Federalist Papers*. Madison expressed his belief in the necessity of such compromise when he insisted that "[n]o man would refuse to quit a shattered and tottering habitation for a firm and commodious building because the latter had not a porch to it, or because some of the rooms might be a little larger or smaller, or the ceiling a little higher or lower than his fancy would have planned them" (Nos. 38, 237). Compromise was crucial to the creation of consensus over the meaning of language in the new Constitution, language that was perceived by the founders as inherently unstable in its reference. Madison argued that all legal meaning was inevitably obscure until the meaning of new laws had been adjudicated.

> All new laws, though penned with the greatest technical skill and passed on the fullest and most mature deliberation, are considered to be more or less obscure and equivocal, until their meaning be liquidated and ascertained by a series of particular discussions and adjudications. No language is so copious as to supply words and phrases for every complex idea, or so correct as not to include many equivocally denoting different ideas. Hence it must happen that however accurately objects may be discriminated in themselves, and however accurately the discrimination may be considered, the definition of them may be rendered inaccurate by the inaccuracy of the terms in which it is delivered. . . .
>
> Here, then, are the three sources of vague and incorrect definitions: the indistinctness of the object, imperfection of the organ of conception, inadequateness of the vehicle of ideas. Any one of these must produce a certain degree of obscurity. The convention . . . must have experienced the full effect of them all.
>
> To the difficulties already mentioned may be added the interfering pretensions of the larger and smaller States. . . . We may well suppose that neither side would entirely yield to the other, and consequently that the struggle could be terminated only by compromise. (Nos. 37, 229)

As a compromising expedient, the three-fifths clause of the Constitution resolved the social conflict over slavery through strategic self-contradiction. The mutual and self-contradictory point on which all at the Convention could agree was that the slave both is and is not a person; that the slave both is property and is not property.

Taken together, the constitutional debates over representation show what is most and least democratic about the framers' respective visions of "the people," and make explicit the central contradiction between rights and race that is the unacknowledged basis for their thinking about political representation, the problem of precisely who may enter the public realm of appearances that is the projected site for democratic due process.[14] Viewed in the tradition of Anglo-American political thought, theories of political representation devolve upon a similar contradiction, even though it has remained unarticulated or developed as such. In *Inventing the People: The Rise of Popular Sovereignty in England and America*, Edmund Morgan points out that the conceptual possibility of effective representation in America depended on the belief in a unified and thus authorizing and sovereign people. He writes, "[T]he sovereignty of the people could be exercised only through representatives who were at once the agents of particular people in particular communities and the wielders of the supreme power that *the* people mysteriously conveyed to them. The viability of the fiction depended, in part at least, on the people of particular communities feeling themselves to be a part of one people, their particular interests not incompatible with the interests of the whole as directed by the assembled wielders of power."[15] At the same time that advocates of proportional representation at the Constitutional Convention affirmed individual autonomy and freedom of choice, many also presented a concept of "the people" that worked against this individualistic premise and argued that the legislature should "mirror" the people's reflection. "The Legislature," as James Wilson put it, "ought to be the most exact transcript of the whole Society"; later he described the legislature as a "portrait . . . excellent in proportion to its being a good likeness" (*Records*, I, 132, 142). Generally speaking, late eighteenth-century liberal writers were relatively confident that they understood the theoretical basis for and saw clear evidence of what Hamilton identified in the *Federalist Papers* as the "surest bond of sympathy" or "strong chords of sympathy" (Nos. 35, 215, 216) that existed between a particular representative and the people.

For liberal philosophers such as John Stuart Mill, the project of defining "the people" was one of trying to reconcile the liberal framework with a developing notion of racial nationalist identity: viewed in these terms, the contradiction between individual and collective identity implicit in theories of representation propounded during the American revolutionary era was rendered in distinctly nineteenth-century, racial nationalist terms. In *Considerations on Representative Government*, Mill refers to a "feeling of nationality"— a feeling he claims is in part the "effect of identity of race and descent"—as the sole basis for group cohesion, which is, in his view, essential to the proper functioning of representative government.[16] What is important to note is that just as Mill invokes a race-based concept, the "feeling of nationality," to articulate his vision of representative government, so in his account of "the public" he argues for the central importance of a morally instructive "feeling" of identification with the public that allows each citizen in turn to assume his public, representative role and responsibilities. "He is made to feel himself one of the public," Mill writes, "and whatever is their interest to be his interest. Where this school of public spirit does not exist, scarcely any sense is entertained that private persons, in no eminent social situation, owe any duties to society except to obey the laws and submit to the government. There is no unselfish sentiment of identification with the public. . . . Thus private morality suffers, while public is actually extinct" (*CRG*, 79–80).

What is the ground for the representative's identification with the public? Are the obligations that unite participants in the public realm of politics assumed by volitional, rational acts of consent, or are they, like ties of race, born into or found as already existing? Mill does not give us answers to such questions. To do so would mean showing how access to the public, as imagined in his treatise on representative government, is ultimately facilitated or impeded by visible particularities such as race, class, and gender.[17] The varied relationships of obligation and difference entailed in this attachment of the representative to the people, the sustained oscillation between what is most and least democratic about the nature of the public, is at the center of Emerson's project in *Representative Men*.

We have seen that the three-fifths clause of the Constitution resolved
the social conflict over slavery through compromise based on strategic self-
contradiction; that the mutual and self-contradictory point on which all at
the Convention could agree was that the slave both is and is not a person;
and that the slave both is property and is not property. Taken as a whole,
Emerson's writings set forth an emerging theory of political relations that
stands as his response to the limitations imposed by the practice of compromise
on the production of founding documents. In 1837, he wrote that "[t]he former men acted and spoke under the thought that a shining social prosperity
was the aim of men, and compromised ever the individuals to the nation. The
modern mind teaches (in extremes) that the nation exists for the individual;
for the guardianship and education of every man. . . . The American Declaration of Independence is a formal announcement of [the new thought] by a
nation to nations, though a very limited expression" (*Early Lectures*, 214).
Paradoxically, however, in *Representative Men*, this professed aversion to political compromise leads Emerson to repeat its contradictory structure in his
uncompromised yoking of opposites. To take just one very important example:
the picture of the representative self that results from Emerson's efforts to
critique the Lockean, liberal concept of property exhibits a striking, central
contradiction between owning and not owning; between boundedness and
boundlessness. In "Uses of Great Men," Emerson emphatically insists that
there are and always will be invisible, uncrossed boundaries between persons:
"There is something deceptive about the intercourse of minds," he writes.
"The boundaries are invisible, but they are never crossed. There is such good
will to impart, and such good will to receive, that each threatens to become
the other; but the law of individuality collects its secret strength: you are you,
and I am I, and so we remain."[18] But only three pages later he demonstrates
that the proper meaning of "the representative" dismantles boundaries between the self and other persons, and that the proper role of the representative
is to effect this equal distribution of spirit, the foundation of what promises
to be an intimate commonwealth of souls:

> No man, in all the procession of famous men, is reason or illumination, or
> that essence we were looking for; but is an exhibition, in some quarter, of
> new possibilities. . . . The study of many individuals leads us to an elemental
> region wherein the individual is lost, or wherein all touch by their summits.
> Thought and feeling, that break out there, cannot be impounded by any
> fence of personality. This is the key to the power of the greatest men,—their
> spirit diffuses itself. . . . [The] union of all minds appears intimate: what gets
> admission to one, cannot be kept out of any other: the smallest acquisition
> of truth or of energy, in any quarter, is so much good to the commonwealth
> of souls. (*RM*, 630–631)

In some respects, Emerson's insistence that we both are and are not property
resembles the compromise reached by the founders in the three-fifths clause
of the Constitution. Both Emerson and the founders designed a rhetoric that

would create a consensus over the meaning of self-ownership, and both resolve conflict by arriving at a self-contradictory formula for representation that precludes the possibility of denial.

The contradiction between owning and not owning that structures Emerson's thinking about the relationship between the representative and the public is expressed at crucial points in his essay by means of his recourse to what I have already identified as two competing nineteenth-century discourses of obligation: the discourse of rights-based, liberal contractarianism and the popular discourse of scientific racialism. The critique enacted in this rhetorical gesture of contradiction is one that works both to transcend and affirm the premises of democracy and racialism. On the one hand, Emerson asserts the necessity of universal access to public, political representation by showing that the effect of the representative is to remove race-based exclusions and barriers between persons and replace the corrupt fascination with a debased form of rights discourse with an apprehension of what Emerson calls "incorruptible goods":

> But if there should appear in the company some gentle soul who knows little of persons or parties, of Carolina or Cuba, but who announces a law that disposes these particulars, and so certifies me of the equity which checkmates every false player, bankrupts every self-seeker, and apprises me of my independence on any conditions of country, or time, or human body, that man liberates me; I forget the clock. I pass out of the sore relation to persons. I am healed of my hurts. I am made immortal by apprehending my possession of incorruptible goods. Here is great competition of rich and poor. We live in a market, where is only so much wheat, or wool, or land; and if I have so much more, every other must have so much less. I seem to have no good, without breach of good manners. Nobody is glad in the gladness of another, and our system is one of war, of an injurious superiority. Every child of the Saxon race is educated to wish to be first. It is our system; and a man comes to measure his greatness by the regrets, envies, and hatreds of his competitors. But in these new fields there is room: here are not self-esteems, no exclusions. (RM, 625)

On the other hand, throughout his meditation on the "Uses of Great Men," Emerson repeatedly and explicitly relies on the conceptual premises of both liberal contractarianism and racialism. Like Mill, Emerson uses these discourses to express the process of identification that constitutes the web of relations in the representative's sphere of life. He writes, "We speak now only of our acquaintance with them in their own sphere and the way in which they seem to fascinate and draw to them some genius who occupies himself with one thing, all his life long. The possibility of interpretation lies in the identity of the observer with the observed" (RM, 619). But whereas Mill does not make explicit his racialism—a racialism that works both to supplement and to critique the democratic notion of rationally assumed obligation as the basis for identification between the representative and the people—Emerson deliberately and directly enlists racialist discourse in his attempt to describe the obligations that attach the representative to the people. "But he must be related to us, and our life receive from him some promise of explanation," he insists. "A sound apple produces seed,—a hybrid does not" (RM, 617).

At the same time that the very idea of the representative registers a universalist move toward transcendence of the body, it also entails Emerson's reliance on the particularities of the body as the ultimate ground for any claims to such a status. This explains Emerson's contradictory aversion and attraction to both racialist discourse and the discourse of political representation at key moments in his argument. Indeed, the proper role of the "representative" self is made visible in the course of Emerson's essay only insofar as Emerson's writing exhibits this dual and contradictory reference to both racialist and democratic discourses—to the language of scientific racialism (chemistry, botany) *and also* that of political representation ("rotation," "vote," "constituency"); the affirmation of obligations to the public that are born into or found as already existing *and also* those that have been contractually consented to:

> The gases gather to the solid firmament: the chemic lump arrives at the plant, and grows; arrives at the quadruped, and walks; arrives at the man, and thinks. *But also* the constituency determines the vote of the representative. He is not only representative, but participant. Like can only be known by like. The reason why he knows about them is, that he is of them; he has just come out of nature, or from being a part of that thing. Animated chlorine knows of chlorine, and incarnate zinc, of zinc. Their quality makes his career; and he can variously publish their virtues, because they compose him. (RM, 619; emphasis added)

In an essay titled "Emerson and the Inhibitions of Democracy," the political philosopher Judith Shklar has pointed out that Emerson resorts to "the representative" as a political metaphor in order to reconcile the possibility of human greatness with his strong commitment to a democratic ethos—what Shklar regards as his unshakable belief in equality:

> The way he coped with [the conflict between greatness and equality] was nothing if not ingenious. The masses of humanity certainly do not exist in order to allow a great person to emerge from their depth to lead and mould them. The great person serves them. And that service is described in the language of democratic politics. The way out of the tension between the sense of the apartness of the great and the claims of humanity was, as in constitutional states, to resort to representation. It is the only way out of the seesaw between anarchy and oppression. Nothing could illustrate more vividly the hold that democratic norms had on Emerson's intellectual imagination. ("Inhibitions of Democracy," 607)

Such an analysis of Emerson's intellectual and imaginative commitment to democratic norms—Shklar's insistence that, despite Emerson's stated discontents with democracy,[19] "the beliefs and practices of American representative democracy constituted an integral moral barrier which he could neither ignore nor cross" ("Inhibitions of Democracy," 601)—fails to account for what I have already documented as Emerson's occasional repudiation of democratic values performed in his recourse to the rhetoric of scientific racialism.

Despite this conceptual limitation, however, Shklar's discussion does end with a question that has a direct bearing on my analysis of the public realm in Emerson's *Representative Men*. Echoing Arendt's critique of Thoreau's appeal to conscience in his performance of civil disobedience, a critique that hinges on the claim that any appeal to conscience is by definition a private matter and as such can never be made public,[20] Shklar proceeds to argue that *Representative Men* is not about politics, even though it is replete with political language and metaphors. By Shklar's account, Emerson's thinking about concepts such as "self-reliance" and "the representative" has nothing whatsoever to do with the public domain.

> *Representative Men* is [not] about politics, which is why the constant intrusion of political language, illustrations, and preoccupations is so striking.

> As an assertion of the independence of private citizens, this is fine, but it loses all value when it is copied, when it is a matter of group life. There is, moreover, something inherently absurd about the projection of the purity of conscience into the public glare. . . . The independence of conscience once it enters the public domain is exploited by less scrupulous political agents ("Inhibitions of Democracy," 612, 613).

The central question of whether and how Emerson's language may be read as political—the connection, posited by Emerson's rhetorical construction of "the representative," between the act of writing philosophy and public, political activism—will be taken up in detail at the end of this book. I will end this chapter with the suggestion that the definition of publicity entailed by Emerson's concept of "the representative" in *Representative Men* is one that blurs distinctions between the private, the social, and the public.[21] The overall effect of such a rendering of the public is that of simultaneously affirming democratic universalisms and racialist exclusions; of facilitating *and* barring access to the public realm.

The centrality of publicity to liberal theories of political representation is immediately visible in the repeated emphasis placed by political philosophers on "the public" as an arena for free speech and rational debate. For liberal writers such as Mill and Dewey, the project of defining political representation and the proper role of representative government devolves upon on their respective assessments of this aspect of the public realm. For Mill, the function of representative governmental bodies is to throw what he calls the "light of publicity" on every act of government; thus it follows that the Parliament, by his account, should be a public arena that allows for the freest possible expressions of opinion, "a place where every interest and shade of opinion in the country can have its cause even passionately pleaded, in the face of the government and of all other interests and opinions" (CRG, 115, 117). Similarly, in *The Public and Its Problems*, Dewey's analysis of publicity derives in part from his definition of representative government as one in which the public has been organized in order to minimize conflict, thereby securing its dominance:

> When a public is generated "[it] arrives at decisions, makes terms and executes resolves only through the medium of individuals. They are officers; they represent a Public, but the Public acts only through them. We say in a country like our own that legislators and executives are elected by the public. The phrase might appear to indicate that the Public acts. But, after all, individual men and women exercise the franchise; the public is here a collective name for a multitude of persons each voting as an anonymous unit. As a citizen-voter each one of these persons is, however, an officer of the public. He expresses his will as a representative of the public interest as much so as does a senator or sheriff. His vote may express his hope to profit in private purse by the election of some man or the ratification of some proposed law. He may fail, in other words, in effort to represent the interest entrusted to him. But in this respect he does not differ from those explicitly designated public officials who have also been known to betray the interest committed to them instead of faithfully representing it.[22]

Observing that "it may be said that not until recently have publics been conscious that they were publics" (*TPP*, 77), Dewey concludes that the primary problem of the public is one of achieving recognition of itself so as to acquire influence in the process of selecting representatives and defining their responsibilities and rights.

Like Mill and Dewey, in *Representative Men*, Emerson repeatedly emphasizes the importance of what he calls "full" expression. But he is always unclear as to precisely where this full expression takes place—whether such moments of expression are, properly speaking, private, social, or public. For example, in "Plato," he writes:

> Children cry, scream, and stamp with fury, unable to express their desire. As soon as they can speak and tell their want, and the reason of it, they become gentle. In adult life, whilst the perceptions are obtuse, men and women talk vehemently and superlatively, blunder and quarrel: their manners are full of desperation; their speech is full of oaths. As soon as, with culture, things have cleared up a little, and they see them no longer in lumps and masses, but accurately distributed, they desist from that weak vehemence, and explain their meaning in detail. If the tongue had not been framed for articulation, man would still be a beast in the forest. The same weakness and want, on a higher plane, occurs daily in the education of young men and women. "Ah! you don't understand me; I have never met with any one who comprehends me:" and they sigh and weep, write verses, and walk alone,—fault of power to express their precise meaning. In a month or two, through the favor of their good genius, they meet some one so related as to assist their volcanic estate; and, good communication being once established, they are thenceforward good citizens. (*RM*, 637)

In this passage, Emerson argues that good communication is a necessary pre-condition for "good citizenship," but the framing context he describes for this communication is one that implicitly blurs the distinction between private, romantic, or social forms of communication and those conventionally asso-ciated with political, public debate. Similarly, in "Uses of Great Men," when he recounts the pleasures of "full" expression associated with the act of reading literary works of genius, Emerson distinguishes such full expression from *private* experience, but does not tell us outright that "full" expression has in fact been made "public."

> What is he whom I never think of? whilst in solitude are those who succor our genius, and stimulate us in wonderful manners. There is a power in love to divine another's destiny better than that other can, and, by heroic en-couragements, hold him to his task. . . . This pleasure of full expression to that which, in their private experience, is usually cramped and obstructed, runs, also, much higher, and is the secret of the reader's joy in literary genius. Nothing is kept back. (RM, 621)

The definition of the public we are left with in *Representative Men* is one that circumscribes a "sphere of thought" that is only tenuously and dubiously related to the sphere of politics: "I count him a great man who inhabits a higher sphere of thought," Emerson writes, "into which other men rise with labor and difficulty; he has but to open his eyes to see things in a true light, and in large relations; whilst they must make painful corrections, and keep a vigilant eye on many sources of error" (RM, 616).[23] The effect of Emerson's blurring of distinctions between the private realm of the household and the public realm of politics is one that simultaneously encourages and bars access to publicity and public action because, by this account, no distinct realm exists beyond the confines of the private. In *Representative Men*, public action is to be found in publications read at home: "Unpublished nature will have its whole secret told," he tells us, "Thus, we sit by the fire, and take hold of the poles of the earth" (RM, 619).

TWO

Property and the Body in Nature

The belief that the discourse of property rights is sufficient to the task of representing the self and the bonds of civil society is a fundamental, well-rehearsed tenet of liberal political thought. The theory of property that best expresses this belief has been put forward by the philosopher John Locke. In his *Second Treatise of Government*, Locke defines the individual as the proprietor of his own person and rightful owner of his body: "[E]very Man has a *Property* in his own *Person*. This no Body has any Right to but himself. The *Labor* of his Body, and the *Work* of his Hands, we may say, are properly his" (Section 27).[1] Locke's description of property as something that comes into being when objects or other aspects of the natural world, originally given by God to mankind in common, have been mixed with a man's labor, is premised on a central claim regarding the private property that every man has in his own body. Viewed in connection with contemporary liberal political philosophies and legal theories, this Lockean preoccupation with private property as delineating bodily boundaries is readily apparent in debates concerning the relationship between the body and the state: for example, the relative degrees of inviolability conferred upon the body by the state, or the question of what counts under a particular system of laws as one person's uncivil, criminal act of trespass with regard to another person's body.[2]

When I spoke earlier of Emerson's picture of the representative self, I suggested that it is strikingly at odds with this liberal, self-owning account of embodied personhood: for Emerson, the self is both bounded and boundless; it is both privately owned and given over to a larger public commonwealth.

This point needs further clarification. This chapter will offer an assessment of three main aspects of the political logic of contradiction in Emerson's thinking about ownership. First, I will try to show that Emerson's recourse to contradiction set forth, as we have seen, in *Representative Men* is in fact the culmination of a sustained critique of the Lockean, liberal notion of property rights unfolded in his early writings. Second, this contradiction between boundedness and boundlessness figures in Emerson's picture of the embodied subject, and is best understood in light of his engagement with ownership as a cultural value, a value he endlessly scrutinizes, cherishes, and resists. In particular, I will situate Emerson's critique within the context of popular discourses on property and the body that proliferated during the ongoing debate over slavery. I will end with the suggestion, to be taken up again in a later chapter, that this critique of property rights inherent in Emerson's contradictory vision of the representative American self in *Nature* contributes to the expression of his nationalism.

On September 20, 1840, Emerson recorded an entry in his journal that exhibits a theory of property. The entry belongs to a series of similar moments in which the relation of ownership is simultaneously embraced and renounced.

> Perhaps after many sad doubting idle days, days of happy honest labor will at last come when a man shall have filled up all the hours from sun to sun with great and equal action, shall lose sight of this sharp individuality which contrasts now so oddly with nature, and ceasing to regard shall cease to feel his boundaries, but shall be interfused by nature and shall interfuse nature that the sun shall rise by his will as much as his own hand or foot do now; and his eyes or ears or fingers shall not seem to him the property of a more private will than the sea & the stars.[3]

Just as in the *Second Treatise* Locke argues that property rights designate a barrier separating the body from (and thereby relating it to) the natural world, so in this passage Emerson describes property that is the product of doubting idleness—labor, in his words, that is not "honest"—as ultimately giving rise to a sharp individuality whose boundaries distance him from nature. But in contrast to Locke's defense of self-owning individualism, in this passage Emerson's state of unwanted individuality, of yearning for unity with the material world, prompts his discovery and articulation of an alternative concept of property. The sun, he tells us, shall be as much his property as his own body, but that body will not be the property of a more private will than the sea and the stars. The meaning for property at which Emerson arrives is twofold and contradictory: at the same time that it opens the possibility of limitless appropriation and calls for the extension of the idea of ownership to remote celestial realms, it also stands as a critique of his proprietary claim on that most private of possessed spaces, the human body.

A second passage from the early writings that registers this curious, contradictory significance Emerson assigns to property occurs in the lecture "Home," delivered in 1838 at the Masonic Temple in Boston.

> The advancing spirit sees how unworthy it is to be immersed in such poor considerations as its bed and board, and to be wounded in every foolish injury that befals [sic] these, and to die daily in the perishing of property and merely local and temporary personal relations. It sees it to be far nobler to hold itself off on cooler terms, and survey the moving drama of life aloof and alone. Then he comes with new rights and with new curiosity into his house to his family, to his household tasks, and relations. . . . Now he is guest in Nature, a guest in his own house, a stranger to his wife and children, a stranger in his own body. . . . For if love and thought be nearness, our bodies are not near us. Open the skin, the flesh, enter the skeleton, touch the heart, liver, or brain of the man, and you have come no nearer to the man than when you were still outside. All this is as strange and foreign to him as to you. You have almost as much property in his body as he has.[4]

Written at the end of 1838, the passage bears the scars of Emerson's grief in the wake of family tragedy: his wife Ellen died of tuberculosis in February, 1831, and his brother Charles in 1836. Property and the fragile human body that perishes are here inextricably linked in Emerson's mind to temporary personal relations. The theory of property put forward in this lecture differs from that of the 1840 journal entry in two major respects. First, whereas Emerson represents himself as idle in the 1840 journal entry, in the lecture passage we witness the activity of mourning and the new self, the "advancing spirit," that represents one constructive response to grief. The realization of this new self derives from a gesture of personal violence risked in dissociation from the family, what Emerson would later in "Self-Reliance" call "shunning." It entails the reduction of intimate relations to property relations, and then the attempt to avoid the wounds and foolish injuries that befall such relations by annihilating the meaning of the property relation itself.[5] The position of ownership occupied by the dissenting guest represents a characteristically Emersonian contradiction: on the one hand, he stands aloof and alone; on the other hand, you have almost as much property in his body as he has. The very claim to the communality of property—"You have almost as much property in his body as he has"—is a statement that simultaneously asserts and effaces the meaning of ownership as a category of thought.

Second, whereas in the 1840 journal entry the Lockean discourse of rights is described as delineating an unwanted boundary that distances the sad, doubting subject from the natural world, in this passage the discourse of property rights is critiqued as a necessary but insufficient expression of intimate relations between persons: in "Home," the issue of property has been more broadly construed as relating to the question of consent to participation in the intimate complexities of a domestic world. Emerson's simultaneous, contradictory invocation and denial of property in this context represents, on the one hand, his desire to express a "nearness" to others even nearer than the proprietary claim he has on his own body, and, on the other hand, his inability to conceive of such nearness in any other terms. Emerson's striking imposition of the vocabulary of rights, commonly associated with the public realm of politics, to render the experience of life in the household—his description of a man who comes with "new rights and with new curiosity into his house"— signals his saturation of the political language of property and social contract with private or commonsense meanings. Although Emerson's use of the family as the primary unit in his model for political relations is in keeping with the social reformers of his day, Emerson's reference to the family model is distinctive insofar as, while his contemporaries were engaged in an ongoing debate as to whether society could be reorganized as a family,[6] he imposed the vocabulary and logic of Lockean, rights-based liberalism upon the structure of the family, imagining the family as a society of contract and consent.[7]

Emerson's steady engagement with rights discourse is visible in the richness and range of his writings on the subject. His early criticisms of the prevailing, highly conventional view of property espoused by his contemporaries were vehement and unceasing. "The great endeavors of man are paralyzed," he wrote in 1838. "They take the law from things; they serve their property . . . and bow the neck and the knee and the soul to their own creation" (*JMN*, VII, 218). One year later, he noted in his journal that "[f]ear, for ages, has boded & mowed & gibbered over property & over social relations. I assure you that obscene bird is not there for nothing. These are great wrongs & need to be revised" (*JMN*, VII, 198). In a lecture titled "Man the Reformer" read before the Mechanics' Apprentices' Library Association in 1841, Emerson insisted that "a sequestration from the sentiments of generosity and love . . . reaches into the whole institution of property, until our laws which establish and protect it, seem not to be the issue of love and reason, but of selfishness."[8] A despairing moment recorded ten years later in his journal discloses his belief in the political necessity and urgency of his attempt to make up a new language and perceptual frame for thinking about ownership: "the subject of education, of art, of religion, [have] come to appear bitter mockeries. The newspaper is only a proclamation & detail of our shames. The very question of property, the house & land we occupy, have lost their sunlight" (*JMN*, XI, 348). For Emerson, the utter incapacity of his contemporaries to examine the question of property disclosed the advanced state of disintegration in human society.

Despite the bitterness of some of his criticisms, it is clear that throughout his life Emerson thought often about the significance of property, for his political philosophy as well as for his imaginative work. In 1843, he noted in his journal that "[a]t the time when Bonaparte appeared military men believed there was nothing new to be done in war. They think the same today of letters, property, labor, & all the rest" (*JMN*, IX, 165); two year later, he observed in the essay "Politics" that "there is an instinctive sense, however obscure and yet inarticulate, that the whole constitution of property, on its present tenures, is injurious, and its influence on persons deteriorating and degrading" (*Essays*, 561). Even as early as 1837, in a lecture series, "Human Culture," Emerson suggested that "[b]efore the steady gaze of the soul, the whole life of man, the societies, laws, property, and pursuits of man, and the long procession of history do blench and quail. Before this indomitable soul ever fresh and immortal the aged world owns its master" (*EL*, II, 219–220).

Taken as a whole, Emerson's intense, early engagement with the critical recuperation of property rights discourse indicates that this project represented a source of endless experimentation and volatile intellectual possibility. "Over thee, over me, over each of these wondrous pilgrims of time, broods away this everlasting Love soliciting us in silent moments to surrender our officious activity to it," he wrote in an 1840 "Address to the People of East Lexington." "In doing thus, the heart is made wise and the tongue inspired. And instead of our former contemptible relations to a plot of ground, or a stock of merchandise, to a few men and a few women to whom we were holden by some tie of interest or of ease, lo! suddenly we belong to the world" (*EL*, III, 329). Emerson's grappling with the problem of what it means to belong to the world and of the dissolution of bodily boundaries that isolate, distinguish, and protect individuals from the world of persons and things is also visible in another lecture, this time on "Religion," delivered three years earlier. Emerson writes, "He that speaks the truth executes no private function of a slender individual will, but the world utters a sound by his lips. . . . Compare all that we call ourselves, all our private and personal venture in the world, with this deep of moral nature in which we lie, and our private good becomes an impertinence, and we take part with hasty shame against ourselves" (*EL*, II, 86–87). Just as in his 1840 journal entry Emerson's description of the self devolves upon a contradiction between privately owning and publicly belonging to the world, so, here, his insistence that our private good is an impertinence to be resisted works simultaneously to affirm and repudiate ownership: by stating the necessity of resisting claims to private property, Emerson implicitly acknowledges the necessary existence of such property.

Moreover, Emerson's odd, consistent rhetorical strategy of self-contradiction is not limited to his early writings. It recurs throughout the course of his entire career. For example, in "Spiritual Laws," published in 1841, property that results from individual production is transformed by Emerson into the infinite productivity and ephemeral good associated with the natural world— what Emerson describes as "his nature." He writes, "What a man does, that he has. . . . Let him regard no good as solid, but that which is in his nature, and which must grow out of him as long as he exists. The goods of fortune may come and go like summer leaves; let him scatter them on every wind as the momentary signs of his infinite productiveness. . . . Everywhere he may take what belongs to his spiritual estate" (*Essays*, 311). In a passage from "Man the Reformer," a lecture read in Boston that same year, Emerson's imagining of limitless appropriation and use threatens the very meaning of property in the body just as it extends the idea of ownership throughout the natural world: "As the farmer casts into the ground the finest ears of his grain, the time will come when we too shall hold nothing back, but shall eagerly convert more than we now possess into means and powers, when we shall be willing to sow the sun and the moon for seeds" (*Essays*, 150). In *Representative Men*, Emerson depicts this rhetorical method of contradiction as the argument of a "balanced soul": "He cannot forgive himself in a partiality, but is resolved that the two poles of his thought shall appear in his statement. His argument and his sentence are self-poised and spherical" (*Essays*, 641).

Taken together, Emerson's various deliberations over the meaning of property culminate in the following 1850 journal entry, which is particularly relevant to the present analysis because it accounts for the contradictory logic of his rhetoric and critique of rights discourse in clear, direct terms. "It occurred yesterday more strongly than I can now state it, that we must have an intellectual property in all property & in all action, or they are naught," Emerson writes. "I must have children, I must have events, I must have social state & history—or my thinking and speaking will have no body and background. But having these, I must also have them not (so to speak), or carry them as contingent and merely apparent possessions to give them any real value."[9] Emerson's parenthetical "so to speak" expresses the inherent difficulty of articulating what appears to be an illogical, self-contradictory theory of property: that possession is a necessary, if inadequate record of existence that embodies voice and thought. Even though he reminds us that "what is of the heart and mind eludes all laws of property" ("Education," *EL*, III, 298), still "there is a Life not to be described or known otherwise than by possession" ("The Method of Nature," *Essays*, 122).[10]

We know that Emerson devoted two terms to reading Locke at Harvard, that Locke is often mentioned in his early writings, and that Locke has generally been thought to be influential in the development of Transcendentalism.[11] What has not been sufficiently noted is that this philosophical engagement with Locke's *Second Treatise* is best understood in light of the popular usage of the Lockean discourse of property rights that prevailed in Jacksonian society. Although Locke's claim that "[t]his no Body has any right to but himself" has been and should be read as presenting a necessary barrier to slavery, a popular version of Locke's analysis of property was habitually invoked as sacrosanct by slaveowners who argued against the compulsory manumission of slaves in the nineteenth century.[12] The fascination with the popular concept of Lockean property that led many to resist the reform efforts of abolitionists manifested itself as the fear expressed for the sanctity of possession. In general, proslavery writers argued that the right to slave property was tantamount to a right to private ownership of material goods, and ownership of slaves was regarded as subject to the same protections Locke assigns to private property.

The habitual slip from Locke's concept of self-ownership as a justification for accumulation and private possession of material goods to the justification of slavery in proslavery argument reflects the contradictory and dual character of the slave's legal status as "chattels personal."[13] In 1832, Thomas Dew, a professor of political law at the College of William and Mary, argued that abolitionist arguments were "subversive of the rights of property" and that emancipation would never be possible unless "slave property were rigidly respected and never taken without full compensation."[14] In his account of debates on the subject of emancipation in the Virginia legislature, the right to ownership was unflinchingly upheld by Dew as an obvious justification for slavery. " 'Man cannot have property in man'—a phrase as full of meaning as, 'who slays fat oxen should himself be fat.' Certainly he may, if the laws of society allow it, and if it be on sufficient grounds, neither he nor society do wrong."[15]

Similar, habitual invocations of property rights also appear in proslavery pamphlets written in the years after the publication of Dew's influential treatise. "[The abolitionists] admit that the slave can only be emancipated by his master. To effect that result, the master must be convinced and conciliated. What measures have they taken to persuade or win him into their views? They have trampled upon his rights—endangered his property . . . ," one pamphleteer argued in 1836. "If any thing be entitled to reverence or regard, it is our sacred Constitution—the barrier which protects us from popular turbulence, from intestine war, from social and political confusion and collision. The consequence of its downfall or of the violation of its provisions, no fancy can adequately conceive. . . . Congress, in this emergency, should prove itself worthy to guard the rights of a free people."[16] A year later, another concerned citizen wrote,

> The owners of slaves have an undeniable right to such property. . . . We suppose all to admit the fact, that every man is justly entitled to his ordinary real and personal property—as the land, goods and chattels of which he is seized and possessed, either by inheritance or purchase. . . . At what era of "moral suasion" do you imagine you could prevail on us to give up a thousand millions of dollars more in the depreciation of our lands, in consequence of the want of laborers to cultivate them? Consider: were ever any people, civilized or savage, persuaded by any argument, human or divine, to surrender voluntarily two thousand millions of dollars?[17]

By the 1850s and early 1860s, the liberal discourse of property rights facilitated the emergence and development of a theoretically coherent, increasingly systematic political philosophy that took on the characteristics of a formal ideology.[18] In *A Defence of the South Against the Reproaches and Incroachments of the North*, published in 1850, the Reverend Iveson Brookes suggests that one of the "ultimate results at which rabid abolitionists aim" is to

> legislate our property from us without compensation. . . . It is the personal, the pecuniary interest (the strongest sort of interest I suppose with some persons at the North, as well as the South) of the master compelling him to use every means necessary to prolong the life and secure the health of his property. . . . How could any person dream that the South would submit ta-

mely to this abolition scheme, which not only deprives her of her pecuniary rights, and her political influence, but threatens her with absolute degrada- tion and final desolation? . . . For this high handed measure of robbery against us would not only inflict upon us personal oppression in depriving us of our just rights and degrading our political standing in the nation, but it would bind our posterity in chains, as well as destroy billions of dollars of their heritage, and lay desolate the fairest region of God's creation.[19]

A year later, another Southern clergyman put forward a similar rights-based argument:

> In the 9th section of the first article, and in the 2nd section of the fourth article, the constitution of the United States recognizes the vested right of the owner, in slave property; which it guaranties [*sic*] against any legislation of the national legislature: and the second section of the first article forbids any State to pass a law impairing contracts which must include destroying vested rights. What court, then, under the supervision of the American con- stitution, would not declare any law null, which should essay to divest me of my slave property without my consent? . . . If we count the hire of half the negroes, and for half the time, with interest, it would mount up to about seven hundred millions, and added to the value of negroes, as above stated, it would swell the sum of loss in the emancipated negroes to ten hundred and thirty-four millions!—and perhaps loss through depreciation of value of land, and interest upon that up to 1927, would raise the loss sustained by the heirs of slave-holders to $1100,000,000 or $1200,000,000 (eleven hun- dred to twelve hundred millions) at least!!!—bestowed on "freedom flung away," as said a negro concerning a vagabond white man who passed him while at work.[20]

In *Slaveholding Not Sinful*, published in 1856, Samuel How observed that "Sla- veholders in the south and the south-west have a legal right to their slaves. The . . . constitution of our country, and the laws of the respective states in which they reside, recognize, assert and guard their right."[21] These combined efforts on the part of apologists to establish a conceptually coherent, legitimate framework for proslavery thought led, in 1860, to the publication of *Cotton Is King and Proslavery Arguments*, a widely disseminated collection of proslavery classics edited by E. N. Elliott.[22]

The use of this popular discourse of property rights in proslavery argu- ment—a usage that pervaded Jacksonian America, North and South alike— fits well with Tocqueville's observation in 1840 that "[i]n no other country in the world is the love of property keener or more alert than in the United States, and nowhere does the majority display less inclination toward doctrines which in any way threaten the way property is owned."[23] In response to the resulting crisis in the referential capacities of rights discourse, one of the first tasks of abolitionist writers such as William Ellery Channing was to question the doctrine of property in persons. In his book *Slavery*, published in 1835, Channing writes as follows:

Now this claim of property in a human being is altogether false, groundless. No such right of man in man can exist. A human being cannot be justly owned. To hold and treat him as property is to inflict a great wrong, to incur the guilt of oppression.

This position there is a difficulty in maintaining on account of its exceeding obviousness. It is too plain for proof. To defend it is like trying to confirm a self-evident truth. . . . The man, who, on hearing the claim to property in man, does not see and feel distinctly that it is a cruel usurpation, is hardly to be reached by reasoning, for it is hard to find any plainer principles than what he begins by denying.[24]

If, as Channing suggests, any assertion against the claim of property in a human being is undermined by its exceeding obviousness, the difficult task of finding an argument in support of this self-evident truth accounts for the sustained, almost obsessive preoccupation with Lockean property that we find in Emerson's early writings. The pervasive, popular conception of property in Jacksonian America not only prompted Emerson's philosophical response to Locke, it also shaped the terms of his engagement with property as a cultural value. In response to Channing's observation concerning the difficulty of any effective argument against slavery, Emerson argues for the necessity of self-ownership while at the same time returning to a sociohistorical context in which the meaning of property is inextricably bound up with a history of enslavement. In the lecture "Politics," first delivered in 1837, he observes that

[i]n a theory of government, this principle lies at the foundation, that property should make the law for property, and persons the law for persons. But to embody this theory in the form of a government is not easy. For persons and property mix themselves in every transaction. The violences upon persons are oftenest for the sake of property as in . . . slavery. . . . No distinction seems to be so fundamental in politics as this of persons and property. Out of an inattention to it arises the whole sophism of slavery. (EL, II, 72–73)[25]

Viewed in these terms, Emerson's clarification of Locke's philosophy, as well as his critical recovery of an ineffective, popularized rights discourse—a discourse that was poised dangerously near the brink of meaninglessness through overuse—had the overall effect of enlarging upon expressive and conceptual possibilities that exist for liberal theory as a whole.

The same intensity of attention Emerson gives to his critique of property rights in the early writings extends to another, closely related intellectual matter: labor, which Locke defined as the source of all property. In his account of the origins of property in the *Second Treatise*, Locke's memorable image for the process of appropriation is one that establishes an intimate connection between property and labor, between ownership and the endless, life-sustaining activity of gathering acorns so as to separate them from the common.

> He that is nourished by the Acorns he pickt up under an Oak . . . , has
> certainly appropriated them to himself. No body can deny but the nourish-
> ment is his. I ask then, When did they begin to be his? When he digested?
> Or when he eat? Or when he boiled? Or when he brought them home? Or
> when he pickt them up? And 'tis plain, if the first gathering made them not
> his, nothing else could. That labour put a distinction between them and
> common. (*ST*, 288)

Although he is deliberately ambiguous as to the precise position of the body
at the moment when first gathering made the acorns his,[26] Locke clearly suggests that physical labor, a natural life process located in the body, is the
origin of property.

In an 1838 lecture titled "The School," Emerson offers the following
account of labor:

> He tills his acre, he plants his tree, and sees with joy the visits of heat and
> moisture to his trees, and pleases himself with the idea of possession. By this
> act of ownership he strangely mixes himself with nature. . . . But the instant
> he separates the image of possession from the tree and the potato field, and
> no longer says "my own"—it loses its piquancy. He presently sees that he
> also is but an instrument like the tree and in the same hands,—a reagent.
> The tree was to grow; he was to transplant and water it; not for him, not for
> it, but for all. (*EL*, III, 40)

The passage represents a critique of Locke's fundamental maxim that to mix
one's labor with nature is the origin of private property in two major respects.
First is the fact that, unlike Locke, Emerson argues that the "act of ownership,"
the mixing of man with nature, may be effected *either* through the laborious
planting of the tree *or* the strikingly unlaborious experience of joyfully seeing
the tree flourish, of pleasing himself with the idea of possession. Second, Emerson critiques the concept of privately owned labor when he describes the
moment at which a man comes to see that his labor and body are not solely
his, but rather that they also constitute a natural instrument, like a tree, that
contributes to a common as well as a private good. This beautiful continuity
between land, tree, and the laboring body has been concealed by the long-
standing, conventional significance of rights discourse—the habit of saying
"my own." By questioning the meaning of such lifeless, mindless speech acts—
a task that is central to his, and indeed any writer's, imaginative work—
Emerson alters our habits of thought about labor as the source of private
property: the laborer's body is pictured here as simultaneously maintaining its
boundaries and as completely merged with the natural world.[27]

Emerson's preoccupation with labor reflects a widespread interest in Jacksonian society and a radical streak of labor reform in antebellum culture and
politics. In nineteenth-century America, the word "labor" represented a broad
spectrum of producing classes: only speculators, bankers, and lawyers were
excluded from this category.[28] By the mid-1820s, pervasive interest led to the

formation of hundreds of new local labor organizations, and in the late 1820s, labor parties were distinct from and even in competition with political parties.[29] In "The Laboring Classes," published in 1840, Orestes Brownson examines the actual condition of the laboring classes "simply and exclusively in their capacity as laborers."[30] That same year, Albert Brisbane published a work titled *Social Destiny of Man; or Association and Re-organization of Industry*, in which he introduces Charles Fourier's model of the ideal society, which hinges upon the concept of "attractive labor."

> We assert, and we will prove, that Labour, which is now monotonous, repugnant and degrading, can be ennobled, elevated and made honourable;—or in other words, that INDUSTRY CAN BE RENDERED ATTRACTIVE! Attractive Industry is the first remedy to be applied to Social evils. . . . We assert, therefore, that the greatest and most important problem which can be proposed to Society . . . is a RE-ORGANIZATION OF INDUSTRY, or a reform in our whole system of Labour. It is here,—in the foundation of the Social edifice, that a reform should commence,—and not in the superstructure, in the administration or the political power.[31]

This glorification of labor was central to Republican ideology and contributed to emerging theories of the good society.

The centrality of labor in Emerson's writings shows his awareness of its usefulness in articulating an ideal model of political relations. In this respect, Emerson's intellectual interests reflect those taken up in works by nineteenth-century political economists. The dignity of labor as it was praised in antebellum culture and politics echoed the conclusions of political economists such as Henry Carey that "*Labour is . . . the sole cause of value.*"[32] In an 1836 treatise titled *Public and Private Economy*, Theodore Sedgwick set forth a critique that entailed the construction of a new category of labor—labor "for the mind"—that purportedly sanctified economy as a religious and moral science:

> There is still another distinction between man and the lower orders of beings, and this is the greatest of all, that he labours for the *mind* and thus while he is laying up treasures on earth he may also by a right use of them, "lay up treasures in heaven" also. Man labours for things that are beautiful to the eye and ear . . . ; he labours to lay up stores for benevolence, for chastity, for hospitality. . . . In proportion as he thinks little of . . . his *animal* appetites and much of his *intellectual*, in that degree is he truly economical man. . . .
>
> *This, then, is one of the great parts of the science of public and private economy; to point out what kind of industry, and what description of labor, is most useful, advantageous, and profitable to man.*[33]

Like Emerson, Sedgwick reveals a particular interest in the significance and function of property. For Sedgwick, the very possibility of intellectual independence may only be realized with the invention of a new idea of property. "Independence is secured by our property," he argues:

and to whom can this consideration be recommended with greater effect than to the American citizen? We have gained our political independence, but there is another, and that is independence of mind.... What a blessing it is, then, to be independent in our conduct and opinions, and not to be obliged to follow the multitude in their political follies.... How it narrows the mind,—what mental slavery it is! ... I mean to show that an immense amount of what people now work for is not property.[34]

In this attempt to reconstitute the meaning of terms in political economy, Sedgwick's project resembles Emerson's: like Emerson, Sedgwick insists that the science of economy must be renovated to meet the needs of an exceptional new world. Sedgwick writes, "Do the people of the United States desire to bring forth the magnificent riches which are to be found in the natural advantages of their country and free government? Then, both rich and poor, must first combine, discard their jealousies and feuds ... turn their backs upon the stupid fashions and follies imported by nearly every packet, and study the proper economy of their own country—this new world."[35]

Emerson's abiding interest in property and labor and much of the conceptual groundwork for his critique of liberalism and utopian model for political relations were inspired very early on in his intellectual life, when he read the works of the political philosopher William Paley as required reading at Harvard College. In a treatise titled *Moral and Political Philosophy*, first published in England in 1785, Paley describes and critiques Locke's concept of property and consent to social contract. The treatise includes an extended account of the history and uses of property and of Locke's famous analysis:

> Moralists have given many different accounts of [the origin of property]....
> [One] says, that each man's limbs and labour are his own exclusively; that, by occupying a piece of ground, a man inseparably mixes his labor with it; by which means the piece of ground becomes thenceforward his own, as you cannot take it from him without depriving him at the same time of something which is indisputably *his*.
> This is Mr. Locke's solution; and seems indeed a fair reason, where the value of the labour bears a considerable proportion to the value of the thing; or where the thing derives its chief use and value from the labor.[36]

Although he accepts the labor theory of value under certain conditions, Paley is also critical of Locke's formulation. And although he does not question the doctrine of property in persons in his argument against slavery, Paley does problematize the meaning of Locke's concept of property when applied to the appropriation and colonization of new-found lands:

> A parcel of unappropriated ground, which a man should pare, burn, plough, harrow, and sow, for the production of corn, would justly enough be thereby made his own. But this will hardly hold ... of taking a ceremonious possession of a tract of land, as navigators do of new discovered islands, by erecting a standard, engraving an inscription, or publishing a proclamation to the birds and beasts.... Nor will even the clearing, manuring, and ploughing of

> a field, give the first occupyier a right to it in perpetuity, and after the cultivation and all effects of it are ceased.[37]

At the same time that he acknowledges, in his discussion of Locke's social contract, the significance of the assembly, election, and construction of a legislature that resulted from revolution, Paley also resolutely maintains his critical stance. Pointing up the distinction between theory and practice, between Locke's political idea and the historical act of establishing the United States of North America, Paley argues that no contract was ever made or entered into in reality, although

> [s]ome imitation of a social compact may have taken place at a *revolution*. The present age has been a witness to a transaction which bears the nearest resemblance to this political idea, of any idea which history has preserved the account or memory: I refer to the establishment of the United States of North America. . . . Yet even here much was presupposed. In settling the constitution, many important parts were presumed to be already settled. The qualifications of the constituents who were admitted to vote . . . were taken from old forms of government. That was wanting, from which every social union should set off, and which alone makes the resolutions of society the act of the individual,—the unconstrained consent of all to be bound by the decision of the majority; and yet without this previous consent, the revolt, and the regulations which followed it, were compulsory upon dissentients.[38]

For Locke, the agreement to enter civil society creates no new individual rights; the right to private and unequal property is brought by men into civil society.[39] Property in one's own person is the primary condition for admission to civil society. Property renders consent to civil society meaningful because consent to the bonds of civil society occurs in exchange for its secure enjoyment. Without property, there can be no major cause for consent: "The great and *chief end* therefore, of Mens uniting into Commonwealths, and putting themselves under Government, *is the Preservation of their Property*" (*ST*, 350–351). The notion of an original social contract, as Locke develops it in his *Second Treatise*, suggests that some sign of consent, the consent of every individual concerned, is prerequisite to legitimate government. "And thus that, which begins and actually *constitutes any Political Society*, is nothing but the consent of any number of Freemen capable of a majority to unite and incorporate into such a Society," Locke writes. "And this is that, and that only, which did, or could give *beginning* to any *lawful Government* in the World" (*ST*, 333). By Paley's account, the consent that Locke clearly deemed essential to just social union was wanting. But although Paley's analysis demonstrates this historical lack, he says nothing that would indicate he had found the concept of consent itself to be problematic. In his discussion of Locke, Paley primarily offers a history of ideas and no critical political theory of his own.

At the beginning of this chapter, I observed that unlike Locke—for whom property facilitates the emergence of a public realm of politics—in the lecture "Home," Emerson defines property rights as extending even to the household, as marking the expression of a man's consent to be a guest in his own home. Here we see that, unlike Paley, Emerson offers a critique of Lockean concepts of property and consent, expressed in his strategic saturation of the political discourse of rights and representation with personal, everyday meanings. Later, when we come to a full consideration of Emerson's philosophy of political obligation, it will be argued that Emerson's critique of liberal concepts such as "social contract" and "consent" results in a description of political life and action that hovers somewhere in between public and private realms. The resulting vision of politics imagined in Emerson's writings—his belief that, to use a popular late-twentieth-century designation, the "personal is political"— is one that not only politicizes the private realm; it also dangerously privatizes the public vocabulary of politics. The potential hazards of such a position are evident in the fact that, for Emerson, worldly, political involvement may be regarded as a matter of sitting and reading at home.

Ultimately, as we shall see, this habitual blurring of the boundary between public and private realms in Emerson's thinking about ownership and political obligation has profound consequences for the development of twentieth-century African-American political philosophies of protest. But for the moment I simply want to raise the suggestion that Emerson's persistent emphasis on ownership and the individual's relation to material nature results in an innovative framework for thinking about the nature of political obligation: the enduring, related questions of contract and consent; the proper basis for thinking about political community; and the ties that bind an individual to the public realm of politics. The critique of property and theory of obligation unfolded in these early writings in turn contribute, in *Nature*, to the development of Emerson's rhetoric and conception of American national identity. To these related issues we now turn our attention.

In 1838, Emerson observed in his journal that "property is somehow intimately related to the properties of man, and so has a sacredness" (*JMN*, VII, 143). His first book, *Nature*, published two years earlier, traces out the full meaning and implications of such an expanded, sacred idea of property. In this work, Emerson develops an original account of the process of laborious appropriation that, for Locke, is the origin of private property in the natural world. Emerson writes, "To a man laboring under a calamity, the heat of his own fire hath sadness in it. Then, there is a kind of contempt of the landscape felt by him who has just lost by death a dear friend. The sky is less grand as it shuts down over less worth in the population" (*Essays*, 11).

At first glance, the suggestive image of a fire whose very heat is full of sadness would seem to designate a concept of property that is roughly analogous to Locke's: a hearth fire, after all, is a natural element that has been laboriously appropriated and removed from nature. But the labor Emerson describes here is not exactly the same as Locke's labor of the body. Although, like Locke, Emerson presents labor as situated deep in the body, intimately bound up with natural, necessary, domestic life processes, the innovative image of labor he renders in the opening pages of Nature is, oddly, that of a mood—the seemingly endless labor of grieving.⁴⁰ Just as in the 1838 lecture "Home" Emerson resorts to the Lockean vocabulary of property and contract to represent intimate domestic relations in the wake of family tragedy, so in this passage the use of quantitative, economic discourse—his account of a friend as "dear"; of the sky as "less grand," shutting down over "less worth in the population"—both represents and enacts the endless process of laboring under a calamity. This laboring, grieving man, Emerson tells us, is like a fire in a hearth: confined in a body whose boundaries distance him from nature, a body whose very life processes wordlessly and endlessly express sadness at the loss, through death, of a dear friend. The overall effect Emerson achieves in this example is to point up simultaneously the insufficiency and the necessity of economic discourse: at the same time he registers contempt for property in the landscape or the fragile human body that perishes, he also communicates his profound incapacity to describe the calamity of death in any other terms.

The centrality of grief—and thus of the constraints and expressive possibilities of economic discourse—to Emerson's project in Nature is immediately evident in his description of this project as one of "enumerating the values of nature and casting up their sum" (Essays, 8). The structure of Emerson's book itself registers his preoccupation with the question of whether, and how, an adequate account of the natural world may be derived from economic discourse: each section in the main body of the text describes a particular use of nature. "Whoever considers the final cause of the world, will discern a multitude of uses that enter as parts into that result," Emerson writes. "They all admit of being thrown into one of the following classes; Commodity; Beauty; Language; and Discipline" (Essays, 12).

The relationship between property, labor, and use is described by Locke in his Second Treatise. "Labour . . . puts the greatest part of Value upon Land," Locke. writes. " 'Tis to [labor] we owe the greatest part of all [Land's] useful Products" (ST, 298). For Locke, only property can be useful. The fact of use implies that an object has already been removed by labor from the natural state in which it once belonged to mankind in common. Although, like Locke, Emerson is interested in the connection between property, labor, and use, he arrives at a fundamentally different definition of these concepts in Nature. Whereas Locke's concept of use marks the existence of property because it can occur only after labor has already transformed nature into valuable, owned objects, Emerson's definition of use does not require that labor has already conferred a value upon natural objects by removing them from the State of Nature. Rather, he argues in Nature that much of what we call property is also natural. In "Commodity," he insists that "Nature, in its ministry to man, is not only the material, but is also the process and result" (Essays, 12).

The claim that property is natural in varying degrees is supported in Nature by Emerson's careful examination of a series of property relations. Each example of property held up for our scrutiny discloses its own subtle but crucial distinctiveness: in every instance, property is associated with a particular process of appropriation and use that is more or less laborious. The less laborious the process of appropriation and use, the closer the object comes to being unowned, held in common in the natural world. This tension between the laboriously appropriated and the natural, the owned and the unowned, registers the contradiction that is central to Emerson's critique of Lockean, liberal rights discourse.

One example of property that exhibits this tension or contradiction between the owned and the natural (or unowned) is defined by Emerson as beauty that is "an object of the intellect" (*Essays*, 18), whose production is associated with poetic experience and imagination.

> The charming landscape which I saw this morning, is indubitably made up of some twenty or thirty farms. Miller owns this field, Locke that, and Manning the woodland beyond. But none of them owns the landscape. There is a property in the horizon which no man has but he whose eye can integrate all the parts, that is, the poet. This is the best part of these men's farms, yet to this their warranty-deeds give no title. (*Essays*, 9)

The passage is striking if we credit Emerson as being aware of Locke's various definitions of property. Locke used the term broadly to refer to "Men's Lives, Liberties and Estates," and to mean "that Property which Men have in their Persons as well as Goods," or he used the term narrowly in the more usual sense of lands and goods (*ST*, 102). The description of poetic property in *Nature* transforms the literal meaning of land in Locke's claim in the *Second Treatise* that "full as the World seems," a man may still find enough and as good land in "some in-land, vacant places of America" (*ST*, 293).[41] The passage juxtaposes the concept of owned land as it was perceived in Jacksonian society with an alternative idea of "property in the horizon," of property in the perpetually unfolding possibility that the American frontier represents.

The habitual, close association of property with vision recurs throughout Emerson's writings. For example, in the 1837 lecture series "Human Culture," Emerson explicitly identifies what he calls "spiritual property" with insight or the labor of seeing:

> He learns that above the merely external rights to the picture, to the park, to the equipage, rights which the law protects,—is a spiritual property which is Insight. The kingdom of the soul transcendeth all the walls and muniments of possession and taketh higher rights not only in the possession but in the possessor, and with this royal reservation, can very well afford to leave the so-called proprietor undisturbed as its keeper or trustee. (*EL*, II, 223)

In 1839 he noted that "[i]t is a noble fact that Heeven refers in his 'Greece,' that in that country every statue & painting was public, it being considered as absurd & profane to pretend a property in a Work of Art,—which belonged to whosoever could see it" (*JMN*, VII, 310), a journal entry that was later

written into the 1860 essay "Wealth": "In Greek cities, it was reckoned profane, that any person should pretend a property in a work of art, which belonged to all who could behold it" (*Essays*, 996). In *Nature*, the labor of the
poet's eye, which integrates all the parts of the landscape, is the origin of
poetic property. The primary difference between Lockean and this poetic form
of labor is, for Emerson, evidenced by the fact that "you cannot freely admire
a noble landscape, if laborers are digging in the field hard by. The poet finds
something ridiculous in his delight, until he is out of the sight of men" (*Essays*,
42).

If possessing a farm in Locke's terms is a model for understanding laws
such as the relation between man and nature, one question that arises is
whether Emersonian property in the horizon differs significantly from material
possession. Property in the horizon resembles Lockean private property insofar
as it is not communal. But the most visible difference between these two
theories of property is the fact that for Emerson the production of such poetic
property is not solely the result of the active process of laborious appropriation.
Although he observes that beauty in nature "seems partly owing to the eye
itself" (*Essays*, 14), Emerson does not describe the process of producing a work
of art as one in which the mind alone actively labors.[42] He observes, "The
beauty of nature reforms itself in the mind. . . . Thus in art, does nature work
through the will of a man filled with the beauty of her first works" (*Essays*,
18, 19). Such natural beauty is presented to, and not created by, the attentive
eye: "To the attentive eye, each moment of the year has *its own* beauty, and
in the same field, it beholds, every hour, a picture which was never seen before,
and which shall never be seen again. The heavens change every moment, and
reflect *their* glory or gloom on the plains beneath" (*Essays*, 15; emphasis
added). For Emerson, these ephemeral phenomena, which express no human
attribute or emotion, belong only to nature itself. "The beauty that shimmers
in the yellow afternoons of October, who ever could clutch it?" (*Essays*, 16).
By Emerson's account, poetic property exhibits a contradiction between the
owned and the unowned or natural that distinguishes it from the concept of
private property elaborated in Locke's *Second Treatise*: such property is both
privately owned and as unowned as any other aspect of the natural world.

Property in the beauty of natural forms, as defined in *Nature*, is analogous
to another form of property referred to by Emerson as "commodity." In a
chapter titled "Commodity," Emerson insists that a commodity is a low form
of use, for the simple reason that it does not entail human labor. We have
seen that for Emerson property is natural in varying degrees, and that the less
laborious process of appropriation and use creates a form of property that
comes closer to being an object in nature, given by God to all men in common. Commodity, in this sense, is completely natural, and not privately
produced or possessed at all. Rather, the existence of commodities is a manifestation of what Emerson identifies as a "divine charity" whose "endless
circulations . . . nourish man" (*Essays*, 12). Whereas Locke sees human agency
as being at the origin of property, at the moment when "[h]is labour hath

taken it out of the hands of nature, where it was common . . . , and hath
thereby appropriated to himself" (*ST*, 289), Emerson describes the creation of
commodities as a process in which "[a]ll the parts [of nature] incessantly work
into each other's hands for the profit of man" (*Essays*, 12). Because commodities represent a "mercenary benefit" that nature works to give charitably to
man, and are not themselves the product or sign of human labor, they are
valuable only with reference to what Emerson describes as a "farther good":
"A man is fed," he insists, "not that he may be fed, but that he may work"
(*Essays*, 13).

Generally speaking, Emerson regards both Lockean property (spelled with
a capital P) and commodity as models of instruction to be used in disciplining
the understanding in intellectual truths. In the chapter "Discipline," he points
out the educative function of property, arguing that "[t]he . . . good office . . .
performed by Property and its filial systems of debt and credit" is the same as
the office performed by nature, namely,

> the discipline of the understanding in intellectual truths. Debt, grinding debt,
> whose iron face the widow, the orphan, and the sons of genius fear and hate;
> —debt, which consumes so much time, which so cripples and disheartens a
> great spirit with cares that seem so base, is a preceptor whose lessons cannot
> be forgone, and is needed most by those who suffer from it most. . . . Whilst
> now it is the gymnastics of the understanding, it is hiving in the foresight
> of the spirit, experience in profounder laws. (*Essays*, 26–27)

Similarly, Emerson writes of commodity that "[a]lthough low, it is perfect in
its kind, and is the only use of nature which all men apprehend. . . . The use
of commodity, regarded by itself, is mean and squalid. But it is to the mind
an education in the doctrine of Use, namely that a thing is good only so far
as it serves that a conspiring of parts and efforts to the production of an end,
is essential to any being. The first and gross manifestation of this truth, is our
inevitable and hated training in values and wants, in corn and meat" (*Essays*,
12, 29). Commodity, like Locke's concept of property, is thus useful as a model
that Emerson uses to describe other forms of property in *Nature*. Emerson refers
to commodity and Lockean property in order to demonstrate their necessity
and insufficiency as expressions for the relation between the individual and
the natural world.[43]

The contradictory invocation and denial of property in the natural world
that characterizes other forms of property in *Nature* also structures Emerson's
thinking about self-ownership. In his introduction, Emerson equates the body
with nature: "Strictly speaking, therefore, all that is separate from us, all which
Philosophy distinguishes as the NOT ME, that is, both nature and art, all other
men and my own body, must be ranked under this name, NATURE" (*Essays*,
8). The act of establishing a right to property in nature is accounted for as
the origin of self-ownership: Emerson does not do away with the idea of self-
possession, but rather assesses the possibilities for what he refers to in "The
School" as a "higher self-possession" than that which Locke envisioned:

In all conversation between two persons, tacit reference is made as to a third
party, to a common nature. That third party or common nature is not social;
it is impersonal; is God. And so in groups wherever debate is earnest and
especially on great questions of thought the company become aware of their
unity; that the thought rises to an equal height in all bosoms, that all have
a spiritual property in what was said as well as the sayer. They all wax wiser
than they were. . . . All are conscious of attaining to a higher self-possession.
(*Essays*, 43)[44]

In *Nature*, Locke's laborious process of appropriation is transformed by
Emerson into a process of making the self, of filling its boundaries by taking
up the world into himself, a process completed not through labor of the body,
but rather through the energy of thought and will. This act of taking up the
world into the self entails a new, expanded meaning for labor. A central
example from *Nature* in which Emerson explores the process of appropriating
a self, the establishment of bodily boundaries that enclose the self-owning
subject from the common, may be found in this most famous of passages. The
theory of property that is the basis for Emerson's model of the self derives
from the question of whether and how the private and beholding eyeball,
synechdochical of the body, may also be collectively owned.

Crossing a bare common, in snow puddles, at twilight, under a clouded sky,
without having in my thoughts any occurrence of special good fortune, I
have enjoyed a perfect exhilaration. I am glad to the brink of fear. In the
woods, too, a man casts off his years, as the snake his slough, and at what
period soever of life, is always a child. In the woods, is perpetual youth.
Within these plantations of God, a decorum and sanctity reign, a perennial
festival is dressed, and the guest sees not how he should tire of them in a
thousand years. In the woods, we return to reason and faith. There I feel
that nothing can befall me in life,—no disgrace, no calamity (leaving me
my eyes), which nature cannot repair. Standing on the bare ground,—my
head bathed by the blithe air, and uplifted into infinite space,—all mean
egotism vanishes. I become a transparent eyeball; I am nothing; I see all: the
currents of the Universal Being circulate through me; I am part or particle
of God. The name of the nearest friend sounds then foreign and accidental:
to be brothers, to be acquaintances,—master or servant, is then a trouble
and a disturbance. I am the lover of uncontained and immortal beauty. In
the wilderness, I find something more dear and connate than in streets and
villages. In the tranquil landscape, and especially in the distant line of the
horizon, man beholds somewhat as beautiful as his own nature. (*Essays*, 10)

In "Democratic Individuality and the Claims of Politics," George Kateb
argues that this passage promotes an end to sociality because it is an example
of the abandonment of what he labels "positive individuality," or the self-
owning, "autonomous person of one's own creating."[45] Kateb labels this new
mode of existence "impersonal individuality," which he defines as "something
beyond individuality or personality or character or even individuation."[46] In
his insistence that the movement in the passage is beyond individuation, be-

yond the social, Kateb places himself within the ranks of the many critics who read the passage as a moment of spiritual transcendence of the material world. What is unique about Kateb's analysis, however, is that he describes the passage as problematic for those who are specifically interested in the issue of self-ownership.

> It may even be that our fuller analysis would find that the accompaniment of positive individuality is such a solemn self-possession that it impedes the growth into impersonal individuality. If the Emersonians do not emphasize the ultimate incompatibility between positive and impersonal individuality, we may. But these writers certainly incline this way. The preference for impersonal individuality over positive individuality would be, in sum, a preference for consciousness over action, for the indefinite over the social . . . , for the true over the fictional.[47]

For Kateb, the difference or incompatibility between these two modes of individuality, the self-possessed and the impersonal, is ultimately done away with by Emerson's preference for the impersonal. As a result, Kateb argues, Emerson prefers consciousness over action.

The possibility of preference for one of two possible modes of individuality, the possibility of a choice between having a self and not having a self, is not in keeping with what I have documented as being the central contradiction in Emerson's theory of property. In Emerson's *Nature*, it is the theory of property (or society, or the individual) he presents that structures his embodied response to the natural world. In the transparent eyeball passage, the moment of appropriating the self is represented as a moment of conversion or spiritual rebirth cast in Emerson's terms. As we shall see in the next chapter, Emerson writes in a tradition of Protestant emblem poets that celebrates infant innocence and vision as a means of experiencing the bliss of eternity. In these poems, the speaker experiences the universe as a disembodied eye, traditionally an emblem of vision focused on heavenly things without the debased mediation of the body.[48] Emerson, however, describes his spiritual state by deploying the image of an actual body part, the eyeball, not simply the more traditional and abstract term "eye." In fact, what is striking about Emerson's image of the transcendent subject, as Christopher Cranch's famous caricature attests, is that it is startlingly, oddly embodied; so much so, that we recognize an eyeball standing barefoot on the common, wearing a hat and suit, as specifically parodic of the Emersonian subject. The parenthetical statement "leaving me my eyes" suggests that even when calamity befalls him—such as we have seen in the 1838 lecture "Home"—the Emersonian guest represents a model of "nearness" to nature and society. Even when the name of the nearest friend sounds foreign and accidental, the infinitesimally thin membrane that envelopes his eye, left to him as property, opens the possibility of representation in the public realm of politics.

The contradiction inherent in such an embodied imagination of the disembodied subject in *Nature*, like the contradiction inherent in the act of saying "I am nothing," is a deliberate and crucial feature of Emerson's thinking about self-ownership.[49] I have said that Emerson does not do away with the idea of self-possession but rather that he assesses the possibilities for a higher form of self-possession than that which Locke envisioned in his description of persons as being possessed of the labor of their bodies. That Emerson constructs a *higher* form of self-possession suggests that his critique inheres in the act of discarding a particular formulation of Lockean ideals while at the same time reaffirming his commitment to those ideals. That "all mean egotism vanishes" does not imply that all egotism vanishes; simply the concept of egotism that existed before Emerson's rediscovery of the term. Although Emerson aspires to universality (and thus to transparency) in his construction of an ideal self in this passage, he also refuses to relinquish particular attributes that characterize this self as unique. In contrast to Locke, whose reference to "Every Man" invokes a relatively abstract and almost allegorical subject, Emerson's vivid description of the self as an eyeball simultaneously raises and obscures the question of its own embodiment.[50]

It is significant that for Emerson the experience of appropriation simultaneously describes a process and something that happens all at once. On the one hand, the statement "I become a transparent eyeball" describes the process of becoming a transparent eyeball, of taking up the world into the self. On the other hand, conversion in this passage is not simply a process by which Emerson gradually fills the membranous boundaries of his being. Rather, his conversion is also something that happens all at once; the newly born self is also something that was there already. In *Nature*, Emerson writes that "the best read naturalist who lends an entire and devout attention to truth, will see that there remains much to learn of his relation to the world, and that it is not to be learned by any addition or subtraction or other comparison of known quantities, but is arrived at by untaught sallies of the spirit, by a continual self-recovery" (*Essays*, 43). At the same time that his insistence on the process of continual self-recovery implies that the self is not durable and that it continually changes, it also implies that the self endures precisely because it can be recovered. The theory of an enduring subject is also expressed in Emerson's claim that his relation to the world is arrived at by untaught sallies of the spirit, which suggests that the self is not made or raised in the imagination as an architect makes and plans, but rather that it is arrived at as something there already. Emersonian conversion is experienced not only as a process of making and becoming; it also happens all at once.[51] This and other important features in Emerson's version of a higher self-possession figured as conversion in *Nature* recur in later work.[52]

The peculiar form of labor used to build and discover the self in *Nature* is one that fits well with the contradictory logic Emerson uses in thinking about self-ownership. For Locke, labor produces the least durable of things, things needed for the life process itself: "The Fruit, or Venison, which nourishes the wild Indian, who knows no Inclosure, and is still a Tenant in common, must be his, and so his, i.e. a part of him, that another can no longer have any right to it, before it can do him any good for the support of his Life" (*ST*, 287). In *The Human Condition*, Hannah Arendt offers this description of Locke's conception of labor:

> Whatever labor produces is meant to be fed into the human life process almost immediately, and this consumption, regenerating the life process, produces—or rather, reproduces—new "labor power," needed for the further sustenance of the body. From the viewpoint of the exigencies of the life process itself, the "necessity of subsisting," as Locke put it, laboring and consuming follow each other so closely that they almost constitute one and the same movement, which is hardly ended when it must be started all over again. The "necessity of subsisting" rules over both labor and consumption, and labor, when it incorporates, "gathers," and bodily "mixes with" the things provided by nature, does actively what the body does even more intimately when it consumes its nourishment.[53]

Emerson's vivid imagining of the self as a transparent eyeball provides ample illustration of the fact that the process of becoming is not laborious in Locke's sense of the word: the continually recovered self is simultaneously the least durable and the most durable of possessions.[54] Private property includes only that which endures; the rest belongs to nature, held by all men in common. The contradictory invocation and denial of private property that characterizes Emerson's thought is, as we might expect, also present in his model of the self-owning subject in *Nature*: the self is both made (that is, owned) and found (that is, unowned, natural). Emerson identifies the labor of appropriation both in gathering and in the heroic act of finding: in the wilderness, he tells us, he finds something more dear and connate than in streets and villages.[55]

The wilderness also functions as a theoretical construct in Emerson's account of the origins of society and the self, and roughly corresponds to Locke's quasi historical State of Nature. The original act of constituting society, in Emerson's terms, is actually an act of recovery; thus social contract is something that has been both made and arrived at. The social contract is arrived at insofar as Emerson's withdrawal into the wilderness makes visible the streets and villages, and the fact of his having already consented to the society and social evil from which he withdraws. The social contract is made insofar as Emerson constructs a new framework for thinking about political community and the problem of obligation. Emerson describes the intimate web of obligations he experiences in the wilderness by using two words: "dear" and "connate." Whereas "connate" implies a relationship of consanguinity and identification, "dear" expresses a bond that is simultaneously economic and sentimental, as if the language of property were both necessary and insufficient to account for experience of so near a relation.

It should probably strike us as odd that the conceptual basis for Emerson's theory of political community occurs to him in a moment of total isolation, crossing the bare common, when the only relationships under examination are proprietary claims he has on his own body and the natural world, not on other persons. For Emerson, the very act of beholding nature establishes property in nature, making nature "his own": "In the tranquil landscape . . . man beholds somewhat as beautiful as his own nature." Beholding, in turn, opens the possibility of the subject's being beholden—that is, seen, indebted, owned. In *Nature*, Emerson asks, "Is not the landscape, every glimpse of which hath a grandeur, a face of him?" (*Essays*, 42). Beholding the face of a nature that is as beautiful as his own, a man comes to behold—that is, to possess—his own face, his own body, his own nature. The reflexive relationship of beholding establishes a self-evident right to self-ownership.

The foregoing analysis suggests that Emerson's analysis of property accounts for various degrees of naturalness in property and thus that property in *Nature* exhibits a tension between the natural or common and the privately owned—the same contradictory invocation and denial of property that occurs, as we have seen, throughout Emerson's early writings. This contradiction within the meaning of property is nowhere more clearly delineated than in Emerson's analysis of a form of property that is neither commodity nor the beauty of natural or artistic forms nor property in one's own person, but rather property that results from a heroic, beautiful action, "beauty . . . which is found in combination with the human will" (*Essays*, 16).[56] In contrast to Locke, who argues that labor combines with nature to create property, in *Nature* Emerson describes will as a source of a beautiful, natural action that is the origin of property: "Every natural action is graceful. Every heroic act is also decent, and causes the place and the bystanders to shine. We are taught by great actions that the universe is the property of every individual in it. Every rational creature has all nature for his dowry and estate. It is his, if he will. . . . In proportion to the energy of his thought and will, he takes up the world into himself" (*Essays*, 16). This natural, graceful action of a heroic figure "entitled to the world by his constitution" (*Essays*, 16) simultaneously celebrates possibilities that are democratically extended to every individual and represents a monarchical, divinely mandated act of appropriation. The fact that Emerson locates and preserves this divine mandate within democratic theory is an important feature of his critique of Locke's refutation of patriarchalism and account of appropriation as effecting the entire removal of property from nature. In contrast to Locke, Emerson offers up a theory of property in which natural phenomena are transformed by the natural act of heroism into artifacts and possessions that nonetheless also remain a part of nature, beyond the realm of privately possessed and thus sordid objects. He writes, "In private places, among sordid objects, an act of truth or heroism seems at once to draw to itself the sky as its temple, the sun as its candle" (*Essays*, 17). In this sense, natural, beautiful action naturalizes—that is, it both consecrates and dismantles—Locke's concept of property.

The critique of Lockean, liberal property rights discourse embedded in

Emerson's description of heroic acts in *Nature* points up the connection between, on the one hand, Emerson's deliberations over the significance of ownership for thinking about individual identity, and, on the other hand, his attempt to show how "representative" acts of heroism or genius contribute to the formation of political community. One year after the publication of *Nature*, in the lecture "Society," he observed that

> [t]he greatest genius is he in whom all other men own the presence of a larger portion of their common nature than is in them. And this I believe is the secret of the joy which genius gives us. Whatever men of genius say, becomes forthwith the common property of all. Why? because the man of genius apprises us not so much of his wealth as of the commonwealth. Are his thoughts profound? so much the less are they his; so much more the property of all. Are his illustrations happy? so feel we does not *his* mind, but *the* Mind illustrate its thoughts. A sort of higher patriotism warms us as if one should say, "That's the way they do things in my country." (*EL*, II, 99)

This notion that a particular vision of the self may be regarded as constitutive of community is, as we saw in the previous chapter, most fully developed in *Representative Men*. But even as early as 1836, Emerson was well aware of the political logic of contradiction in all its aspects—its significance for his critique of Lockean rights discourse and theory of the "representative" as well as his development of a coherent, effective nationalist vision and rhetoric. In *Nature*, this logic is revealed to us full-blown in a vivid and disturbing passage, which depicts Columbus's appropriation of the New World:

> When a noble act is done,—perchance in a scene of great natural beauty . . . are not these heroes entitled to add the beauty of the scene to the beauty of the deed? When the bark of Columbus nears the shore of America;—before it, the beach lined with savages, fleeing out of their huts of cane; the sea behind; and the purple mountains of the Indian Archipelago around, can we separate the man from the living picture? Does not the New World clothe his form with her palm-groves and savannahs as fit drapery? (*Essays*, 16, 17)

The critique of Locke articulated in this passage hinges upon what by now should be a familiar contradiction between owning and not owning. Just as in his journal Emerson explores a meaning for property that simultaneously opens the possibility of limitless appropriation (even the sea and stars) *and* threatens the right to ownership of his own body, so, here, he asks whether we can "separate the man from the living picture," a rhetorical question that works simultaneously to affirm the integrity of Columbus's bodily boundaries *and* to dissolve those boundaries, rendering Columbus inseparable from the living picture he appropriates. Emerson's critique of Locke's refutation of patriarchalism hinges on this self-contradictory description of Columbus's inheritance of America: although the act of imperialist appropriation occurs in a setting not unlike Locke's State of Nature, Columbus's claim to America has not been labored for in Locke's terms, because such a right to property must also be arrived at or found. The contention that Columbus is inseparable from the living picture he beholds naturalizes the act of imperialist expansion, because possession of the New World has thereby been depicted and justified as the self-evidently rightful possession of the body.

What is most important and disturbing to notice is the way in which Emerson strategically enlists racialist discourse in this passage: the contradiction between owning and not owning that is central to his critique of Locke has been here put forward as a contradiction between a rights-based and a racialist vision of the American self. Emerson's racist rendering of "savages" registers this enlistment of nineteenth-century, scientific, Anglo-Saxonist discourse to represent Columbus's self-evident, natural superiority over the pre-Columbian inhabitants and possessors who flee their huts of cane. The image suggests that Columbus's divinely mandated, monarchical right to property in the New World's fit drapery works against Emerson's democratic claim that the universe is the property of every person in it.[57]

The obvious, gross incompatibility between, on the one hand, Emerson's racist depiction of "savages" whose Lockean rights to property are violated and, on the other hand, his claim that the rights Columbus bears are democratically extended to every man dramatizes the imaginative and psychological pressures exerted by this contradictory logic, which force Emerson to negotiate a tense, tenuous, rhetorical settlement between his democratic, antislavery convictions and his racial nationalism, between what is most and least democratic about his political thought. The same rhetoric of contradiction that is central to Emerson's critical recuperation of democratic ideals in the early writings also functions to justify a violent, imperialist, nationalist act of expansion. At the same time that this aversive gesture of critique situates Emerson at the brink of egocentric absolutism and enacts a disavowal of democratic society, it also presents an open invitation for Emerson's return, or renewed aspiration to, democracy.[58] Only a state of aversion that represented a perpetual flight from and return to property and the body, only a method of argument that exhibited the two poles of Emerson's thought, could express such a contradictory relation between the conflicting claims of rights and racialist consanguinity.[59]

Louis Hartz once observed that the basic ethical problem presented by liberal society is not "the danger of the majority which has been its conscious fear, but the danger of unanimity, which has slumbered unconsciously behind it."[60] My interest here is in Emerson's deployment of the logic of contradiction as a deliberate engineering of unanimity—a critique of ownership that enlists a rhetoric of racialism and a symbology of feudalism that Hartz fails to account for in his important and now classic assessment of American liberalism.[61] In the previous chapter, I tried to show how the concept of "the representative" expresses a particular vision of the public realm, and that it simultaneously instates and erases boundaries that exist, not between the self and the material world, but rather between the self and other persons. I want to conclude this chapter with the suggestion, to be elaborated at a later point, that Emerson's depiction of Columbus as a "representative" self forms the basis for a concept of identity that is specifically national.

The erasure of individuality implicit in the idea of "the representative" in *Nature*—a phenomenon that Emerson did not describe in explicit, theoretical terms until more than a decade later in *Representative Men*—makes visible the imaginative effects of that quintessentially American taboo, the age-old nightmare of miscegenation. The effect of this prohibition in *Nature* is to restore a precarious symbolic order that reverberates with self-contradictory political meanings. Emerson's racist invocation of difference—his deliberate exclusion of "savages" from the public, political space of representation, the new nation symbolized by Columbus—is an act of mimesis that simultaneously endorses and enacts the exclusions built into the formula for political representation arrived at by the framers of the Constitution. In *Nature* and, as we shall see, throughout Emerson's writings, contradiction produces an effective rhetoric and conceptual framework for cohesion that is both democratic and racist; a nation that is simultaneously depicted as quintessentially democratic, infinitely permeable, and expansive, and as patently exclusive and homogenous: as irreducibly white and male as Columbus's body.[62]

We now arrive at the compelling logic of contradiction in Emerson's writings: the same, repeated affirmation of rights to sacred property that works to promote nationalist, racist exclusions from political representation also invites the possibility of a more perfectly democratic public realm.

THREE

The Poetics of Contradiction

Religious and Political Emblems in "The American Scholar"

Technology discloses man's mode of dealing with Nature," wrote Marx, "the process of production by which he sustains his life, and thereby also lays bare the mode of formation of his social relations, and of the mental conceptions that flow from them. Every history of religion . . . that fails to take account of this material basis, is uncritical." A truly scientific description of material culture should not simply discover, by analysis, "the earthly core of the misty creations of religion." Instead, Marx prescribes that we systematically deduce the connection between our various modes of association and the content of our religious beliefs—the development, as he puts it, "from the actual relations of life the corresponding celestialised forms of those relations."[1]

Unlike Marx's writings, which highlight this insistent secularism, Emerson's political philosophy exhibits an intimate but not uncritical engagement with religious language and ideals. Having traced out the political logic of Emerson's thinking about identity and ownership, we are now in a position to see that Emerson's method of contradiction in early works such as *Nature* is fundamentally different from that to be found either in Christian gospel or in Marxism. The contradiction that lies at the heart of Emerson's political critique is a contradiction between what Cornel West calls "human nature" and "human practice": like the Christian, Emerson affirms the existence of natural attributes (such as the depravity or dignity of persons), but his historicism also resembles the historicism posited by Marxism insofar as Emerson affirms both the material contingency and the inevitable perfectability of the human.[2]

Part II of this book will investigate the major conceptual ramifications of Emerson's adaptation of religious terms to his task of writing political philosophy. There we shall see that his juxtaposition of existing, contradictory liberal and religious discourses on obligation situate these discourses in a novel relationship of mutual supplementarity and critique. At the same time that Emerson affirms the importance of friendship or race as a basis for representing political ties that are born into or found as already existing, he also affirms the conceptual necessity of Lockean, contractual obligations that are creatively and voluntarily assumed by acts of rational consent. Although Emerson's enlistment of religious discourse is in keeping with writings by other American reformers of his day,[3] his manipulation of this discourse is distinctive insofar as the deliberate juxtaposition of religious concepts with more traditionally political, Lockean concepts that we find throughout his writings underscores their necessity and insufficiency as vehicles for his utopianism. The resulting self-contradictory model of political identity and obligation Emerson arrives at is one he designates as "double-consciousness."

The larger political and cultural significance of Emerson's enlistment of religious discourse will be most evident in Part III, in which we consider his availability to subsequent critiques undertaken by twentieth-century African-American philosophers. For the moment, however, I propose to broaden our understanding of Emerson's recuperation of Christian concepts by pointing out two important, previously unexamined literary, religious, and popular iconographical traditions that profoundly shaped his critical method of contradiction. The following chapter will show that in his early writings Emerson invented a constellation of emblems that register his grappling with the related questions of ownership and political community, as well as the significance of scholarly labor, the role of the intellectual, in the improvement of public life. By reconstructing the cultural history of Emerson's emblematics, I will call attention to his strategic mediation between two distinct and related iconographical resources. On the one hand, Emerson recognized the applicability of a seventeenth-century tradition in Protestant poetics and iconography, which emerged in a popularized form during the nineteenth century, for the expression of his utopian vision. On the other hand, he also drew from a proto-nationalist, secular emblematics that was associated both with American Freemasonry and with the development of patriotic symbols during the revolutionary era. As a result of his negotiation between these two traditions, the emblematics we find in works such as "The American Scholar" discloses the interpenetration of liberal and religious meanings; the invasion of politics into what Protestant poets conceived of as the essentially private act of constructing a relationship between the self and God. The critique of religion and property Emerson puts forward in this 1837 address is thus strikingly different from, but no less systematic than, the critique Marx would develop some thirty years later.

The Protestant emblem poem is a literary kind invented in the seventeenth century whose genealogy can be traced back at least to Andrea Alciati's *Emblemata* of 1531.[4] An emblem poem comprises elements that call attention to the poem's materiality because they are both seen and read: a picture, a motto, and a poem. Each poem represents an inextricable relation between words and things, and each element of the poem, the read and the seen, functions to explicate or illuminate the other. Whereas the picture in an emblem poem is generally referred to as its "body," the verbal elements that explicate the body and are explicated by it are called the "soul." In sacred-emblem books, the meaning of an emblem poem inheres in the relationship among the body of the emblem, the poem, and the rhetorical conceit that appears in its motto. As the well-known emblematist Francis Quarles remarked to the reader in his preface to *Emblems*, published in 1635, this rhetorical conceit is not the product of human wit but is rather the true wit of God's word. It is an important characteristic of emblems that their meanings are arrived at or found, and not made: "An Emblem is but a silent parable," Quarles writes. "Let not the tender eye check, to see the allusion to our blessed SAVIOR figured in these types."[5] Whereas the verbal element in an emblem poem represents the fallen, laboriously narrative aspects of human existence, the pictorial element represents aspects that are ideal and spiritual, each image calling our attention to some declaration of God's will, expressed in correspondence with a natural fact. Together these elements enact the drama of salvation.

George Herbert's emblem poem "The Altar" is called a "shaped" poem because it exhibits its writing, which takes the form of an altar, as a picture to be seen as well as read:

> A broken ALTAR, Lord, thy servant rears,
> Made of a heart, and cemented with tears:
> Whose parts are as thy hand did frame;
> No workman's tool hath touched the same.
> A HEART alone
> Is such a stone,
> As nothing but
> Thy pow'r doth cut.
> Wherefore each part
> Of my hard heart
> Meets in this frame,
> To praise thy Name:
> That, if I chance to hold my peace,
> These stones to praise thee may not cease.
> O let thy blessed SACRIFICE be mine,
> And sanctify this ALTAR to be thine.[6]

Herbert's poem represents a humanly imperfect effort on the part of the speaker to lie perfectly still and wait for a gift of salvation from God. The generic form of the emblem poem itself is one that allows Herbert to explore the features and expressive possibilities of this receptive position and to convey two fundamental facts about the relationship between the self and God.[7] First, any effort to be perfectly receptive and thus to merit or earn God's grace is itself a form of rebellion. Even the initiating, verbal act of offering up the self to God is a rebellious deed, because in so doing God's servant (or broken altar) rears up and declares his distance from the divine master.

Herbert dramatizes the inherently rebellious nature of such a poetic as-sertion of personhood by emphasizing his poem's narrativity—the fact that his rendering of the self coheres only through the work of our human understand-ing. When we read through the poem, the speaker describes himself as trapped in a fallen, hardened state; bound up by the inescapable logic of language. His heart is a solitary stone that will be creatively cut and shaped into a beautiful, poetic, loving expression of praise only by God's powerful will: "Wherefore each part/ Of my hard heart/Meets in this frame,/ To praise thy Name" (ll. 9–12). If, however, we stop reading and only see the poem, we free the speaker from this narrative prison, allowing him to "hold [his] peace" (l. 13). Viewed in these terms, "The Altar" coheres both as a logical and as a visual unity.

The contradiction between the read and the seen exhibited in Herbert's poem registers a second crucial fact about the relationship between the self and God: namely, that although the state of grace is clearly preferable to a fallen state, the structure of the emblem poem as a whole also affirms the value of the fallen and the human. Only the relationship between the poem's verbal and visual elements, and neither element alone, expresses the Christian premise that an individual must fall in order to be saved and that "grace" has meaning for us only as it stands in relation to a concept of difference from God.

The value of the fallen self is an idea that is central to many Protestant emblem poems, such as Christopher Harvey's "Sacrifice of the Heart." The concluding lines of Harvey's poem, written fourteen years after Herbert's "The Altar," disclose Harvey's formal, conceptual, and stylistic indebtedness to Her-bert: "LORD, be my altar, sanctify/Mine heart thy sacrifice." Like Herbert's "The Altar," Harvey's poem specifically deals with the sacrament of the Lord's Supper, a sacrament that reveals the immanence of God in a fallen, material world. Both poems explore the meaning of salvation, of Christ's sacrifice for man's sin, as a gift of infinite price. Both poems are in the tradition of emblem books representing "schools of the heart," a tradition in which the humble heart is represented as undergoing purgation from sin and sanctification by God as a fit sacrifice before receiving the gift of grace (figure 3.1). And in both poems, the speaker simultaneously describes and enacts a "sacrifice of praise" in which the heart that was God's in the first place is once again given back to God.

What is most important to notice is that in both Harvey's and Herbert's poetry—and, indeed, in any Protestant emblem poem that represents a sac-rifice of the heart—the language of possession takes on the burden of express-ing its own necessity and insufficiency. If receiving God's gift is a sacrifice of the self, it is a sacrifice of a peculiar kind, because a heart given by God that

The representation of a sanctified heart with whom
the Father, Son, and Holy Spirit have made their
abode .

Figure 3.1. Emblem of a "Sanctified Heart." From Peter Bauder,
The Spiritual Mirror, or Looking Glass (Newburyport, Mass., 1844).
Courtesy Harvard College Library.

is given back to God is not a meaningful form of sacrifice. Although in absolute terms grace is God's gift, the only way of thinking about salvation that
is logically comprehensible to us is as an economic exchange in which salvation has been labored for and earned. The self must exist before its selfhood
or difference from God can be sacrificed.

The poetics of contradiction we find at work in Protestant emblem poems precisely enacts this peculiar sacrifice of praise. In Herbert's and Harvey's poems, the speaker constructs a fallen, declarative, narrative rendering of the self in order to make the difference between the fallen and saved self, the before-and-after stages of conversion, comprehensible. A poem that lacked this narrative of a self-owning subject and retained only the pictorial element of the emblem poem could not be a poem about sacrifice, or about anything else.

There is little evidence that any emblem books such as Francis Quarles's *Emblems* (1635), Geoffrey Whitney's *A Choice of Emblems and Other Devises* (1586), or Christopher Harvey's *School of the Heart* (1647) ever reached New England during the seventeenth century. However, there are strong indications that the emblems themselves were familiar to New Englanders because they were incised, carved, or otherwise transmitted on colonial silverwork, stonemasons' work, and wood engravings.[8] The iconographic vocabulary used in the *New England Primer* educated Massachusetts Puritans to think of the world in emblematic terms. The visual vocabulary of the emblem tradition deeply influenced the poetry of Edward Taylor and exerted a vigorous iconographical influence well into the nineteenth century, when it is known to have been used by writers such as Poe and Dickinson.[9]

Emblems also appeared in popular literature that pervaded nineteenth-century American culture. The influence of this emblem tradition was so strong that in 1836, a year before Emerson delivered "The American Scholar," poems by Francis Quarles were included for publication in a popular gift book titled *The Book of Gems: The Poets and Artists of Great Britain*. Emblems contained in James Thurston's *Religious Emblems*, first published in London in 1810, reappeared twenty-eight years later in an emblem book published in Boston by James Thomas. And the widespread popularity of William Holmes and John W. Barber's *Religious Emblems* (1846) marked the revival and codification of the Protestant emblematic tradition in America. Emblems were also widely used in children's literature. John Bunyan's *A Book for Boys and Girls* (1686), published in Philadelphia as *Divine Emblems* (1794); John Wynne's *Choice Emblems . . . for the Improvement and Pastime of Youth* (1814); *A New Hieroglyphical Bible, for the Amusement and Instruction of Children* (1818); *The Juvenile Almanac; or, Series of Monthly Emblems* (1831); *The Little Child's Present* (1838); and *Moral Emblems: A Gift from Aunt Ann* (1838) are only a few titles from a vast juvenile literature that constituted an important source of popular emblemism in nineteenth-century America. The pervasiveness of the popular iconography of this emblem tradition is evident in the fact that, in addition to its appearance in children's literature and on gravestones, it was transmitted on objects ranging from scientific treatises (such as *Lectures on Natural Science . . . An Illustration of Chronology by Natural Emblems* [1830]) to maps (such as Joseph Ingraham's *An Historical Map of Palestine . . . Interspersed with More Than Two Hundred Vignettes and Emblems . . .* [1828]).

Specific references to this religious, literary, and popular emblem tradition recur throughout Emerson's early writings. For example, many of the emblematic images he uses in "Self-Reliance"—images such as the "leaning willow" and "bended tree," or the reference to "Fortune's wheel" in the closing lines of the essay—were commonplace in the popular "farewell" iconography associated with the nineteenth-century moral and religious emblem.[10] In the "Language" section of *Nature*, Emerson describes his indebtedness to the natural world as the origin of all words and things that convey a "spiritual import":

> It is not words only that are emblematic. It is things which are emblematic. Every appearance in nature corresponds to some state of mind, and that state of mind can only be described by presenting that natural appearance as its picture. An enraged man is a lion, a cunning man is a fox, a firm man is a rock, a learned man is a torch. A lamb is innocence; a snake is subtle spite; flowers express to us the delicate affections. Light and darkness are our familiar expression for knowledge and ignorance; and heat for love. Visible distance behind and before us, is respectively our image of memory and hope. (*Essays*, 20–21)

In the course of my previous remarks concerning Emerson's critical recuperation of Lockean, democratic notions of property, personhood, and the public realm, I have repeatedly emphasized that this political critique entails Emerson's methodical saturation of political discourse with contradictory personal or private meanings. We saw this in *Nature*, when he enlisted the discourse of rights to render a scene in domestic life, and, similarly, when he enlarged Locke's conception of labor to accommodate for moods such as doubtfulness or grief. The special applicability of the religious emblem tradition to effect Emerson's critical negotiation between public and private meanings is even more apparent when we consider that the appeal of popularized, nineteenth-century versions of these emblems as American cultural artifacts derived largely from the fact that they accommodated for meanings that were both radically private and absolutely public. To take just two isolated, illustrative examples: emblems that appeared on children's samplers and on gravestones conveyed individual as well as traditionally religious, symbolic meanings.

Emerson's personalizing of what was traditionally a public, universal, religious iconography reenacts this popular democratic aspect of emblem-making and brings the process of invention itself into sharp relief. At the same time that he derives what he calls his "picturesque language" (*Essays*, 23) from a universal, publicly recognized emblematic tradition, Emerson also suggests in *Nature* that the significance of each emblem he constructs is highly personal; that the meaning of natural forms are both created by the poet and, as in the emblematic tradition, found as the declarations of God's will.[11] "Have mountains, and waves, and skies, no significance but what we consciously give them, when we employ them as emblems of our thoughts?" he asks. "The world is emblematic. . . . The laws of nature answer to those of matter face to face in a glass. . . . This relation between the mind and matter is not fancied by some poet, but stands in the will of God, and so is free to be known by all men" (*Essays*, 24).

Although, as I showed in the previous chapter, Emerson's imagining of himself as a transparent eyeball clearly registers his attempt to confront the philosophical problematics of ownership, this image should not simply be read in light of his engagement with Locke's *Second Treatise* and popular discourses on property and the body that proliferated in nineteenth-century debates over slavery. It also calls our attention to Emerson's appropriation of a religious and literary iconography developed by seventeenth-century Protestant poets,[12] and demonstrates Emerson's manipulation of a widely pervasive iconography of the eye that figured prominently in New England literature and culture, especially in gravestone carving.[13]

The message of these Protestant emblems is neither obscure nor difficult. The sole purpose of making such artifacts was to exhibit the faith of the person who wrote or embroidered or carved them. Just as emblem poems by Herbert, Harvey, Traherne, and Vaughan are written to express the fundamental Christian belief that we are humanly limited to understanding ourselves and our bodies in terms of ownership and also that we do not own them because we are guardians of assets belonging to God, so Emerson's writing expresses his faith in a particular meaning for property.[14] The end result of this sustained engagement with religious sources in the transparent eyeball passage is an innovative, transformative critique of both religious and liberal renderings of the self. In *Nature*, and throughout his early writings, Emerson deliberately juxtaposes contradictory religious and Lockean or economic accounts of the self so that they stand in a mutual relationship of supplementarity and critique: the traditionally emblematic, disembodied, celestial eye also stands on the bare common as an owned body part, the eyeball.

The systematic attribution of political, secular significances to conventionally religious emblems that we find in Emerson's early writings calls attention to another important source of his emblematics, namely, the emblematics of American Freemasonry. The eye was a familiar, primary symbol associated with this secret fraternal organization, and appeared in Jeremy Cross's immensely popular book *The True Masonic Chart*, published in 1819. Cross hoped that *The True Masonic Chart* would do away with the improper classification of masonic emblems. He worked in collaboration with Amos Doolittle of Connecticut, whose engravings established the standard designs for the American Masonic symbolism that would continue to figure on masonic aprons, furniture, stonemasons' work, china, needlework, and in other aspects of American culture (figures 3.2 and 3.3). This widespread use of masonic emblems in America dates back to the revolutionary era, when Freemasonry was a vehicle for the popularization of liberal ideals associated with the struggle for independence. As one commentator has noted, "It is not surprising . . .

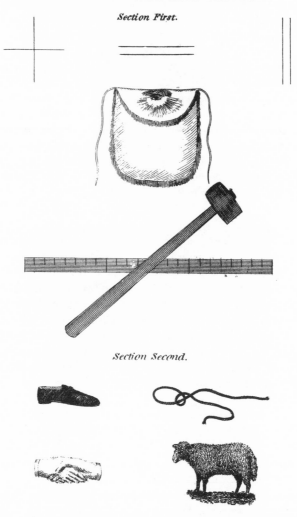

ENTERED APPRENTICE DEGREE.

Section First.

Section Second.

Figure 3.2. Masonic emblems. From Jeremy Cross, *True Masonic Chart* (New Haven, 1826). Courtesy American Antiquarian Society.

that an extremely close relationship exists between the development of patriotic symbols and the use of Masonic symbols in American decorative arts."[15] The close connection between Masonic and nationalist emblematics in the nineteenth century is evident in the popularity of the image of George Washington wearing a Masonic apron and in the presence of the Masonic eye on

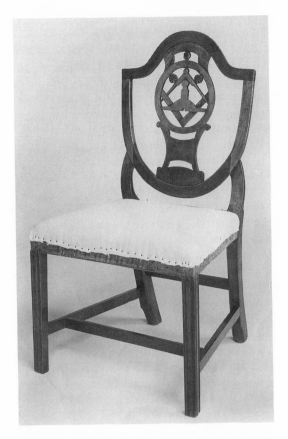

Figure 3.3. Masonic emblems on a Hepplewhite side chair. Massachusetts, c. 1785–1795. Courtesy Bernard & S. Dean Levy, Inc., New York.

the Great Seal of the United States, first adopted in 1782 and appearing on the dollar bill (figure 3.4).

Viewed from the context of nineteenth-century American culture, the boundaries between the moral, Masonic, and emergent nationalist emblematics are often blurred: the willow, traditionally associated with the moral emblem tradition, was also used to express the ideals and teachings of Freemasonry and, in some cases, appeared as a national symbol.[16] Cross included a broken column, which derives from the moral or religious iconography and is not, strictly speaking, Masonic, as part of his *Masonic Chart* (figure 3.5).[17] In general, Masonic emblematists attributed a moral significance to the forms associated with classical architecture, and this may have contributed to the increasing popularity of classical forms that culminated in the emergence of a

Figure 3.4. George Washington wearing a Masonic apron. Engraving by George Edward Perine, published by Moore and Co., New York, c. 1860. Courtesy Museum of Our National Heritage, Gift of Mr. Alfred M. Braga, 79.10.

national style of architecture ("Masonic Imagery," 9). Masonic engravers often drew on popular religious emblematics to express the moral dimension of these architectural forms: the conventional Christian iconographical figures of Faith, Hope, and Charity often adorned the columns that appeared on objects such as Masonic aprons (figures 3.6 and 3.7).

The convergence of the religious and the Masonic iconographic traditions in Emerson's writings is clearly marked in his construction of the upright subject as a column at the end of the essay "Self-Reliance":

Our dependence on these foreign goods leads us to our slavish respect for numbers. The political parties meet in numerous conventions. . . . In like manner the reformers summon conventions, and vote and resolve in multi-

Figure 3.5. Broken column included as a Masonic emblem. From Jeremy Cross, *True Masonic Chart* (New Haven, 1826). Courtesy American Antiquarian Society.

tude. Not so, O friends! will the God deign to enter and inhabit you, but by a method precisely the reverse. It is only as a man puts off all foreign support, and stands alone, that I see him to be strong and to prevail. He is weaker by every recruit to his banner. Is not a man better than a town? Ask nothing of men, and in the endless mutation, thou only firm column must presently appear the upholder of all that surrounds thee. (*Essays*, 281–282)

Figure 3.6. Masonic apron with all-seeing eye emblem and figures of Faith, Hope, and Charity adorning columns. Artist unknown, c. 1820. Courtesy Museum of Our National Heritage, 79.74.9. Photograph by John M. Miller.

The column represents a model of self-transformation that is simultaneously religious and political. On the one hand, the anticolonial rhetoric Emerson deploys in conjunction with the emblematic column—his insistence that a man must "[put] off all foreign support"—recalls the Masonic iconographical tradition associated with the development of liberal ideals during the revolutionary era (figure 3.8). On the other hand, this incorporation of the emblematics of American Freemasonry also works against the symbolic resonances of the column in the context of a popular moral and religious iconographic tradition. Emerson and his readers would have recognized the column as part of this larger system of allegorical and typic devises that per-

Figure 3.7. Open Lodge Certificate with figures of Faith, Hope, and Charity. Line and stipple engraving, published by Samuel Maverick, New York, 1823. Courtesy Museum of Our National Heritage, 85–18. Photograph by David Bohl.

vaded nineteenth-century literature and culture. The image of a female figure standing beside a column derives from Ripa's "Constantia." It recurs in an 1810 version of the emblem, which was reproduced in James Thomas's collection *Religious Emblems*, published in Boston in 1838 and which conflates the secular pillar of Justice with an image of the holy cross (figure 3.9). In another collection of religious and moral emblems edited by William Holmes and John W. Barber, first published in 1846, an emblem of "Fortitude and Constancy" reproduces the popular images of a column and an upright body (figure 3.10).

The conventional nineteenth-century religious significance attached to the column refers to the value of virtuous opposition associated with a holy cause. That Emerson purports to provide a method by which God will "deign to enter and inhabit you" in his essay, just as the sacred emblem poem provides, as we have seen, a structure that allows the poet to explore the possibility of a perfectly receptive position meriting salvation, demonstrates the special generic applicability of the emblem poem to Emerson's view of the self. His persistent mediation between the religious and Masonic significances of the column in "Self-Reliance" expresses the invasion of politics into the

Figure 3.8. Masonic column emblems. From Jeremy Cross, *True Masonic Chart* (New Haven, 1826). Courtesy American Antiquarian Society.

highly personal task of establishing a relationship between the self and God: cast in Emerson's terms, salvation or the entrance of God into the self involves the conception of a new, more perfect web of political obligations.

Emerson's systematic merging of traditional Masonic and Christian iconographies to mobilize contradictory meanings that are simultaneously political and personal results in the vivid, innovative emblematics we find in "The American Scholar," a Phi Beta Kappa oration delivered at Harvard in 1837. In this address, Emerson explicitly refers to the process of emblem-making in his discussion of Swedenborg: "He pierced the emblematic or spiritual char-

Figure 3.9. Emblem of "Constancy." From Rev. James Thurston, *Religious Emblems* (London, 1810). Courtesy Harvard College Library.

acter of the visible, audible, tangible world. Especially did his shade-loving muse hover over and interpret the lower parts of nature; he showed the mysterious bond that allies moral evil to the foul material forms, and has given in epical parables a theory of insanity, of beasts, of unclean and fearful things" (*Essays*, 69–70). Viewed in these terms, emblems are expressive vehicles that allow the poet to immerse himself fully and freely in an intense experience of the natural world, and to reemerge knowledgeable but morally unscathed.

The obvious sexual connotations in Emerson's description of the way emblems mediate Swedenborg's experience and depiction of nature's "lower parts"—allowing the writer, as it were, to hover over, interpret, and "pierce" any foul, unclean, and fearful forms that he may encounter in the natural world—also emerge in the following passage, which underscores the significance of Emerson's own practices as an emblematist.

> Fear always springs from ignorance. It is a shame to [the scholar] if his tranquillity, amid dangerous times, arise from the presumption, that, like children and women, his is a protected class; or if he seek a temporary peace by the diversion of his thoughts from politics or vexed questions, hiding his head like an ostrich in the flowering bushes, peeping into microscopes, and turning rhymes, as a boy whistles to keep his courage up. So is the danger a danger still; so is the fear worse. Manlike let him turn and face it. Let him look into

Figure 3.10. Emblem of "Fortitude and Constancy." From Rev. William Holmes, *Religious Emblems and Allegories* (London, 1868). Courtesy Harvard College Library.

its eye and search its nature, inspect its origin,—see the whelping of this lion,—which lies no great way back; he will then find in himself a perfect comprehension of its nature and extent; he will have made his hands meet on the other side, and can henceforth defy it, and pass on superior. The world is his, who can see through its pretension. (*Essays*, 65)

At first glance, the passage seems to exhibit an altogether private and thus unpoetic pictorial language, signaling a failure of Emerson's imagination. As readers we are inundated with a confusing, arbitrary array of images: a flowering bush, an ostrich, a microscope, a lion, and an altogether obscure reference to a body position in which the hands are made to meet on the other side. Upon closer inspection, however, we can see that these images constitute a visual vocabulary that bears coherent reference to a widely recognized iconography associated with a popular tradition in religious emblem literature. Attention to these iconographic resources immediately opens Emerson's dense, obscure emblematic vocabulary to new, more substantive readings.

One visual referent for most of these images may be found in the popular iconography for "Prudence and Foresight," represented by an emblem in the

Holmes and Barber collection (figure 3.11). The emblem represents a woman peeping into a telescope, which signifies the uses of Prudence in the life to come. She stands before a rosebush, and sees a serpent lying behind it. Behind her lurks a hungry lion, which she also sees reflected in the mirror she holds. The epigraph that accompanies the emblem is from Ephesians (v. 15): "See that ye walk circumspectly." The conventional icongraphy presents us with a constellation of erotically charged symbols of sexual danger (serpent, lion, bush) that depict Prudence at a moment of absolute stasis, and in a position where any bodily movement forward or backward will result in a dangerous moral lapse. As a result, Prudence must simultaneously wield telescope and mirror, in order to see that she walks circumspectly.

Although Emerson could not have seen the Holmes and Barber emblem, which was published almost a decade after he wrote "The American Scholar," he would have been familiar with the popular iconography from which this emblem of "Prudence and Foresight" was drawn. The radically altered significance of Emerson's pictorial vocabulary results from the series of changes he makes to the conventional iconography, a few of which I will briefly examine here.

First, in Emerson's version, the female body and flowering bush have been displaced by the image of the scholar, represented as an ostrich hiding his head in the bushes. Prudence's fear of sinful, omnipresent threats to her virginity has thereby been transformed by Emerson into the scholar's ignorant fear of dangers involved in any intimate encounter with nature or politics. Second, Emerson's deliberate substitution of the scholar's microscope for Prudence's telescope suggests that the scholar has foregone experience of his own sexual nature—experience which, as we have seen, Emerson celebrates as absolutely necessary to Swedenborg's and his own success as a writer—in order to practice this myopic, studious avoidance of political and sexual life. As a result, he has been reduced to the unmanly activity of peeping—the shame-faced, limited pleasures of the voyeur.[18] Third, whereas the conventional emblem exhorts us to follow the prudent example of a woman who is trying to protect her body and soul from the hazards of sexual trespass, Emerson's exhortation to scholarly publicity is an exhortation to manhood. The scholar, to be manlike, must cease to peep through microscopes and instead look danger directly in the eye.

Finally, whereas the conventional religious iconography refers to the personal dangers associated with sinning, Emerson's emblematics articulates a meaning for dangers that are simultaneously private and public. He suggests that the scholar's avoidance of public life not only poses a danger to the scholar himself but also to America's realization as an ideal political community. This exhortation to participation in the public realm is also a reconceptualization of that realm: Emerson's critique of traditionally political concepts of property and personhood entails his strategic enlistment of a religious, private, inwardly meditative, and thus feminized discourse. This enlistment is evident in Emerson's deployment of the traditional religious

Figure 3.11. Emblem of "Prudence and Foresight." From Rev. William Holmes, *Religious Emblems and Allegories* (London, 1868). Courtesy Harvard College Library.

iconography of "circumspection" to represent the self in this passage. Whereas in the popular iconography the woman gazes in the mirror so that she can see the lion behind her, in "The American Scholar" the mirror has been replaced by the curious reflexivity of the male subject's gaze in the heroic act of appropriating a self. Both the scholar's eye and the lion's eye are reflected in and constructed by the scholar's gaze; both "its" nature and "his" nature are possessed in the activity of circumspection. In the previous chapter, we saw that the perfect receptivity and labor of vision accomplished by the emblematic eyeball in *Nature* resulted in the discovery and appropriation of a self within the confines of a transparent membrane. Likewise, in "The American Scholar," the labor of appropriating a self has been depicted as circumspection, the activity of looking all around as a means of constituting the self.

That Emerson deliberately adapts the poetics and iconography of Protestant emblem literature for the purposes of political critique is evident in his reference to another emblematic figure intimately related to circumspection: "comprehension." The image for comprehension is represented in Emerson's address as an obscure, barely articulated reference to the body. Looking into the eye of danger, Emerson tells us, the scholar will find a perfect comprehension of its nature and extent: he will have made his hands meet on the other side. Comprehension, like circumspection, is an appropriative act through which the scholar makes an external, material nature his own.

There is strong evidence to suggest that the emblem of comprehension Emerson describes in his address derives from Francis Quarles's *Emblems, Divine and Moral*, a collection of emblem poems published in 1635 that was widely read during the time Emerson wrote "The American Scholar."[19] One poem in particular explores the limits of the rational, logical labor of human understanding, expressed by economic language, to communicate divine truths. The poem's central subject is that of comprehension, defined by Quarles as the endless, laborious activity of desiring and accumulating worldly goods.

> O HOW our widen'd arms can overstretch
> Their own dimensions! How our hands can reach
> Beyond their distance: How our yielding breast
> Can shrink to be more full, and full possest
> Of this inferior orb!
> ....
> We make art servile, and the trade gentile,
> (Yet both corrupted with ingenious guile,)
> To compas Earth, and with her empty store
> To fill our arms, and grasp one handful more:
> Thus seeking rest, our labours never cease,
> But, as our years, our hot desires increase:
> Thus we, poor little worlds! with blood and sweat,
> In vain attempt to comprehend the great:
> Thus, in our gain, become we gainful losers,
> And what's enclosed encloses the enclosers.[20]

The traditional iconography Quarles deploys in the picture accompanying the poem—an iconography that emerged in a modified form in the nineteenth century—displays an emblematic body position. The figure pictured in the emblem wraps his arms around a globe, trying to extend them so that his hands meet on the other side (figures 3.12 and 3.13).

Taken as a whole, Quarles's poem demonstrates that any attempt to comprehend the great will result in loss, because any appropriative act, or any conceptualization of experience in terms of economic gains and losses, will ultimately lead to a state of terrible entrapment within the confines of our own logic. Comprehension is enslavement to a system of thought that is a limited, human creation; as such, it is insufficient to describe or lead us to God's grace. But just as emblem poems by Herbert and Harvey disclose the necessity, as well as the insufficiency, of economic language and human understanding in thinking about the relationship between the self and God, so Quarles points out the necessity and also the insufficiency of comprehension to render salvation meaningful in human, fallen terms. As in many other Protestant emblem poems, in this poem Quarles presents a critique of ownership.

Figure 3.12. Emblem of "Comprehension." From
Francis Quarles, *Emblems, Divine and Moral* (London, 1839). Courtesy Harvard College Library.

In his reference to hands that will have been made to meet on the other
side, Emerson represents a body position similar to Quarles's position of comprehension. For Emerson, as for Quarles, the position of comprehension represents an act of appropriation that is the origin of private property: the
enclosure of the natural world, performed by the emblematic body position of
comprehension, corresponds to the scholar's possession of nature in himself.
For Emerson, as for Quarles, comprehension is as necessary in the appropriation of a world and a self as it is in the move toward the transcendence and
repudiation of property. Only by comprehending nature, by both enclosing it
from the common and finding it in himself, will the scholar be henceforth
able to defy it.

The applicability of the religious iconography to the task of writing political philosophy becomes more apparent when we consider that Emerson's
adaptation of the emblem of comprehension stands as a critique of the theory
of property put forward in Locke's *Second Treatise of Government.* The emblematic figure of comprehension refers to an act of appropriation and enclosure that corresponds to Locke's account of laborious gathering as the origin
of property in nature and in the self. Like Locke's image of gathering, Emer-

Figure 3.13. Emblem of "The World Made Captive," showing a modified, nineteenth-century version of "Comprehension." From Rev. James Thurston, *Religious Emblems* (London, 1810). Courtesy Harvard College Library.

son's image of hands that will have been made to meet on the other side represents the body's act of encircling and absorbing nature. But the critique of Lockean property inherent in Emerson's emblem of comprehension raises the question of the precise position of the body at which the material world has been appropriated as private property, thereby pointing up a critical ambiguity in Locke's analysis.

The point of focus for Emerson's critique is Locke's idea of first gathering as the sole point of origin for private property:

> He that is nourished by the Acorns he pickt up under the Oak, or the Apples he gathered from the Trees in the Wood, has certainly appropriated them to himself. No Body can deny but the nourishment is his. I ask then, When did they begin to be his? When he digested? Or when he eat? Or when he boiled? Or when he brought them home? Or when he pickt them up? And 'tis plain, if the first gathering made them not his, nothing else could. That labour put a distinction between them and the common.[21]

Like Locke's subject, whose claim to existence and property is grounded in a condition of endless labor, Emerson's subject also labors and possesses— the world, we are told, is his—but such possession does not entail labor in Locke's sense of the word. For Emerson, the body displayed in a position of comprehension is in a position that corresponds to but differs radically from the gathering, appropriating body of the *Second Treatise*. Just as in Protestant emblem poetry grace is represented as that which is both understood as earned and experienced as given by God, so in "The American Scholar" Emerson shows us that at the moment of comprehension property in the self is both laboriously made *and* found. The scholar, he tells us, will then have *made* his hands meet on the other side; he will then also *find* in himself a perfect comprehension of danger's nature and extent. Given what we already know about the poetics of contradiction at work in Emerson's writings on property, we are now in a position to state that Emerson recognized the special applicability of a seventeenth-century tradition in Protestant poetics for the expression of his political critique, a tradition that also represents a significant cultural and literary backdrop to Locke's writing of the *Second Treatise*. The important cultural work performed by this Protestant poetics was thus not only to open the conceptual possibility of Locke's formulation of property,[22] but also to shape Emerson's developing critical approach to Locke's thought.

The political critique represented by the emblem of comprehension requires Emerson's sustained oscillation between Lockean democracy and Filmer's absolutism as contradictory but equally necessary poles of thought. Just as in *Nature* the critique of rights discourse expressed in Emerson's imagining of Columbus as a representative American self simultaneously promotes democracy *and* imperialist expansion, so in "The American Scholar" the concept of self and community envisioned by the Emersonian iconography of comprehension is simultaneously democratic and imperialist. That Emerson's rendering of a fully comprehended, bounded and boundless, private and public self involves his systematic merging of the vocabularies of democratic representation and monarchical, divine right is evident in his observation that "[t]he private life of one man shall be a more illustrious monarchy,—more formidable to its enemy, more sweet and serene in its influence to its friend, than any kingdom in history. For a man, rightly viewed, comprehendeth the particular natures of all men. Each philosopher, each bard, each actor, has only done for me, as by a delegate, what one day I can do for myself. . . . The human mind cannot be enshrined in a person, who shall set a barrier on any one side to this unbounded, unboundable empire" (*Essays*, 67). Just as in *Nature* Emerson's critique of self-owning personhood celebrates Columbus's representative act of appropriating a new world, so in "The American Scholar" this political critique devolves on the image of the scholar's representative act of appropriating nature—including all other human natures—as his own. "[The scholar] shall see, that nature is the opposite of the soul, answering to it part for part," Emerson insists. "One is seal, and one is print. Its beauty is the beauty of his own mind. Its laws are the laws of his own mind. . . . So much of nature as he is ignorant of, so much of his own mind does he not yet possess" (*Essays*, 56).[23]

Emerson's critique of property and personhood in "The American Scholar" results in his invention of a constellation of emblems that communicate his utopian vision of America as a nation. Just as the Preamble of the

American Constitution works to ordain and establish (on both a federal and a national level) its own creation of a nation, so Emerson's address exhibits a compelling, self-evident emblematic vocabulary of the body that ordains and establishes a proposed model of political community. Emblematic images of the body pervade, substantiate, and are in turn explicated by Emerson's theoretical claims in his address. Taken together, this iconography registers Emerson's critique of Lockean, liberal notions of social contract and rational, voluntary consent; by raising the question of how, and in accordance with what model of ownership and of association, it may be said that we own each other.

In recent years, historians have noted that states or related social groups often invent political symbols that affirm and register national identity.[24] These national emblems do not simply express political identity; rather, they are a means by which an individual confronts the very question of political identity—the recognition of a national emblem as one's own is an act that constitutes the self as citizen. At the end of his address, Emerson emblematizes the act of political association as action, as the movement of an entire nation as one body: "We will walk on our own feet; we will work with our own hands; we will speak our own minds," he writes. "A nation of men will for the first time exist, because each believes himself inspired by the Divine Soul which also inspires all men" (Essays, 71). This utopian emblem of association and national unity appears an even more fitting and hopeful conclusion when we consider the fact that Emerson opens his address with a strikingly dystopic emblem: the dismembered body. "The state of society is one in which the members have suffered amputation from the trunk, and strut about so many walking monsters,—a good finger, a neck, a stomach, an elbow, but never a man" (Essays, 54). As an emblem of chaos and disunity, the dismembered body was central to a political iconography that was immensely popular during the Revolutionary era among those who were critical of the British government's American policies. For example, Benjamin Franklin's engraving "MAGNA Britannia: her Colonies REDUC'D," was originally printed at the end of 1765 or the beginning of 1766, widely distributed throughout England and America on note cards, and subsequently reproduced in modified form in America, France, England, and Holland (figure 3.14).

The model of association articulated by Emerson's emblematics is most visible at the point where he imagines his entrance into the public realm as his entrance into a circle of scholars.

> The world,—this shadow of the soul, or other me, lies wide around. Its attractions are the keys which unlock my thoughts and make me acquainted with myself. I run eagerly into this resounding tumult. I grasp the hands of those next me, and take my place in the ring to suffer and to work, taught by an instinct, that so shall the dumb abyss be vocal with speech. I pierce its order; I dissipate its fear; I dispose of it within the circuit of my expanding life. So much only of life as I know by experience, so much of the wilderness have I vanquished and planted, or so far have I extended my being, my

Figure 3.14. Engraving of "Magna Britannia, Her Colonies Reduc'd." By Benjamin Franklin, c. 1766. Courtesy The Library Company of Philadelphia.

dominion. I do not see how any man can afford, for the sake of his nerves and his nap, to spare any action in which he can partake. It is pearls and rubies to his discourse. (*Essays*, 60)

Following the philosophical maxim that "speech is what makes man a political being,"[25] we may readily interpret the iconography of this passage as being intimately bound up with political matters. Just as in his discussion of Swedenborg Emerson points out the uses of emblems as allowing the shade-loving muse to safely hover over and pierce the tangible world, so here he uses emblems to pierce the order of the dumb abyss, making it a political, public realm that is vocal with his own speech.

Setting aside for the moment the highly problematic meaning for "action" put forward in this passage, we can see that the passage critiques the Lockean contractarianism that prevailed in nineteenth-century America. Here, as elsewhere in his address, Emerson merges traditional religious and political iconographies and so invents a new vocabulary for imagining personhood and political association. In an early lecture titled "Doctrine of the Hands" delivered in 1837, Emerson noted that "[a] man in view of political economy is a pair of hands,"[26] and two years later, in a lecture titled "The Protest," he wrote, "How generous and noble is the position of the young! . . . This sovereign freedom . . . , this as yet uncommitted hand, unpledged vote."[27] The iconography of the handshake was also included in Cross's *Masonic Chart* and appeared on nineteenth-century gravestones, as well as in seventeenth-century poems such as Vaughan's "The Match" to signal Vaughan's literary inheritance of Herbert's poetry (figure 3.15).[28]

Cast in Emerson's terms, the emblem of grasping hands represents a suggestive critique of Lockean contractarianism in three major respects. First, as a contract, a handshake lies somewhere in between public, political discourse and the highly personalized discourse used in the conduct of daily social life; it is both a contract and not a contract. Second, the concept of property invoked by Emerson's iconography is one in which property in another person implies that the possessor is also possessed by his appropriated object: the grasping hand is also grasped. The mode of possession designated by Emerson's image of the enclosure of a common nature by a circle of scholars is both individual and communal, and it is a mode that requires each individual in society to belong to every other.

What is perhaps most striking about Emerson's iconography of the handshake as a model of political association is the fact that it simultaneously invites and places safe constraints upon the scholar's experience of his own and other people's bodies. The image suggests that some intimate encounter with physical nature must necessarily accompany and mark the scholar's entry into public life, because such physicality is the inevitable culmination of laborious self-cultivation—the scholarly cultivation of a mind, as Emerson puts it, "braced by labor and invention" (Essays, 59). Viewed in these terms, scholarly life is and should always be a life devoted to bodily, public labor. Emerson writes:

> There goes in the world a notion, that the scholar should be a recluse, a valetudinarian,—as unfit for any handiwork or public labor, as a penknife for an axe. The so-called "practical men" sneer at speculative men, as if, because they speculate or *see*, they could do nothing. I have heard it said that the clergy,—who are always, more universally than any other class, the scholars of their day,—are addressed as women. . . . Action is with the scholar subordinate, but it is essential. Without it, he is not yet man." (Essays, 60).[29]

The account of such "wider activity" Emerson puts forward in his address is one that lies beyond what he calls "popular judgments and modes of action" (Essays, 63). Premising his claims on this new, expanded definition of action, Emerson insists that the scholar is capable of contributing to social change.

Henry Nash Smith once sharply criticized Emerson's "American Scholar" for promoting a meaning for "action" that subordinates life and actual social reform to the merely literary exercise of imagining.[30] The question of Emerson's views on reform will be taken up at length in the next chapter. For the moment, it is enough to note that throughout his address, Emerson's imagining of political action is accomplished only in his move to the emblematic. The highly problematic definition of public labor and action which we find throughout his writings precisely derives from his recourse to this emblematics. As we have seen, the iconography of association Emerson develops is one that

Figure 3.15. Gravestone carving with Masonic emblems. Cambridge, Massachusetts, 1841. Courtesy Mt. Auburn Cemetery. Photograph by Orlando Patterson.

represents the *social* occasion of the scholar's engagement with other scholars in their jointly conceived academic pursuits as an act of *political* association or participation in an ideal public realm.

The question of whether, and how, the scholar's handshake may be conceived of as public, political action calls our attention back to the account of publicity Emerson develops in *Representative Men*. Just as Emerson's definition of the public in *Representative Men* circumscribes a sphere of thought that hovers somewhere in between privacy, sociality, and publicity, so in "The American Scholar" we are left with a meaning for scholarly labor that simultaneously encourages and precludes the scholar's capacity for political action because, by Emerson's account, no distinct public realm exists beyond the confines of the private. Public action and social reform, as Emerson pictures them in "The American Scholar," are also private, invisible, meditative, and religious matters. Such acts of resistance against the tyranny of mind, such harboring of secret presentiments, are revolutionary only because Emerson promises that, in the end, they will be deemed "most acceptable, most public, and universally true" (*Essays*, 64). In this troubling sense, patience *is* political activism. "Patience,—patience," he tells us, "with the shades of all the good and great for company; and for solace, the perspective of your own infinite life; and for work, the study and communication of principles, the making those instincts prevalent, the conversion of the world" (*Essays*, 70–71).

PART II

Political Obligation

FOUR

"Self-Reliance"

The Ethical Demand for Reform

In an early version of the essay "Politics," first delivered as part of an 1837 lecture series, "The Present Age," Emerson promised that "the philosophy of property if explored in its foundations would open new mines of practical wisdom which would in the event change the face of the world. . . . It would go deep into the ethics and touch all the relations of man" (EL, II, 79). Whereas in previous chapters I discussed Emerson's deliberation over the meaning of "ownership," in this chapter I consider the ethical consequences of his critique. The transformed meaning for property Emerson arrives at in his writings also results in a new way of thinking about the "obligations" or relations that bring individuals together in society.

Reading through Emerson's early statements about social reform, I argue that his systematic merging of political and religious discourses in "Self-Reliance" has the effect of equating "political" obligation with a personal, moral, and legally unenforceable obligation to resist conformity as a means of bettering society as a whole.[1] For Emerson, the political and social commitment to nonconformity should be hidden deep within every citizen and expressed through acts of self-reliant thinking. What is most striking and paradoxical about this strategic personalizing of our obligation to resist conformity is that it ultimately results in a reactionary vision of reform as "inaction" or "sublime prudence," a view that ultimately dismantles any real possibilities for visible public protest.

Emerson's relationship to reform movements in general and to the abolitionist movement in particular has long been recognized as problematic.[2] His first public address on the question of slavery, delivered in November

1837 was described by abolitionists as disappointingly "cool and philosoph-ical,"[3] and Emerson's private reaction to having written to President Van Buren about the Cherokee Indians discloses a strong ambivalence toward any act of public philanthropy.[4] In general, this ambivalence reflects Em-erson's attempt to come to terms with his own project as a philosopher and poet, a project he clearly regards as being fundamentally at odds with the programs for reform variously adopted by his contemporaries. Unmoved by plans for Brook Farm, he noted to himself in 1840, "Shall I raise the siege of this hencoop & march baffled away to a pretended siege of Bab-ylon? It seems to me that to do so were to dodge the problem I am set to solve" (JMN, VII, 408).

During the course of my previous remarks on the critique of ownership undertaken in Emerson's early writings, I suggested that he viewed slavery as a fundamental, theoretical failure to comprehend the meaning of "prop-erty" and "labor." As we have seen, Emerson's preoccupation with these matters was shared by some of his more radical contemporaries, such as Albert Brisbane and Orestes Brownson—and his critical reflections on property and labor reflected an abiding interest in political economy that was inspired early on in his life, when he first read William Paley's *Moral and Political Philosophy* (1785) as required reading at Harvard College. The task of making a better world, as he then saw it, was one of inventing a poetic idiom and philosophical framework that would accommodate for his imagining of a more perfectly democratic public realm.[5] In the years before 1844—the year of Emerson's address on the British West Indian Emanci-pation that inaugurated his public participation in the antislavery move-ment—this scholarly project of fashioning a poetics of philosophical critique marks the extent of his involvement in the related problems of slavery, democratic life, and social reform.[6]

Emerson's belief in the revolutionary potential of philosophy and poetry is visible in his 1840 lecture "Reforms." At one point, he notes with assurance that the doctrine of labor, rightly and philosophically construed, would put an end to slavery. "The labor of society ought to be shared by all and in a community where labor was the point of honor the vain and the idle would labor. What a mountain of chagrins, inconveniences, diseases, and sins would sink into the sea with the uprise of this one doctrine of labor. Domestic hired service would go over the dam. Slavery would fall into the pit" (EL, III, 264). Just as in "The American Scholar" Emerson castigates the scholar for hiding in the bushes and turning rhymes to keep his courage up, so in "Reforms" he would criticize the poet for a fanciful retreat from involvement in work that is "due today":

> Our modes of living are not agreeable to our imagination; we suspect they are unworthy. We accuse our daily employments; they appear to us unfit, unworthy of the faculties we spend upon them. In conversation with a man whom we highly esteem we apologize for our employments, we speak of them

with shame. The fancy flies from the work that is due today to its various fairylands, to some agreeable hope, some object of affection, some foreign residence, some passage of poetry (*EL*, III, 258).

One clear advantage to the idea of reform Emerson develops over the course of these early years—his belief in the efficacy and sufficiency of poetry and philosophical critique as effective forces for social change—is that it simultaneously allowed him to nurture his literary genius and to justify his rejection of popular reform movements. In 1844, he privately observed that his proper work in remedying social evil should derive from his particular capacities and broadly conceived role as a scholar and poet.

> In the actual world, the population, we say, is the best that it could yet be. Its evils, as war & property, are acknowledged, which is a new fact, & the first step to the remedying of them. But remedying is not a work for society, but for me to do. If I am born to it, I shall see the way. . . . Though it is an imperfect system & noxious, yet I do not know how to attack it directly, & am assured that the directest attack which I can make on it, is to lose no time in fumbling & striking about in all directions, but to mind the work that is mine, and accept the faculties & openings which my constitution affords me. (*JMN*, IX, 85)

The problem with existing reform movements, by Emerson's account, is that they lack poetic and philosophical insight: they do not retain what he calls "the purity of an ideal" and thus do not present a "poetic image to man" (*EL*, III, 259).[7] The value of current reform movements consists solely in the poetically inspiring, philosophical conclusions one is able to draw from them. Inquiring into the nature of such efforts, Emerson observes that "[t]he political questions, of Banks; of the limits of Executive power; of the right of the people to instruct their representative of the tariff; of the treatment of Indians; of the Boundary Wars; the Congress of Nations; are all pregnant with ethical conclusions" (*EL*, III, 257). The proper use of these popular movements is to furnish the scholar with new matter for deliberation and self-cultivation. Just as in "The American Scholar" Emerson celebrates the scholar's representative, literary act of appropriating other people's works of genius as his own, so in "Reforms" he contends that the best way to deal with reformers is, as it were, to eat their words—to take possession of their heroic acts and causes by imaginatively and laboriously shaping them into forms that express a genius that is altogether new.

> What then is our true part in relation to these philanthropies? Let us be true to our principle that the soul dwells with us and so accept them. The one doctrine we urge under many forms is the sacred. Accept the reforms but accept not the person of the reformer nor his law. . . . If you take the reform as the reformer brings it to you he transforms you into an instrument. It behoves you to receive into a willing mind, every trait, every bold stroke which is drawn. Let the Age be a showman demonstrating in picture the needs and wishes of the soul: take them into your private mind; eat the book

and make it your flesh. Let each of these causes take in you a new form, the form of your character and genius. (EL, III, 260)

Emerson's stated interest in the activity of philosophical critique as being tantamount to a physical deed of self-insertion into the public realm is no-where more clearly, memorably, and problematically set forth than in the essay "Self-Reliance."[8] Given what we already know about Emerson's early writings on the subject of reform, many key concepts he adduces in "Self-Reliance" should by now be familiar. In this 1841 essay, as in his lecture "Reforms" delivered a year earlier, Emerson insists on the importance of scholarly phil-osophical critique as revolutionary, public action. Warning his readers against the devastating social effects of the popular fascination with Locke's concep-tion of property,[9] Emerson prescribes instead the revolutionary work of "self-reliance," the critical exploration of property in its foundations—a philosophical critique that would, by his account, inevitably bring about a change in our arbitrary, retrograde modes of association and perception. "It is easy to see that a greater self-reliance must work a revolution in all the offices and relations of men; in their religion; in their education; in their pursuits; their modes of living; their association; in their property; in their speculative views" (Essays, 275).

This description of philosophizing as revolutionary, public action is ac-complished rhetorically by means of Emerson's imposition of the discourse of rights onto the scene of intellectual inheritance. In "Self-Reliance," he com-pares the dangerous effects of intellectual idolatry to the experience of living under an oppressive political regime. The urgency of Emerson's claims regard-ing the mind- and world-altering power of Locke's daunting analysis and clas-sification of property is evident in this striking invocation of rights. Any person, he says, who attempts to reject the conventional view of property embraced by the majority is in effect pronounced a legal alien who has been dispossessed of his right to see:

> Every mind is a new classification. If it prove a mind of uncommon activity and power, a Locke . . . it imposes its classification on other men and lo! a new system. In proportion to the depth of the thought, and so to the number of the objects it touches and brings within reach of the pupil, is his compla-cency. . . . The pupil takes the same delight in subordinating every thing to the new terminology, as a girl who has just learned botany in seeing a new earth and new seasons thereby. . . . But in all unbalanced minds, the classi-fication is idolized, passes for the end, and not for a speedily exhaustible means, so that the walls of the system blend to their eye in the remote horizon with the walls of the universe; the luminaries of heaven seem to them hung on the arch their master built. They cannot imagine how you aliens have any right to see,—how you can see. (Essays, 276–277)

Just as in "The American Scholar" Emerson proposes that the scholar's retreat from publicity poses a danger not simply to himself but to society as a whole, so in "Self-Reliance" he warns that the popular adulation of Locke's coherent, tenacious point of view has already resulted in a dangerous lack of greatness or perfection in society. "Our age yields no great and perfect persons. We want men and women who shall renovate life and our social state, but we see that most natures are insolvent, cannot satisfy their own wants, have an ambition out of all proportion to their practical force, and do lean and beg day and night continually" (*Essays*, 274–275).

Emerson's insistence on the viability of philosophical critique as revolutionary action in "Self-Reliance" calls our attention to another attribute of reform that is referred to throughout his early writings. As a mode of philosophical critique that works actual, revolutionary changes in society, "self-reliance" also involves a special process of reform that Emerson designates as "self-cultivation" or "self-culture." "[Men] measure their esteem of each other by what each has, and not by what each is," Emerson writes. "But a cultivated man becomes ashamed of his property, out of new respect for his nature" (*Essays*, 281). Whereas in the *Second Treatise* Locke argues that the act of appropriating Nature is the origin of private property, Emerson's reference to the cultivated man who is ashamed of his property refers to the critique of self-ownership put forward in his early writings. In "Self-Reliance," the term "cultivation" simultaneously expresses an agricultural meaning and bears reference to the origin of self-possessed subjectivity, the moment when every man must take himself as his portion: "There is a time in every man's education when he arrives at the conviction that envy is ignorance: that he must take himself for better, for worse, as his portion: that though the wide universe is full of good, no kernel of nourishing corn can come to him but through his toil bestowed on that plot of ground which is given him to till" (*Essays*, 259).

The model of self-possessed individuality that results from Emerson's description of social reform as "self-cultivation" in "Self-Reliance" is best understood in the context of Emerson's early writings on the subject of culture. Unlike Locke, who regards the process of appropriation as one of first gathering, of mixing labor with nature, Emerson imagines appropriation and the origin of self-ownership as the activity of "self-culture." "In hard times, cultivate yourself," he wrote in 1839. "And you cannot lose your labor. A just man, a wise man is always good property; the world cannot do without him be the fashions or the laws or the harvest what they may" (*JMN*, VII, 297). In a lecture series on "Human Culture" delivered two years earlier, Emerson elaborates on a concept of self-culture that he regards as being intimately bound up with a person's fundamental right to embodied self-possession. "His own Culture—the unfolding of his nature, is the chief end of man. . . . The true culture is a discipline so universal as to demonstrate that no part of a man was made in vain. We see men who do nothing but cipher—dot and carry one;—others, who can only fetch and carry; others who can only write or speak; how many who hardly seem to have a right of possession to their legs, their shoulders, and who get the least service out of their eyes" (*EL*, II, 215).

The unequivocal commitment to the idea of cultivation expressed throughout Emerson's early writings reflects a broader intellectual trend. Of the various efforts put forward by his contemporaries to promote self-culture as an instrument of social reform, Emerson would undoubtedly have been most struck by William Ellery Channing's 1838 lecture devoted to the subject. In his introduction, Channing defines self-culture as "the care which every man owes to himself, to the unfolding and perfecting of his nature."[10] Many of the concerns Channing raises in his lecture are similar to those Emerson himself would take up, as we have seen, in his deliberations over the meaning of reform. For example, like Emerson, Channing develops a concept of self-culture that represents a critique of the popular fascination with ownership and material success as the primary basis for thinking about personhood.[11] In chapter 2, we saw that Emerson critiques Locke's fundamental maxim concerning the mixture of bodily labor with nature: according to Emerson, even the activity of joyfully watching a tree grow would be tantamount to laboring and making that tree his own. Like Emerson, Channing's critique of self-ownership involves a new, expanded meaning for labor. In his lecture on self-culture, Channing broadens the traditional conception of labor to accommodate for self-possession that results from a process of self-cultivation pictured as one of inward, spiritual unfolding.

> To cultivate any thing, be it a plant, an animal, a mind, is to make it grow. Growth, expansion is the end. Nothing admits culture, but that which has a principle of life, capable of being expanded. He, therefore, who does what he can to unfold all his powers and capacities, especially his nobler ones, so as to become a well proportioned, vigorous, excellent, happy being, practices self-culture. . . . In a wise self-culture all the principles of our nature grow at once by joint harmonious action, just as all parts of the plant are unfolded together. (*Self-Culture*, 15)

Another point of similarity necessarily follows from this: like Emerson, Channing believes that any useful theory of labor must also account for scholarship. Just as in "The American Scholar" Emerson insists that only a mind braced by labor and invention will lend itself to a public, as well as a private, good, so Channing contends that "almost all labor demands intellectual activity, and is best carried on by those who invigorate their minds; so that the two interests, toil and self-culture, are friends to each other" (*Self-Culture*, 67–68).

Of all the various attributes of self-culture that emerge over the course of Channing's analysis, two are of particular consequence for Emerson's subsequent theorizing of social reform. First, that the practice of self-culture, insofar as it unfolds the affectionate nature in persons, represents a critique of Locke's contractarianism—the cherished, liberal premise that political obligations that constitute the public realm are necessarily assumed by volitional, rational acts of consent. As Channing himself puts it, "Self-culture is Social, or one of its great offices is to unfold and purify the affections, which spring up instinctively in the human breast, which bind together husband and wife, parent and child, brother and sister; which bind a man to friends and neighbors, to his country, and to the suffering who fall under his eye, wherever they belong" (*Self-Culture*, 23).[12] The framework that evolves from such a notion of obligation is also explicitly nationalist. Just as in "The American Scholar" Emerson depicts the scholar's involvement in public life both as the inevitable result of his intellectual development and as a necessary first step toward realizing America's promise, so in his analysis of self-culture Channing concludes that true self-culture necessarily entails an awareness of public spirit and the obligation to work toward the fulfillment of American national destiny.

> The individual is called to determine measures affecting the well-being of millions and the destinies of posterity. He must consider not only the internal relations of his native land, but its connexion with foreign states, and judge of a policy which touches the whole civilized world. He is called by his participation in the national sovereignty, to cherish public spirit, a regard to the general weal. A man who purposes to discharge faithfully these obligations, is carrying on a generous self-culture. (*Self-Culture*, 50–51)

The critique of contractarianism embedded in Channing's description of self-culture leads to a second facet in his concept of reform that profoundly shaped Emerson's own deliberations on the subject. By Channing's account, the advantage of self-culture as a program for reform is that it imposes clear constraints on possibilities for making any real changes in actual social arrangements:

> Undoubtedly there is insecurity in all stages of society, and so there must be, until communities shall be regenerated by a higher culture, reaching and quickening all classes of the people; but there is not, I believe, a spot on earth, where property is safer than here, because no where else is it so equally and righteously diffused. . . . Property is more in danger from those who are aspiring after wealth, than from those who live by the sweat of their brow. I do not believe, however, that the institution is in serious danger from either. All the advances of society in industry, useful arts, commerce, knowledge, jurisprudence, fraternal union, and practical Christianity, are so many hedges round honestly acquired wealth, so many barriers against revolutionary violence and rapacity. (*Self-Culture*, 56–57)

The doctrine of self-culture presents the securest means of bringing about reform, for the simple reason that by emphasizing the importance of personal, moral, and spiritual change it presents a safeguard against the violent danger to property associated with the more traditional, familiar idea of revolution as public action. Thus Channing concludes that any public outcry against the rapacity of the working classes, and all the fearful criticisms of reform regarding the subversion of property rights are entirely unfounded and merely "calumnious" (*Self-Culture*, 56).

Like Channing's political critique in *Self-Culture*, the critique of contractarianism in Emerson's essay shows how the fulfillment of a moral and personal obligation to become self-reliant is central to the orderly process of institutional reform. Such an obligation, Emerson argues, requires that each person obey a universal law hidden deep within their private heart: "To believe your own thought, to believe that what is true for you in your private heart is true for all men—that is genius" (*Essays*, 259).[13] What Emerson suggests is that such an inner, transformative experience of belief is not only evidence of genius; it is also a means of improving society as a whole.

The law of the heart Emerson describes in "Self-Reliance" is clearly at odds with what the political philosopher Nancy Rosenblum has recently identified as the prevailing, nineteenth-century romantic response to liberalism.[14] In *Another Liberalism: Romanticism and the Reconstruction of Liberal Thought*, Rosenblum argues for an unequivocal, prevailing opposition to legal formalism as being a primary feature of the critique of liberalism undertaken by Romantic writers. Whereas, viewed historically, the liberal commitment to legal formalism came about in the attempt to prevent the arbitrariness of political tyranny, Rosenblum argues that "[t]he romantic law of the heart makes faithfulness to feelings the measure of all things. Under its reign, actions spring from impulses, not purposes. They are lovely and sincere, not dutiful or instrumental."[15] By Rosenblum's account, this romantic, anarchic tendency toward self-absorption—the romantic writer's impulsive, purposeless obedience to what Rosenblum defines as a privately experienced law of the heart—is destined for failure. Given Rosenblum's reliance on such facile generalizations,[16] it comes as no surprise when she concludes that, ultimately, the most compelling critiques of this law of the heart have been articulated by "romantic sensibilities who come to see that consistent obedience to spontaneous and purely personal feelings is impossible. Perhaps, given the romantic anarchist's self-absorption, only failures perceived from within can chasten and provide impetus for reconciliation with liberalism" (*Another Liberalism*, 49). For such impossibly anarchic sensibilities, Rosenblum insists, the distress of unbridled sentiment will be brought to an end only in what she describes as the saving "Relief of Legalism" (*Another Liberalism*, 53).

In contrast to Rosenblum's description of the Romantic anarchist's resistance to liberal, legal formalism, Emerson enlists legal discourse in order to rhetorically equate "political" obligations with those that are moral, social, and personal. The primary motivation for doing this is his claim that the fulfillment of such duties cannot be institutionally enforced or "told" from without. Emerson makes this point in a difficult passage that shows a distinction between "reflex" and "direct" standards for duty:

> You may fulfil your round of duties by clearing yourself in the *direct*, or in the *reflex* way. Consider whether you have satisfied your relations to father, mother, cousin, neighbour, town, cat, and dog; whether any of these can upbraid you. But I may also neglect this reflex standard, and absolve me to myself. I have my own stern claims and perfect circle. It denies the name of duty to many offices that are called duties. But if I discharge its debts, it enables me to dispense with the popular code. If any one imagines that this law is lax, let him keep its commandment one day. . . .
>
> High be his heart, faithful his will, clear his sight, that he may in good earnest be doctrine, society, law to himself. (*Essays*, 274)

When we fulfill our duties to the community or town in which we live in a thoughtlessly habitual or "reflex" way,—duties, that is, to our neighbors, father, mother, cousins—Emerson says that we are not fulfilling obligations that are, properly speaking, social or civil. A duty that is considered by us to be "satisfied" simply because we are no longer being "upbraided" by relatives or barked at by our dog is not a relationship of obligation assumed necessarily and only to human beings. By contrast, Emerson says, the "direct" way of fulfilling duties involves a far sterner claim and list of commandments than normative social etiquette. As we shall see, in "Self-Reliance" Emerson creates an "ordinary" or common-sense vocabulary of obligation that draws on meanings that are simultaneously political (or legal) and religious (or moral). Throughout this essay, Emerson insists that only persons who have achieved a "direct" fulfillment of their duties are members of a truly civil and humane society—what he describes in this passage as a perfect social circle.

Before turning to Emerson's systematic merging of religious and political discourses, we should first note in more general terms that the vocabulary for obligation he invents in "Self-Reliance" reverberates with meanings that are simultaneously legal or philosophical and, as Stanley Cavell uses the term, "ordinary."[17] Examples of Emerson's creation of a language that resonates with legal and ordinary meanings abound in "Self-Reliance." At times this convergence of legal and ordinary meanings is expressed in the simple act of punning. "No law can be sacred to me but that of my nature. Good and bad are but names very readily transferable to that or this; the only right is what is after my constitution, the only wrong what is against it" (*Essays*, 262). And: "As great a stake depends on your private act to-day, as followed their public and renowned steps. When private men shall act with original views, the lustre will be transferred from the actions of kings to those of gentlemen" (*Essays*, 268). Similarly, Emerson broadens the familiar legal concept of "trust" so that it also accommodates an ordinary, common-sense meaning when he describes the embodied experience of self-trust that necessarily accompanies any person's act of self-reliance. "Trust thyself," Emerson writes. "Every heart vibrates to that iron string" (*Essays*, 260). "With the exercise of self-trust, new powers shall appear" (*Essays*, 275).

The transformation of contractarian discourse that we find in Emerson's essay is best understood in the context of American legal history. As Tocqueville noted in 1845, the boundary between ordinary and legal language in America was habitually blurred in debates over political issues. "There is hardly a political question in the United States which does not sooner or later turn into a judicial one. Consequently the language of everyday party-political controversy has to be borrowed from legal phraseology and conceptions. As most public men are or have been lawyers, they apply their legal habits and turn of mind to the conduct of affairs. Juries make all classes familiar with this. So legal language is pretty well adopted into common speech." (*Democracy in America*, 270). Tocqueville's observation concerning the general adoption of legal language into common speech was especially true in the field of contract law. Although the codification of contract law and the discovery of a general theory of contract did not occur until the late nineteenth century, this century has nonetheless been called the "golden age of contract" by legal historians, and the terms of contract theory were very much in circulation when Emerson was writing "Self-Reliance." The blurred boundary between ordinary and legal meanings of terms relating to contract was facilitated by the field's distinctive lack of technicality. As Lawrence Friedman has observed, "In general, the law of contract was not as technical as land law or civil procedure. It had little jargon of its own. Its rules were few and departed less from common sense than the rules of other fields of law."[18]

Emerson's merging of ordinary language and legal discourse in "Self-Reliance" is part of what I have suggested is an even larger project: namely, his critical recuperation of Locke's political vocabulary of social contract in the *Second Treatise of Government*. The frequent and almost frantic punning on legal words—such as "trust," "constitution," and "act"—in Emerson's essay seems to offer him the freedom and benefits of restoring to legal language an ordinary, commonsense meaning that shows a connection with everyday use and life, but the far more threatening, negative net effect of punning is that it undermines the referential capacities of legal terms and leave unresolved the questions of how the process of self-transformation relates to actual political realities such as constitution writing. For example, the manipulation of ordinary and legal meanings leads to Emerson's obscure, rhetorical question concerning the origins of the self and civil society: "Who is the Trustee? What is the aboriginal Self, on which a universal reliance may be grounded?" (*Essays*, 268). "Trustee" is a familiar legal concept that is also central to the political philosophy and account of obligation developed by Locke in the *Second Treatise*. In particular, Locke uses the legal idea of "trust" to describe the people's relationship to government. Whereas people are contractually related to each other in society, they are not contractually obliged to government, which comprises trustees and thus can be dissolved when governors fail in their trust.

Less familiar than "trust," the concept of "reliance" was also commonly defined in nineteenth-century contract law as a potential source of liability, and referred to a relationship associated with the existence of a contract, whether implied or actual. Read in this context, Emerson's description of "self-reliance" not only designates, in the ordinary sense, dependence on one's own powers, judgment, and ability, it also represents a legal idea. The concept of "self-reliance" represents a privately reflexive but also social and contractual relationship—the self relying on itself—that the individual makes and authorizes as doctrine, society, and law to himself. Emerson's obscure pun on the contractarian concept of "reliance" in "self-reliance" implies his central criticism of Locke's theory of social contract, a theory that was called upon time and again in public debates to legitimize slavery and a debased system of property relations. "And so the reliance on Property, including the reliance on governments which protect it, is the want of self-reliance," he observes. "Men have looked away from themselves and at things so long, that they have come to esteem the religious, learned, and civil institutions as guards of property, and they deprecate assaults on these, because they feel them to be assaults on property" (*Essays*, 281).

Because society has degenerated to its present, uncivil state—a society in "conspiracy against the manhood of every one of its members"—Emerson warns that in truth we are not a society at all but rather a "joint-stock company, in which the members agree, for the better securing of his bread to each shareholder, to surrender the liberty and culture of the eater" (*Essays*, 261). By Emerson's account, the stultifying effects of this pervasive fascination with property range from a dangerous impoverishment of original thought and expression to the bizarre, terrible fact that he can find no evidence of legitimate society: "now we are a mob" (*Essays*, 272).[19] America is a mob, not a society, because the security of property to which men presently aspire results in the surrender (and not the safeguarding) of individual liberties.

Emerson's systematic merging of political and religious discourses on obligation in "Self-Reliance" is most obvious at points at which his critique of Locke's theory of social contract extends to Locke's justification of the people's right to rebellion and dissolution of government. In the *Second Treatise*, Locke makes the argument that legislators who endeavor to reduce a people to slavery have put themselves in a state of war with the people, and that under these conditions, the people have a right to establish a new legislative such as they think fit. In "Self-Reliance," Emerson's recasting of Locke's right to rebel—and, specifically, his deliberate merging of legal, contractarian discourse and the religious, honorific discourse of divine right—are found in his reference to "receipt of benefits," a central concept in nineteenth-century contract law.[20] But in contrast to the prevailing view of contract, in Emerson's essay the benefits of contract have been paid with honor instead of money:

> The world has been instructed by its kings, who have so magnetized the eyes of nations. It has been taught by this colossal symbol the mutual reverence that is due from man to man. The joyful loyalty with which men have everywhere suffered the king . . . to walk among them by a law of his own, make his own scale of men and things, and reverse theirs, pay for benefits not with money but with honor, and represent the law in his person, was the hieroglyphic by which they obscurely signified their consciousness of their own right and comeliness, the right of every man. (*Essays*, 268)

Read as a response to Locke's *Second Treatise*, the juxtaposition of "benefits" with "reverence" in this passage expresses a critique of William Barclay's treatise on absolutism, the key passage cited by Locke to show Barclay's concessions to resistance. But whereas Barclay relies on religious concepts such as "reverence" to describe the proper posture of even a rebellious people toward their monarch,[21] Emerson retains the honorific ideal of reverence in order to show how access to such a divine right is due to every citizen as the democratic "benefit" of social contract, and thereby transforms the traditional posture of reverence toward a monarch into a democratic, contractual relationship that also extends a divine, mutual right of reverence to every man.[22]

We can see that throughout his essay Emerson's intimate engagement with Locke's political language and justification for rebellion produces an expanded notion of obligation: cast in Emerson's terms, Locke's political obligation to rebel is rhetorically equated with a personal, moral, and social obligation to resist conformity through acts of self-reliant thinking. But here we must pause and make note of an important paradox: namely, that the result of Emerson's broadening of the obligation to reform, and his strategic personalizing of political language, is that he ultimately dismantles any real possibilities for visible public protest.

Just as Locke promotes his justification of the right to rebellion and dissolution of government on the grounds that it is "*the best fence against Rebellion, and the probablest means to hinder it*" (*ST*, 415), so Emerson offers up a theory of "self-reliance" that motivates, justifies, and enacts a revolution in all the offices and relations of men at the same time that it signals the end of revolution. The saturation of political language with religious and commonsense meanings in Emerson's essay has the effect of severely limiting its referential capacities beyond the realm of the personal. Whereas Locke insists on the essentially conservative nature of his justification of the right to rebellion by arguing that "[t]his slowness and aversion in the people to quit their old Constitutions has ... kept us to ... our old Legislative ..." (*ST*, 414), Emerson describes self-reliance as a new, "political" definition of rebellion that includes aversion to any conformity in all spheres of life. As Emerson famously puts it, "The virtue most in request is conformity. Self-reliance is its aversion" (*Essays*, 261). Paradoxically, this broadened, Emersonian definition of the obligation to reform has the net effect of limiting possibilities for public action and protest.

The convergence of political and religious discourses on obligation in "Self-Reliance" and the dismantling of possibilities for effective, meaningful forms of public action—including public expressions of protest against slavery—are evident in one of Emerson's most provocative, controversial inquiries into the ethical demand for reform:

> Expect me not to show cause why I seek or why I exclude company. Then, again, do not tell me, as a good man did to-day, of my obligation to put all poor men in good situations. Are they *my* poor? I tell thee, thou foolish philanthropist, that I grudge the dollar, the dime, the cent, I give to such men as do not belong to me and to whom I do not belong. There is a class of persons to whom by all spiritual affinity I am bought and sold; for them I will go to prison, if need be, but your miscellaneous popular charities; the education at college of fools; the building of meeting-houses to the vain end to which many now stand; alms to sots; and the thousandfold Relief Societies; —though I confess with shame I sometimes succumb and give the dollar, it is a wicked dollar which by and by I shall have the manhood to withhold. (*Essays*, 263)

In "An Emerson Mood," Stanley Cavell has explored Emerson's transformation of religious discourse in this passage:

What Jesus required of one who would follow him Emerson requires of himself in following his genius. . . . He would not give money to the poor, who are not *his* poor, for the reason that Jesus will not give words but in parables, because to those who have ears to hear and hear not, and do not understand, it is not given to know the mysteries of the kingdom of heaven; because 'for whosoever hath not, from him shall be taken away even that he hath' (Matthew 13:12–13). Hard sayings; but no harder than the fact that he is the one he is and that each of us is the one each of us is."[23]

Given what we now know about Emerson's creation of a rhetoric of obligation in "Self-Reliance," we can also see how the question "Are they *my* poor?" simultaneously invokes a broad concept of "political" obligation that extends to legally unenforceable personal, moral, and social duties—while at the same time dismantling possibilities for public action.

What is also important to note is that Emerson's rhetorical, ambiguous mode of reference to slavery in this passage—"[t]here is a class of persons to whom by all spiritual affinity I am bought and sold"—stages on a discursive level his ambivalence about joining the abolitionist movement. Just as, in his early years, Emerson persistently justified his reluctance to join existing reform movements by asserting his freedom to develop his poetic genius as work that is "due today," so in this passage he refuses to assume the social consequences and responsibilities associated with literal language that would have expressed a clear, unequivocal stand against slavery. Refusing, at this time, to speak directly about the outrages of slavery, he opts instead for the pleasures and freedoms of ambiguity—the freedom to trope.

The unanswered philosophical queries raised by the ambiguity of Emerson's rhetoric include the important question of whether he is in any way—personally, socially, or politically—obligated to help slaves, and, further, whether these slaves are "persons." Emerson's profound ambivalence toward black American slaves is registered in the fact that we can never be sure they are included in the unidentified "class of persons" with whom Emerson says he shares a spiritual affinity. We know that Emerson says he "will" go to prison for any person to whom he has been, metaphorically speaking, enslaved or "bought and sold." But the point is that he never did—publicly, visibly, literally—go to prison, and so the question of whether he shares a spiritual affinity with black American slaves is left wide open. Indeed, the rhetorical ambiguity of the passage is such that it leaves open the question of whether Emerson knows anyone who is not, metaphorically speaking, enslaved—and this, in turn, raises the possibility that the family and townspeople around him are no more than barking dogs, not human at all. Realizing the crazy implications of this rhetoric, we might feel compelled to interpret the phrase "go to prison" metaphorically, as an image that stages Emerson's retreat into rhetorical ambiguity—into the bounded safety of poetic language that alludes to but ultimately steers clear of direct, literal reference to social realities such as slavery.[24]

I have suggested that Emerson transforms Locke's political language of obligation and justification for rebellion in order to offer up a new, broadened definition of "political" obligation to reform that extends to our personal, moral obligation to invisibly change ourselves as a means of improving society as a whole, but that the net effect of this broadening of our obligation to change society is that it severely limits possibilities for public protest against slavery. Another difficult and rhetorically fraught example of this paradox may be found in Emerson's racialist exhortation "Let us enter into the state of war, and wake Thor and Woden, courage and constancy, in our Saxon breasts" (*Essays*, 273). Whereas in the *Second Treatise* Locke makes the argument that legislators who endeavor to reduce a people to slavery have put themselves in a state of war with the people and that under these conditions the people have a right to establish a new legislative such as they think fit, in "Self-Reliance" Emerson's call to revolution contains veiled references to American slavery that suggest a broader, personal and social obligation to change society and new conditions for justified rebellion, in light of the fact that the black slaves who had been put in a state of war with legislators were never legally defined as "persons." But, in characteristic fashion, the net effect of Emerson's rhetoric is to hobble any real attempts at institutional reform precisely when he is most adamant. Paradoxically, in "Self-Reliance" Emerson calls upon the revolutionary premises of Anglo-Saxonism and uses its inflammatory, racialist rhetoric to suggest that citizens have been subjected to enslavement by the State and that the proper conditions for dissolution of government apply— but in so doing he effectively blinds his readers to any clear recognition of racial diversity in America.[25]

The rhetorical constraints Emerson places on exhortations to revolution-ary action in "Self-Reliance" are best seen in his writings on prudence as an attribute of persons engaged in the project of reform. The transformed signif-icance Emerson assigns to prudence emerges in his portrait of "Man the Re-former." Just as in "The American Scholar," Emerson transforms the traditional moral iconography of Prudence in order to convey the importance of the scholar's engagement in public life, so, in this 1841 lecture on reform, he insists on the necessity of "sublime prudence" in realizing social change. "The mediator between the spiritual and the actual world should have a great prospective prudence. There is a sublime prudence, which is the very highest that we know of man, which, believing in a vast future,—sure of more to come than is yet seen,—postpones always the present hour to the whole life; postpones talent to genius, and special results to character" (*Essays*, 149, 150).

The exhortation to sublime prudence articulated in this passage seems even more apt and compelling as a response to Locke's philosophy when we consider that Locke himself discusses prudence in connection with his pro-posed justification for dissolution of government in the *Second Treatise*. But whereas Emerson recuperates the moral concept of prudence in developing his model for reform, Locke unequivocally dismisses any peace that would result from prudence, which Locke associates with passive obedience to tyranny. In Locke's view, given conditions of injustice, such a prudent peace would be analogous to the unacceptable peace preached by Ulysses in Polyphemus's cave.

> If the innocent honest Man must quietly quit all he has for Peace sake, to him who will lay violent hands upon it, I desire it may be consider'd, what a kind of Peace there will be in the World, which consists only in Violence and Rapine; and which is to be maintain'd only for the benefit of Robbers and Oppressors. . . . *Polyphemus's* Den gives us a perfect Pattern of such Peace, and such a Government, wherein *Ulysses* and his Companions had nothing to do, but quietly to suffer themselves to be devour'd. And no doubt *Ulysses*, who was a prudent Man, preach'd up *Passive Obedience*, and exhorted them to a quiet submission, by representing to them of what concernment Peace was to Mankind; and by shewing the inconveniencies might happen, if they should offer to resist *Polyphemus*, who had now the power over them. (*ST*, 417)

Viewed in the context of his early writings on reform, Emerson's celebration of sublime prudence registers a definition and justification of scholarship—the solitary, introspective activities of philosophical critique and poetic imagining—as public action. In an 1841 essay, "Prudence," Emerson insists that "[p]oetry and prudence should be coincident. Poets should be lawgivers; that is, the boldest lyric inspiration should not chide and insult, but should announce and lead, the civil code, and the day's work" (*Essays*, 362). Likewise, in his early lecture "Reforms," Emerson explicitly renders a connection between what he calls "highest" prudence and social reform, between health of the body (both individual and collective or political) and revolutionary change:

> Temperance when it is only the sign of intrinsic virtue is graceful as the bloom on the cheek that betokens health, but temperance that is nothing else than temperance is phlegm or conceit. But if the connection of this asceticism with the highest prudence is considered and its connexion with that health and that beauty which is now rather the exception than the rule of human nation . . . , it becomes at once an object of interest to the philosopher and from its elegance worth the thought of every pure and refined spirit. (*EL*, III, 262–263)

Later in the same lecture, the concept of sublime or highest prudence is brought forward to register Emerson's blurring of distinctions between philosophy, poetry, and public action. Just as in "The American Scholar" Emerson concludes with the suggestion that patience, rightly viewed, constitutes a viable mode of political activism, so here he upholds the ideal of prudence to justify his own commitment to inaction and withdrawal into solitary passivity. Prudence and patience, when performed with deep piety, represent public acts of reform:

> In regard to all these projects of reform it appears that the individual should use them and not be used by them. To the young man diffident of his own ability and full of compunction at his unprofitable existence the temptation

is always great to lend himself to these movements and as one of a party accomplish what he cannot hope to effect alone. But he must resist this degradation of a man to a measure. "Will you not come to this convention and nominate a Temperance, an Abolition, a Peace, a Church ticket? Let me show you the immense importance of the step."—Nay, my friend, I do not work with these tools. The principles on which your church and state are built are false and a portion of this virus vitiates the smallest detail even of your charity and religion. Though I sympathize with your sentiment and abhor the crime you assail yet I shall persist in wearing this robe, all loose and unbecoming as it is, of inaction, this wise passiveness until my hour comes when I can see how to act with truth as well as to refuse. A patience which is grand, a brave and cold neglect of the offices which prudence exacts so it be done in a deep, upper piety, a consent to solitude and inaction which proceeds out of an unwillingness to violate character, is the century which makes the gem. (EL, III, 265–266)

Once again, in this passage Emerson arrives at a personal solution to the question of social reform by equating acts of reform with those of philosophical critique and poetic making. Because the founding, Lockean principles of property and contract are false, he says, civil society, in order to be rebuilt, must first be reimagined from the ground up. This broad claim regarding the significance of scholarship for public and private life is predicated on a definition of poetry and philosophy as testimony of the soul. "It is the eternal testimony of the soul in man to a fairer possibility of life and manners than he has attained that agitates society every day with the offer of some new amendment" (EL, III, 259). Such testimony, he argues, is not simply a flight of poetic fancy; it is a form of daily, social agitation that results in (and here he uses a word that is powerfully deceptive, laden with explicit legal connotations) some new "amendment" that is as spiritual as it is institutional.

The question of whether any testimony of the soul (however deep and true) counts as political activism, of whether and how Emerson's reference to agitation and amendment relates to the actual consequences of political reform, leads us back to what is most striking—and also most problematic—about Emerson's concept of public action. Just as in "The American Scholar" Emerson's adaptation of a conventional moral and religious iconography produces a concept of public action that also accommodates for what have traditionally been conceived of as private and social activities, such as handshaking and patient scholarship, so in "Reforms" he expands the concept of public action to include even solitary inaction:

Why should we be cowed by the name of action? 'T is a trick of the senses, no more. We know that the ancestor of every action is thought. The poor mind does not seem to itself to be anything unless it have an outside badge, some Gentoo diet or Quaker coat, or Abolition Effort or a great donation or a high office or, anyhow, some wild contrasting action to testify that it is

somewhat. The rich mind lies in the sun and sleeps and is Nature. To think
is to act. (*EL*, III, 267–268)

If the invisible activity of thought is action, then the inactive should win our
new respect: "We must learn to respect inaction more than prodigious activity
without," he writes. "Action and inaction are alike to the true" (*EL*, III, 266,
267).

The meaning for public action put forward in "Self-Reliance" and
throughout Emerson's early writings on reform—his demand that the philos-
opher-poet quit his foreign residence and, by means of some public performance, show that he has taken up residence in society—registers what is most
reactionary and paradoxical in Emerson's thinking about reform. As Emerson
sees it, true reform consists in a self-making act of consent to a society of
one—a prudent, patient act of consent to solitude and inaction.[26] He writes,
"I cannot consent to pay for a privilege where I have an intrinsic right"
(*Essays*, 263). Whereas in "The American Scholar" Emerson imagines his
passage into the public realm, a realm inhabited by scholars, as being marked
by the visible, symbolic action of handshaking, in "Reforms" he imagines his
own act of reform—a self-reliant expression of consent to participation in
public life—as being entirely solitary and invisible. Cast in Emerson's terms,
the related activities of reform and consent to civil society should always be
invisible. Viewed in the public eye, he says, such acts of consent should always
appear as inactive as a loose, unbecoming robe.[27] In this sense, the critique of
social contract and consent undertaken in "Self-Reliance" serves almost to
negate the existence of a world of politics outside the self—a self Emerson
pictures as being entirely self-sufficient, society to itself.

Emerson's claim that social change may be brought about by becoming
self-reliant suggests that the formation of a more perfect society and social
contract can be accomplished by only one person, provided that the person
is "representative." In "Prudence," Emerson writes, "Though your views are
in straight antagonism to theirs, assume an identity of sentiment, assume that
you are saying that which all think, and in the flow of wit and love roll out
your paradoxes in solid column, with not the infirmity of a doubt. . . . Assume
a consent, and it shall presently be granted, since, really, and underneath their
external diversities, all men are of one heart and mind" (*Essays*, 366–367).
This critique of the democratic idea that "consent" may be purely voluntary
and rational is characteristic of all of Emerson's early writings insofar as in
this passage Emerson affirms sentimental values at the expense of democratic
values—"identity of sentiment" amid diversity is affirmed at the expense of
rational voluntarism—in order to ensure social cohesion.[28] Emerson's insistence on the importance of "assuming what others assume"—something that
Whitman, following Emerson, clearly depicts in "Song of Myself" as being the
primary task of the poet—implies that the obligation to reform cannot be
assumed by an act of consent that is purely rational and voluntary. In the
next chapter, we will explore Emerson's critique of traditional theories of

"consent" in more detail. For the moment, it is enough to note that Emerson's critique of consent is central to his reactionary definition of reform—namely, reform that begins and ends with "self-reliance."

In conclusion, Emerson's writings on the subject of reform show his belief in the efficacy and sufficiency of poetry and philosophical critique as forces that would ultimately lead to institutional change. This interest in philosophical critique as being tantamount to a physical deed of self-insertion into the public realm is memorably stated in "Self-Reliance." In this essay, Emerson's systematic merging of political and religious discourses has the effect of equating "political" obligation with a personal, moral, and legally unenforceable obligation to resist conformity as a means of bettering society as a whole. For Emerson, the political and social commitment to nonconformity should be hidden deep within every citizen and expressed through acts of self-reliant thinking. What is most striking and paradoxical about this strategic personalizing of our obligation to resist conformity is that it ultimately results in a reactionary vision of reform as "inaction" or "sublime prudence," a view that ultimately dismantles any real possibilities for visible public protest.

It is difficult to see how such a reactionary idea of reform could have influenced someone as radical and politically active as Martin Luther King Jr. In the concluding chapter of this book I show that King's definition of reform is the opposite of Emerson's insofar as it requires visibility and public action. But depite this critical point of difference, King's thinking about the obligation to change ourselves as a way of improving society—for example, his definition of the "ethical demand for integration" as including social and moral obligations that are not legally enforced by the state—clearly derives from Emerson's philosophy of obligation in "Self-Reliance." The fact that King himself was well aware of the uses and limits of Emersonianism is evident in the famous sermon "Transformed Nonconformist," in which King, in an effort to combat the deadening conformity of racism, quotes and creatively interprets Emerson's exhortation to nonconformity in "Self-Reliance." Drawing on Emerson's philosophy and rhetoric as conceptual resources, King presents self-reliance as a quintessentially American value that involves the obligation to commit *both* personal acts of self-transformation *and* public acts of civil disobedience.

FIVE

Locating the Limits of Consent in "Friendship"

ction registers the connectedness of persons in public space. The reality of any single action is entirely dependent on the fact of its visibility and the presence and reactions of others.[1] In *The Human
Condition*, Hannah Arendt is trying to make this same basic point when she
excludes any biologically driven and thus "hidden" activities traditionally associated with the household from her definition of political action.[2] The Greek
polis, in her account, is a place in which all bodily action in political life
(including violent action) has been reduced to talk:

> In the experience of the *polis*, which not without justification has been called
> the most talkative of all bodies politic, and even more in the political phi-
> losophy which sprang from it, action and speech separated and became more
> and more independent activities. The emphasis shifted from action to speech,
> and to speech as a means of persuasion rather than the specifically human
> way of answering, talking back and measuring up to whatever happened or
> was done. To be political, to live in a polis, meant that everything was
> decided through words and persuasion and not through force and violence."
> (*The Human Condition*, 26)

Despite its glaring insufficiency as a representation of cultural life, the explan-
atory power of Arendt's description of the polis is nonetheless considerable.[3]
Warning us that action is impossible in isolation, Arendt also reminds us that
even the strongest and most superior of men have been reduced to impotent
inaction because they failed to create the community necessary for taking an
initiating step into public life. "History is full of examples of the impotence

of the strong and superior man who does not know how to enlist the help, the co-acting of his fellow men. His failure is frequently blamed upon the fatal inferiority of the many and the resentment every outstanding person inspires in those who are mediocre" (*The Human Condition*, 189).[4]

Of the many human activities Arendt confines to the domestic world is "companionship of the human species." Because such companionship springs merely from a biological need, she says, it is not properly political action, but rather "merely social," "a limitation imposed upon us by the needs of biological life, which are the same for the human animal as for other forms of animal life" (*The Human Condition*, 24). This description of companionship as consisting solely in the gratification of drives represents a fundamental flaw in Arendt's catalogue of political actions and obligations because it precludes any consideration of friendship as a primary source of human relatedness in civil society.[5]

Thus far in my discussion of Emerson's theory of political obligation I have argued that his systematic merging of religious and political discourses results in an expanded concept of obligation as being both voluntarily assumed and involuntarily grounded in the body—an idea of obligation that extends even to the ethical demand for social reform. Inquiring into the nature of the obligation to improve public life, in "Self-Reliance" Emerson effectively critiques Lockean contractarianism by describing civil acts of resistance in private and social as well as public terms. The vision of political action that emerges is one that accounts for traditionally apolitical activities such as handshaking, patient scholarship, and aversion to conformity in all spheres of life. Real, enduring social reform thus entails not only a change in law but also a change of heart.

In this chapter, I propose to show that Emerson's writings on friendship represent a further elaboration of his political critique. My analysis will emphasize four main points concerning the larger significance of Emerson's theory of friendship. First, Emerson was initially drawn to thinking about religious ideas about friendship in his effort to imagine a more perfect theoretical model of political obligation than that developed by liberal contractarians such as Hobbes and Locke. Second, the definition of obligation that arises out of Emerson's theory of friendship and critique of contractarianism not only underscores the limits of rational, voluntary consent as a political concept but also contributes to his construction of a coherent, innovative model of American national identity. Third, despite his early interest in friendship as a means of envisioning political community, by the mid-1850s Emerson had abandoned friendship as a viable model of obligation and instead placed increasing emphasis on the importance of "race" as an expression of American national cohesiveness and distinctiveness. Finally, I will show how the all but neglected philosophy of friendship as obligation put forward in Emerson's writings is in turn critiqued by Thoreau, who in *A Week on the Concord and Merrimack Rivers* systematically traces out the significance of friendship for the developing expression of American nationalism.

Emerson's journals show that he was fascinated by the subject of friendship well before he officially began his career as a writer and lecturer. The running commentary on the meaning of friendship in the early journals demonstrates the extent to which he associated friendship with the experience of deep religious feeling. For example, the centrality of religious faith to Emerson's vision of friendship is evident in Emerson's July 14, 1831, journal entry, in which he notes that "Ellen wondered why dearest friends, even husband and wife did so little impart their religious thoughts. And how rarely do such friends meet. Here I sit alone from month to month filled with a deep desire to exchange thoughts with a friend who does not appear—yet shall I find or refind that friend?" (JMN, III, 272). Elsewhere he asks, "The bounds of friendship, where are they?... It transmutes blood to ichor and transubstantiates flesh" (JMN, VI, 250). And in 1834 he insisted that "[i]f friendship were perfect there would be no false prayers" (JMN, IV, 299).

The religious significance of friendship is also closely examined by Emerson in a number of sermons he delivered over the course of his ten years' experience in the pulpit. In these semons, he develops a theory of obligation that devolves upon the ideal of friendship upheld in the teachings of Christ. Many of the special attributes of friendship that are brought forward in Emerson's characterization are worth mentioning here. First, and most important of all, is the fact that Christ's friendship to man is a gift from God. As Emerson observed in one sermon delivered on January 10, 1830, at the Second Church in Boston, "I will only specify one of the foreign helps whereby God most signally assists the human mind; that is, by friends. Shall we then esteem corn and wine and oil the gift of God, and not esteem our friends as his special and highest gift?"[6] The obligations inherent in our friendship with Christ are not at all based on rational self-interest. Rather, they are expressed in what Emerson speaks of in another semon, delivered the previous year, as our "reciprocal regard," "a lively affection like that borne to a venerated friend, yet exalted and peculiar in its strain," which these words "authorize us to feel and to express toward ... the character and the living spirit of the great Founder of the Christian Religion" (Sermons, LXII, 118).

Because the model of Christian obligation Emerson discovers in his sermons is based on affection, reverence, love, and, ultimately, human "kindness," it is clearly much less hierarchical than the relationship of obligation that exists between servant and master. Looking at Christ's statement that "[h]enceforth I call you not servants, for the servant knoweth not what his Lord doeth; but I have called you friends, for all things that I have heard of my Father, I have made known to you" (John 15:15), Emerson asks, "And is it not also most reasonable that they who, by the practice of his commandments ..., should be continually drawn closer to him in affection; that obedience should be raised into reverence, and reverence should ripen into love, that in the progress of a virtuous mind ... [it] should perceive that God had confined it to no low bounds, but had urged it in the spirit of a solemn confidence to feel for its moral Saviour, the kindness not of a servant but of a friend" (*Sermons*, LXII, 120).

Despite the fact that obligations arising out of friendship to Christ are visibly less hierarchical than those which exist between servant and master, they nonetheless entail strictest obedience to God's law. The obligations that love for Jesus inspires are much stronger than those of mere respect for the law. Even very good men often mistake respect for this deep and equal love, which, above all, may be evident in friendship based on a spirit of trust.

> I am led to make these remarks because I am persuaded that not only do men generally rather respect than love religion, but it seems to me that very good men incline to a certain diffidence and a separation of their religious views from common feelings and the cheerful common speech of men, which is alien to the spirit of trust and deep and equal love which the character and professions of Jesus ought to inspire. As in the relations of earthly friendship civility will never be received as a return for love, so in heavenly things respect is a bad substitute for devotion. (*Sermons*, LXII, 119)

The same loving obligation that binds us to Christ, he says, also binds us together as an entire community of Christian brethren. "I believe, my Christian brethren, that no good man can read or hear these words without sincere satisfaction. For this language is not confined to the twelve disciples to whom it was first addressed, since Jesus has himself in the context extended its signification to all his church by declaring the conditions of his friendship. 'Ye are my friends, if ye do whatsoever I command you'" (*Sermons*, LXII, 118).

Examples of the similarity between friendship with Christ and friendship between Christian brethren are most clearly illuminated in Emerson's description of the relationship that develops between teachers and their students. The obligations associated with this form of educative friendship are examined in a sermon first preached at the anniversary celebration of the Boston Female Asylum on September 23, 1831.[7] In this sermon, Emerson deals with the proper objects and ends of education and deliberately characterizes the bond of friendship between teachers and their students as being fundamentally different from but nonetheless essential to the eventual development of the child's friendship with God. Like Christ's friendship to man, Emerson says, the teacher's friendship with his students requires, first and foremost, a love of children. "To teach children, you must have the love of children. A good teacher must be the child's friend" (*Sermons*, CXXVIII, 229), he insists. Education involves a loving process of possessing one's students, showing them faith in God: "You must aim to give them this inward strength by actually possessing them with love, and faith, and resolution. It will not do to cleanse the outside of the cup" (*Sermons*, CXXVIII, 229). Like Christ, the teacher must be aware at every moment of his great responsibilities and "grave trust" (*Sermons*, CXXVIII, 226) as a teacher. He has to know, and let the young student know, that the ultimate source of all learning is God.

> Under the light of Christianity it is the aim of education to convince the child in its own experience that truth is better than falsehood; that kindness is better than selfishness; that it is better to be useful than useless; to make known to the young learner by his own consciousness, the unmeasured extent of powers of his own soul; and when he first feels the awful delight of this possession, to unfold to him that it is God who gave, nay, who is now giving its powers, to make him feel that goodness and truth have never been left alone in the world, but that God always provides for the instruction and salvation of his youngest child; that Jesus Christ was born and died to teach and save it, and to spread out before its wondering eye the sublime employment and opportunities of an endless duration. (Sermons, CXXVIII, 228)

Although Emerson extends the Christian model of obligation to accommodate earthly friendship among Christians, he also notes that friendship with Christ is fundamentally different from religious brotherhood. Whereas the bonds that constitute Christian community are to some degree constructed by acts of voluntary consent, the loving bonds of friendship to Christ are in every instance involuntarily assumed. In order to show this involuntary nature of our obligation to Christ, Emerson once again points to the friendship that develops out of the educational process. The obligations associated with such friendship are qualitatively different from those of "kindness" owed to all our fellow men, because it involves "particular claims" to friends that we are at liberty to select. Emerson writes, "Whilst most of our duties lie at our door and are not to be chosen, a certain extent of choice is allowed us in regard to others. Whilst we owe the duty of kindness to all our fellow men, we are left at liberty to select for ourselves those few whom we are willing to engage in a strict friendship" (Sermons, CXXVIII, 226). Although the world "teems" with "a crowd of benevolent projects ... [that] demand our sympathy and respect" (Sermons, CXXVIII, 226), Emerson insists that the obligations associated with educative friendship are both loving (or involuntary) and assumed by reasoned acts of voluntary consent. In this account, the ideal Christian community that derives from educative friendship is one in which an intimate, voluntarily chosen circle of friends constitutes a distinctive subset of the human race, set apart from the rest of civil society made up of "all our fellow men" (Sermons, CXXVIII, 226), toward whom we involuntarily feel the claims of kindness.

Ultimately, Emerson's invocation of the religious ideal of friendship with Christ as the primary ground for earthbound obligations between Christians results in a developing theory of obligation as "spiritual affinity"—a theory that simultaneously points up the necessity and the insufficiency of Lockean, liberal notions of consent because such ties of affinity can never be assumed by acts of consent that are wholly volitional or rational. Just as in "Self-Reliance," Emerson depicts the ethical demand for acts of reform—his obligation to aid "my poor"—as being predicated on spiritual affinity, so in his thinking about friendship Emerson considers obligations grounded in spiritual affinity to be uppermost. In his account, the obligations that bind him to an imagined, perfect friend are fundamentally similar to religious obligations insofar as they are not, strictly speaking, rationally or voluntarily assumed. "God cannot be intellectually discerned," he wrote in 1831. "The feast is pleasant, but its joys have no afterlife. . . . Why not follow out the great idolatry, no, the great penchant of the human mind for friendship? Is it not beautiful, this yearning after its mate—its mate I mean by spiritual affinities and not by sex?" (JMN, III, 274).

Although in the early 1830s Emerson's writings about friendship focused primarily on the related matters of faith and the nature of his relationship to God and Christian brethren,[8] by the late 1830s, he had shifted his point of focus, moving from the question of *religious* obligations and spiritual affinity to the question of *political* obligations that exist not between the self and God but among persons in civil society. Just as in early works such as "The American Scholar" and "Self-Reliance" Emerson arrives at a concept of political obligation by merging religious and liberal discourses, so in his writings on friendship he eventually critiqued and transformed the Christian, religious model of obligation in an attempt to account for the ties of citizenship. This conceptual sea change in Emerson's writings about friendship reflects his life-altering turn away from the ministry and his subsequent embrace of a new-found calling and identity as a lecturer and writer. The centrality of friendship to Emerson's developing model of political relations is evident as early as 1835, when he remarked in his journal that "[s]ociety is the imitation of friendship" (JMN, XII, 40). The secular, political meaning Emerson assigns to friendship is even more explicit in an early lecture titled "Society," delivered two years later at the Masonic Temple in Boston. "Let us now enumerate in order the particular forms of society," Emerson asks in this lecture: "the society of marriage; of friendship; of power (the State); of philanthropy; of opinion (sect or party); of bodies (mobs); of minds (eloquence)" (EL, II, 102).

Like the concept of friendship presented in Emerson's sermons, in the lecture "Society" friendship is described as being closely associated with the educational process and aspiration to knowledge of a divine law. However, in this lecture the education Emerson describes is far more broadly defined than it was in the sermon he preached at the anniversary celebration of the Boston Female Asylum. Whereas in the sermon Emerson praises earthly friendship only insofar as it functions as an illustrative vehicle in developing a child's friendship with and absolute obedience to God, in the lecture "Society" he describes the intellectual benefit of friendship as an inherent, worldly, and social good. "See how joyfully the presence of a friend worketh upon the intellect," he writes. "A man is jaded and malcontent and his mind seems to him empty and its power of producing thought, quite gone. The arrival of a friend tempts thoughts and emotions out of their dark corners, so that instantly he is rich, eloquent, and hopeful, by the mere activity of his own mind" (EL, II, 101). Unlike the earlier sermon, which emphasizes the benefits of education conferred by the teacher on mind of the student, in this lecture

Emerson argues that the reverse is also true—that the benefits of education pass from student to teacher: "Every intellectual man cannot fail to have observed that after reading has become stale and certain thoughts, truisms, the meeting with a young person who has a lively interest in his speculations, shall revive the faded colors, and restore the price of thought," he insists. "This is the foundation in nature, of Education" (*EL*, II, 101).

Thus, in addition to being an expression of Emerson's deep religious feeling, by the late 1830s and early 1840s the concept of friendship had also come to suggest possibilities that were as political and social as they were privately devotional. This importance of friendship as a solution to the problem of political obligation and as a vehicle for Emerson's utopianism is readily apparent in an 1843 journal entry in which he notes that "[i]t will no doubt appear after twenty years that the circle of friends with whom we stand connected, was a sort of masonic fraternity strictly bound, only we are impatient of the slow introductions of Destiny and a little faithless, and think it worth while to venture something" (*JMN*, IX, 22). Indeed, Emerson recognized the important conceptual linkage between friendship and the problem of political obligation as early as 1826, when he observed in his journal that

> You love your friend for your sake, not for his own, might say Hobbists and wolves, for you would not have that good fortune befall him that should raise him above your reach of your society. I please myself that I can dimly see how it would gratify me to promote the very good fortune of my friend. In God's name what is in this topic? It encourages, exhilarates, inspires me. I feel that the affections of the soul are sublimer than the faculties of the intellect. I *feel* immortal. (JMN, III, 25)

The passage is remarkable not just because it powerfully conveys the almost bewildering excitement Emerson experienced in his discovery of friendship as a topic that would inspire the act of writing. It also sets forth a series of related topics that would motivate his exploration of the penchant of the human mind for friendship and explicitly points to his emerging theory of political obligation, a theory that reconciles Hobbesian claims of self-interest with a Christian faith in the affections of the soul. For Emerson, imagining the utopian possibilities of friendship spurs him to imagine a complex vision of political relations and a theory of political obligation he will return to and continue to develop over the course of his entire career.

The theoretical first premises of Emerson's utopian theory of obligation as friendship are put forward as early as 1839, in the lecture "Private Life," which he delivered as part of a winter lecture series, "The Present Age." He observes in this lecture:

> We walk alone in the world. Friends such as we desire are dreams and fables: but a sublime hope cheers ever the faithful heart that elsewhere in other regions of the universal power souls are now acting, enduring, and daring which can love us and which we can love. We may congratulate ourselves that the period of nonage, of follies, of blunders, and of shame is passed in

solitude, and when we are finished men, we shall grasp heroic hands in heroic hands. (EL, II, 254)

Viewed as a critique of liberal contractarianism, the theory of political relations unfolded in this passage is explicitly and systematically developed, as we have already seen, in "The American Scholar," an address delivered three years earlier. Just as in "The American Scholar" Emerson imagines his entrance into civil society as the symbolic act of grasping hands and thus entering into a circle of scholars, so in "Private Life" the emblematic handshake represents an affirmation and critique of liberal contractarianism. But whereas in "The American Scholar," an Emerson imagines this perfect, public realm in nationalist terms as being composed of specifically American scholars, in "Private Life," he imagines instead a cosmopolitan and global but also intimate circle of friends who have been educated to the point that they experience political obligations, which they express in heroic acts of faith and love for one another.

Taken together, Emerson's various, fragmented descriptions of friendship constitute an innovative philosophy of political obligation that contributes to the larger critique of Lockean liberalism unfolded in the early writings. "There are two purposes with which we may seek each other's society," he privately observed in 1834:

> For finite good as when we desire protection, aid in poverty, furtherance in our places, even political societies and philanthropical. All have relation to present well being. But there is a desire of friends for the sake of no mercenary good small or great. There is a seeking of friends that thoughts may be exchanged, sympathies indulged, and a purity of intercourse established that would be as fit for heaven as it is for earth. The object of this intercourse is, that a man may be made known to himself to an extent that in solitude is not practicable. Our faculties are not called out except by means of the affections." (JMN, IV, 270-71)

The significance of Emerson's idea of friendship as a critique of Locke's contractarianism is visible as early as 1830, when Emerson argued that the first and most important attribute of any true friendship is that, like Christ's friendship to man, it represents God's most special and highest gift to humankind. But this theme persisted well after his abandonment of the pulpit and commitment to an imaginative, secular ethos. In 1839, the same year he left the ministry, Emerson noted in his journal, "If you visit your friend, why need you apologize for not having visited him and waste his time and deface your own act? Visit him now. Let him feel that the highest love has come to see him in thee its lowest organ. . . . Be a gift and a benediction. Shine with real light, and not with the borrowed reflection of gifts" (JMN, VII, 192–193); and in 1840 he wrote, "Not by wealth and a city-consequence, not by skill in arts nor by the manners and address of the world could I, if these I had, bring any gift worthy of the acceptance of friendship, but only out of a deeper magazine whereto cities and bankers cannot go, out of the realms of an un-broken peace, of loving meditation, of a habitual conversation with nature" (JMN, VII, 516). Later that same year, Emerson made another entry in his journal that deliberately and explicitly spells out the connection between friendship, the divine gift of grace, and the critique of material ownership:

> I went to a wedding and the Lord said unto me where is thy gift? And I looked and saw that there was nothing in my hand. Then I thought of twenty useful or shining things, and remembered all that I had seen in the gold-smith's windows, and considered what book or gem or trinket I might buy. But the Lord said, These are no gifts for thee: thy desire for these is not thy desire, but the desire of others in thee: look thou back on the city and people thou has left. The gift which thou canst bring and which thy friends expect at thy hands is that which thou canst offer them. I have given thee a door of the Soul to keep: go in thereat, and hearken to what shall be told thee, for never man stood in that place before; and then go to thy friends, and tell them what thou knowest. They shall hearken to thee, and shall forget all that they ever knew. My word is all that thou shalt carry in thy hand. (JMN, VII, 520)

The repeated claim that true friendship is a gift from God forms the basis for what I have described in previous chapters as Emerson's habitual blurring of boundaries that exist between the self and others. For Emerson, friendship presents the possibility of access into even the secretest of moods: "The wise man has no secrets," he observed in 1836. "Secrets belong to the individual, local. He strives evermore to sink the individual in the universal. The friend who can bring him into a certain mood has a right to all the privacies that belong to that mood" (JMN, V, 187). Four years later, he wrote, "Hast thou friends? Do bright eyes and leading souls approach thee once and again, and now in companies? They so inform thee of the fact that you are not your own but a public and sacred property which it were profane in you to hinder in its effect or to degrade to base uses" (JMN, VII, 400).

Emerson's firm belief that his own divine right to property in other per-sons derives from the fact that his friends are gifts from God is most clearly and powerfully articulated in the 1841 essay "Friendship," first published in *Essays: First Series* in 1841:

> I awoke this morning with devout thanksgiving for my friends, the old and the new. Shall I not call God the Beautiful, who daily showeth himself so to me in his gifts? I chide society, I embrace solitude, and yet I am not so ungrateful as not to see the wise, the lovely, and the noble-minded, as from time to time they pass my gate. Who hears me, who understands me, becomes mine,—a possession for all time. Nor is nature so poor but she gives me this joy several times, and thus we weave social threads of our own, a new web of relations; and, as many thoughts in succession substantiate themselves, we shall by and by stand in a new world of our own creation, and no longer strangers and pilgrims in a traditionary globe. My friends have come to me

unsought. The great God gave them to me. By oldest right, by the divine affinity of virtue with itself, I find them, or rather not I, but the Deity in me and in them derides and cancels the thick walls of individual character. (*Essays*, 343)

In this passage, Emerson's cancellation of the walls of individual character, his repudiation of a friend's claim to self-ownership, establishes his claim to a divine right to property in his friend and opens the possibility of limitless appropriation. The critique of individual property rights that is central to the political utopia Emerson imagines—his vision of society as an intimate web of relations, an association of friends in which each friend represents a gift given to him by God—forms as sound a conceptual basis for an imperialist act of appropriation as it stands as an expression of his desire for a society constituted by acts of friendship and love.

When I spoke earlier of Emerson's vision of the self, I suggested that his critique of Locke's model of the self and civil society is structured on a simple, central contradiction between owning and not owning. Likewise, in "Friendship," the contradiction between owning and not owning is used to express an ideal relationship between persons in society. For Emerson, friendship threatens the boundary that constitutes even that most private of possessed spaces, the human body: "I must feel pride in my friend's accomplishments as if they were mine,—and a property in his virtues," he insists. "I feel as warmly when he is praised as the lover when he hears the applause of his engaged maiden. We overestimate the conscience of our friend. . . . Our own thought sounds new and larger from his mouth" (*Essays*, 343). On the one hand, Emerson repudiates the concept of property as insufficient to account for obligations that arise out of the bonds of friendship:

> Leave it to girls and boys to regard a friend as property. The only reward of virtue is virtue; the only way to have a friend is to be one. You shall not come nearer a man by getting into his house. If unlike, his soul only flees the faster from you, and you shall never catch a true glance of his eye. . . . Late,—very late,—we perceive that no arrangements, no introductions, no consuetudes or habits of society, would be of any avail to establish us in such relations with them as we desire,—but solely the uprise of nature in us to the same degree as in them; then shall we meet as water with water; and if we should not meet them then, we shall not want them, for we are already they. (*Essays*, 351, 352)

At the same time, however, that he repudiates the concept of property as insufficient to account for the bonds of friendship, Emerson also argues for the theoretical necessity of the claim to ownership. Paradoxically, the dissolution of property that the act of friendship entails is also one that preserves and justifies the significance of the liberal claim to ownership: "Let us even bid our dearest friends farewell, and defy them," he writes. "Ah! seest thou not, O brother, that thus we part only to meet again on a higher platform, and only be more each other's, because we are more our own?" (*Essays*, 353).

Emerson's imagining of a political community of friends not only stands as a critique of liberal contractarianism, it also represents a critique of theories of obligation and association put forward in traditional philosophical works that explore the meaning of friendship as a category of political thought. The earliest known treatise in Greek on the subject of friendship is found in Plato's *Lysis*.[9] As commentators have noted, Socrates' rhetorical virtuosity and elaborately wrought characterization of friendship in the central dialogue of this treatise has the effect of leaving many readers more confused than enlightened about the meaning of friendship.[10] Perhaps the most unequivocal statement we can make about this dialogue is that the dramatic action represented in the course of Socrates' narrative demonstrates the efficacy of his highly seductive pedagogical method. Indeed, Socrates' own lengthy speculations about the relationship between friendship and desire in the *Lysis* are all the more persuasive in light of the fact that during the course of the dialogue he enacts a seduction of the young student, Lysis.[11] And although Socrates never explicitly addresses the problem of political obligation in his discussion of friendship, the general relevance of political obligation to Plato's *Lysis* is more readily apparent when we consider the fact that Socrates was ultimately tried and executed for his friendship with and alleged corruption of the young.

The connection between the subject of friendship and the problem of political obligation is more explicitly articulated in the eighth and ninth books of Aristotle's *Nicomachean Ethics*.[12] For Aristotle, friendship is not only natural and necessary in all times of life; it is also a powerful means of achieving political order. In this treatise, Aristotle insists that good legislators have had more care for friendship than for justice:

> [F]riendship would seem to hold cities together, and legislators would seem to be more concerned about it than about justice. For concord would seem to be similar to friendship and they aim at concord above all, while they try above all to expel civil conflict, which is enmity. Further, if people are friends, they have no need of justice, but if they are just they need friendship in addition; and the justice that is most just seems to belong to friendship. (*Nicomachean Ethics*, 9.11.23–28)

Aristotle's commentary on friendship in the *Nicomachean Ethics* addresses the problem of political obligation in two respects. First is his suggestion that different types of friendship may be associated with particular political systems—kingship fosters paternal friendship, a king's friendship to his subject; aristocracy is associated with a form of friendship that is analogous to the friendship of man to woman, one which "reflects virtue, in assigning more good to the better, and assigning what is fitting to each" (*Nicomachean Ethics*, 9.65.24–25); and timocracy produces a brotherly form of friendship that exists between citizens who are "meant to be equal and decent, and so rule in turn and on equal terms" (*Nicomachean Ethics*, 9.65.28–29). Second, Aristotle argues that different types of friendship create different forms of obligation: "Must one accord [authority in] everything to his father, and obey him in everything?" he asks. "Or must he trust the doctor when he is sick, and should he vote for a military expert to be general? Similarly, should someone serve his friend rather than an excellent person, and return a favour to a benefactor rather than do a favour for a companion, if he cannot do both?" (*Nicomachean Ethics*, 10.51.23–27).

Friendship continued to be an occasional preoccupation of writers who flourished in the Hellenistic world,[13] but the most influential classical theory of friendship, and one that directly confronted the problem of political obligation, appeared only in late Republican Rome. In his famous essay on friendship, *Laelius De Amicitia*,[14] Cicero established what would become the prevailing view of friendship in discussions of political obligation until the innovative and modern notion of friendship invented in the writings of Montaigne. For Cicero, as for many writers who followed him, friendship represented a valuable support of virtue and political loyalty. In *De Amicitia* he insists that friendship cannot exist except among good men, that no better thing has been given to man by the immortal gods, and that, indeed, the obligations that unite individuals in bonds of friendship are considerably stronger than those associated with the bonds of kinship:

> For it seems clear to me that we were so created that between us all there exists a certain tie which strengthens with our proximity to each other. Therefore, fellow countrymen are preferred to foreigners and relatives to strangers, for with them Nature herself engenders friendship, but it is one that is lacking in constancy. For friendship excels relationship in this, that goodwill may be eliminated from relationship while from friendship it cannot; since, if you remove goodwill from friendship the very name of friendship is gone; if you remove it from relationship, the name of relationship still remains. Moreover, how great the power of friendship is may most clearly be recognized from the fact that, in comparison with the infinite ties uniting the human race and fashioned by Nature herself, this thing called friendship has been so narrowed that the bonds of affection always unite two persons only, or, at most, a few. (*De Amicitia*, 129)

At the same time, however, that he demonstrates the value of friendship as a support to political loyalty, Cicero also insists upon one fundamental law of friendship—namely, that obligations arising out of friendship are in every case inferior to civic obligations. "Therefore let this law be established in friendship: neither ask dishonourable things, nor do them, if asked," he writes. "And dishonourable it certainly is, and not to be allowed, for anyone to plead in defence of sins in general and especially of those against the State, that he committed them for the sake of a friend" (*De Amicitia*, 151).

The classical, Ciceronian view of friendship prevailed in the tradition of political thought that extends up to the Renaissance, when Michel de Montaigne's radical critique of this tradition established what we now recognize as the modern conceptual framework for thinking about friendship and the problem of political obligation.[15] "What we ordinarily call friends and friendships are nothing but acquaintanceships and familiarities formed by some chance or convenience, by means of which our souls are bound to each other," Montaigne observes. "In the friendship I speak of, our souls mingle and blend with each other so completely that they efface the seam that joined them, and cannot find it again. If you press me to tell why I loved him, I feel that this cannot be expressed, except by answering: Because it was he, because it was I."[16] Montaigne's "Of Friendship" marks a significant break from the Ciceronian tradition because in this essay he argues that obligations arising out of the bonds of friendship supersede and demonstrate the limits of civic obligations: in contrast to Cicero, Montaigne argues that we are friends before we are citizens or subjects.

What is most important to notice about Montaigne's essay is that it bears a striking similarity to Emerson's early writings on the subject of friendship insofar as, like Emerson, Montaigne uses friendship to critique the Lockean, liberal concept of obligations that are assumed by acts of rational, voluntary consent. Elaborating on his point that Laelius and Blossius "were more friends than citizens," Montaigne explicitly frames this question of obligation as the question of whether the notion of voluntary consent has any applicability to actions motivated by the judgments of a true friend. Montaigne compares Blossius's statement that he would obey his friend Laelius even if such obedience entailed acts against the state with Montaigne's own rationale for answering "yes" to the question "If your will commanded you to kill your daughter, would you kill her?"

> For that does not bear witness to any consent to do so, because I have no doubt at all about my will, and just as little about that of such a friend. It is not in the power of all the arguments in the world to dislodge me from the certainty I have of the intentions and judgments of my friend. Not one of his actions could be presented to me, whatever appearance it might have, that I could not immediately find the motive for it. Our souls pulled together in such unison, they regarded each other with such ardent affection, and with a like affection revealed themselves to each other to the very depths of our hearts, that not only did I know his soul as well as mine, but I should certainly have trusted myself to him more readily than to myself. (OF, 140)

Emerson's own writings on friendship show that he persistently returned to and grappled with the characterization of friendship set forth in Montaigne's essay.[17] As early as 1838, in a lecture titled "The Heart," Emerson quoted extensively from a passage in Montaigne's essay in which Montaigne insists upon the validity and effect of obligations associated with friendship as a means of demonstrating the limits of political obligations imposed by the State.

> There is no more remarkable example in modern times of a thorough and noble friendship than that of Montaigne and Stephen de Boece, described

to us in the most engaging lines by Montaigne himself. Montaigne proceeds to intimate the laws of this amity.

> When Lealius in the presence of the Roman Consuls who, after they had sentenced Tiberius Gracchus, prosecuted all those who had any familiarity with him also, came to ask Caius Blosius, who was his chiefest friend and confident, how much he would have done for him? And he made answer, 'All things.' 'How! All things!' said Laelius. 'And what if he had commanded you to fire the temples?'—'He would never have commanded me that,' replied Blosius.—'But what if he had?' said Laelius. 'Why if he had, I would have obeyed him,' said the other. Those who accuse this answer as seditious, do not well understand the mystery nor presuppose that he had Gracchus's will in his sleeve both by the power of a friend and the perfect knowledge he had of the man. They were more friends than citizens, and more friends to one another than either friends or enemies to their country, or than friends to ambition and innovation. Having absolutely given up themselves to one another, either held absolutely the reins of the other's inclination, which also they governed by Virtue and guided by the conduct of Reason (which also without these it had not been possible to do) and therefore Blosius's answer was such as it ought to be. If either of their actions flew out of the handle, they were neither (according to my measure of friendship) friends. (*EL*, II, 290–291)

The sheer length of the quotation taken from Montaigne in Emerson's attempt to articulate the connection between friendship and political obligation is itself a highly uncharacteristic expression of intellectual dependency on Emerson's part. But what is perhaps even more striking is the way in which Emerson also critiques Montaigne in "The Heart." Immediately following his recitation of Montaigne, Emerson observes:

> But alas! In relation again to *the actual state of society* it will appear on much experiment that one cannot enter intimately, lovingly into familiarity with numbers of men, that great waste of time and great waste of peace would be incurred and endless chagrins. Wisdom seems to teach us to make no great effort in the matter but let societies form as will. Say, "Here am I, a complex human being. Welcome to me all men, all creatures. Welcome each to your part in me. You shall have conversation and such cooperation as the natural sympathy you form with me demands. It is easy to conceive that tomorrow I may encounter a person who shall command my entire being. But now welcome the wise man to his part; the kind man to his; the forward and the mean man to all he can get also. (*EL*, II, 291; emphasis added)

At first glance, Emerson's reference to the "*actual* state of society" would seem to indicate that he is putting forward a cultural critique of Montaigne's philosophy of friendship. But the relative conceptual inadequacy of this critique is evident in the fact that it devolves, in the end, upon a simple language game. The pun on the word "state" is here used, rather unconvincingly, to show that Emerson's exploration of the human penchant for friendship results in a definition of obligations that are simultaneously social and political. Emerson's vision of a more perfect state, organized by sacred ties of friendship, is more effectively represented in an 1840 journal entry in which he observes that "[w]e should be very rich if we could speak the truth, for since that is the law of our progress, in proportion to our truth we should coin the world into our words. If we, dear friends, shall arrive at speaking the truth to each other, we shall not come away as we went. We shall be able to bring near and give away to each other the love and power of all the friends who encircle each of us, and that society which is the dream of each shall stablish itself in our midst, and the fable of Heaven be the fact of God" (*JMN*, VII, 513).

The critique of Montaigne that forms the basis for much of Emerson's thinking about friendship as political obligation is nowhere more fully and explicitly unfolded than in his essay "Friendship." At one critical jucture in his argument, Emerson repudiates Montaigne's thesis concerning the essentially apolitical nature of friendship by arguing instead that the ties of citizenship should be identical to those of friendship.

> My author says,—'I offer myself faintly and bluntly to those whose I effectually am, and tender myself least to him to whom I am the most devoted.' I wish that friendship should have feet, as well as eyes and eloquence. It must plant itself on the ground, before it vaults over the moon. I wish it to be a little of a citizen, before it is quite a cherub. We chide the citizen because he makes love a commodity. It is an exchange of gifts, of useful loans; it is good neighborhood; it watches with the sick; it holds the pall at the funeral; and quite loses sight of the delicacies and nobility of the relation.... The end of friendship is a commerce the most strict and homely that can be joined; more strict than any of which we have experience. (*Essays*, 348)

In contrast to the idea of friendship established in Montaigne's essay—and indeed, in contrast to concepts of friendship presented in an entire tradition of classical and modern political thought—Emerson argues in "Friendship" that obligations arising out of friendship are in fact political obligations; that friendship exists not only as a threat or support to obligations that bind citizens to the state, but that the bonds of friendship are actually constitutive of the state.

Emerson's critique of Montaigne—in particular, his recourse to friendship as an alternative to rationally assumed, contractual obligations that draw citizens together, binding them to the state—is visible as early as 1834, when Emerson observed in his journal that

> [i]t occurs that the distinction should be drawn in treating of Friendship between the *aid of commodity*, which our friends yield us, as in hospitality, gifts, sacrifices, & c. & which, as in the old story about the poor man's will in Montaigne, are evidently esteemed by the natural mind (to use a cant word) the highest manifestations of love; and secondly, the spiritual aid— far more precious and leaving the other at infinite distance,—which our

friends afford us, of confession, of appeal, of social stimulus, mirroring ourselves. (JMN, IV, 271)

Like Montaigne, Emerson distinguishes between obligations associated with
"the aid of commodity" (what Montaigne calls "convenience") and the intimate expression of obligations entailed in the friendly act of offering up spiritual aid, which blends individual souls with each other so completely that
they efface the seam that joined them.

Even more important is the fact that, despite his fundamental differences
with Montaigne regarding the public, political relevance of obligations arising
out of friendship, Emerson's examination of friendship as a critique of liberal
contractarianism—his effort to point out the limits of consent as a useful,
coherent political concept—is similar to the critique of consent set forth in
Montaigne's essay. But whereas Montaigne makes no mention of friendship
as a Christian ideal, Emerson's critique of consent devolves upon his systematic merging of liberal and religious discourses on obligation. Just as in his
early sermons on the subject, Emerson's definition of friendship as political
obligation required his reconciliation of the Lockean, liberal claim to rational
self-interest with an abiding Christian faith in the affections of the soul, so
in the essay "Friendship" he would present a model of political obligation
that, like the sacrament of the Lord's Supper, would reveal the immanence of
God in a fallen, material world. Drawing on the same rhetorical strategies
developed, as I have already tried to show, in seventeenth-century Protestant
emblem poetry, conveys in "Friendship" Emerson the necessity and the insufficiency of the idea of ownership in order to imagine this new mode of
political association and assumption of political obligations among persons.

On the one hand, Emerson suggests that the obligation to perform mutual
acts of sacrifice, which is the only mark of true friendship, is comprehensible
only if liberal concepts of ownership and voluntary, rational consent are preserved: "We must be our own before we can be another's," he writes (Essays,
351). "Friendship requires that rare mean betwixt likeness and unlikeness, that
piques each with the presence of power and of consent in the other party. . . .
Let him not cease an instant to be himself. The only joy I have in his being
mine, is that the not mine is mine. . . . There must be very two, before there
can be very one" (Essays, 350). On the other hand, in "Friendship," Emerson
also insists that true friends can never own themselves and thus voluntarily
consent to their act of association because each represents a divine gift given
for the enjoyment of the other. At the same time that he shares Locke's
analysis of consent as economic exchange—that is, consent that is manifested
as the rational and self-interested assumption of political obligations—Emerson also reveals the limitations of such an account of the relationship that
exists between friends.

> So I will owe to my friends this evanescent intercourse. I will receive from
> them, not what they have, but what they are. They shall give me that which
> properly they cannot give, but which emanates from them. But they shall

not hold me by any relations less subtle and pure. We will meet as though we met not, and part as though we parted not. (*Essays*, 354)

Emerson's use of the word "emanate" in this passage recalls the emblematic handshake he imagined in "The American Scholar" and "Private Life" to express both an affirmation and a critique of social contract. The Lockean social contract results first in the formation of a political association and then in the establishment of a liberal government. The first stage results in a relationship of obligation between members of the political community, while the second results in a relationship of obligation between each citizen and the liberal state. For Locke and other liberal theorists, the creation and justification of these self-assumed political obligations in every case entail the citizen's free and rational consent, the free and rational act of choosing to be put under political authority.[18] By contrast, Emerson observes in "Friendship" that "[w]e talk of choosing our friends, but friends are self-elected" (*Essays*, 350).

Emerson's attempt to underscore the limits of consent as the basis for political obligation in "Friendship" centers primarily on a particular form of consent described by Locke in the *Second Treatise*—namely, consent that is "tacit." Philosophers of consent have long debated the question of whether "express consent" to a given political system—consent,that is, which is manifested as deliberate, voluntary acts such as pledges of allegiance or active participation in politics—is a realistic account of how obligations are undertaken in liberal society. Many liberal writers have attempted to solve this problem and maintained voluntarist justifications for political obligation by arguing that there is a kind of silence that represents "tacit consent through residence," a phrase Locke himself uses in Section 119 of the *Second Treatise*.

> There is a common distinction of an express and a tacit consent, which will concern our present Case. No body doubts but an *express Consent*, of any Man, entring into any Society, makes him a perfect Member of that Society, a Subject of that Government. The difficulty is, what ought to be look'd upon as a *tacit Consent*, and how far it binds, *i.e.* how far any one shall be looked on to have consented, and thereby submitted to any Government, where he has made no Expressions of it at all. And to this I say, that every Man, that hath any Possession, or Enjoyment, of any part of the Dominions of any Government, doth thereby give his *tacit Consent*, and is as far forth obliged to Obedience to the Laws of that Government, during such Enjoyment, as any one under it; whether this his Possession be of Land, to him and his Heirs for ever, or a Lodging only for a Week; or whether it be barely travelling freely on the Highway; and in Effect, it reaches as far as the very being of any one within the Territories of that Government.[19]

Emerson's "Friendship" is full of references to tacit consent. But whereas Locke defines such consent in terms of possession and enjoyment of any government's dominions—even when such consent is expressed as free travel on a public highway—Emerson views consent as the intimate and silent assumption and recognition of obligations that exist between persons in society.

"How many persons we meet in houses, whom we scarcely speak to, whom yet we honor, and who honor us!" he writes. "How many we see in the street, or sit with in church, whom, though silently, we warmly rejoice to be with! Read the language of these wandering eye-beams. The heart knoweth" (*Essays*, 341). Later in the essay he observes, "What is so great as friendship, let us carry with what grandeur of spirit we can. Let us be silent,—so we may hear the whisper of the gods" (*Essays*, 352). And: "I cannot afford to speak much with my friend. If he is great, he makes me so great that I cannot descend to converse" (*Essays*, 353).

Emerson's critique of Locke's theory of tacit consent has two main facets. First, whereas Locke and other liberal philosophers define tacit consent as being wholly voluntary, Emerson's thinking about this special form of consent is that it is never purely self-interested, rational, or voluntary. Challenging Locke's fundamental premise, Emerson insists that the experience of mutual enjoyment—enjoyment that directly follows from the act of assuming the obligations of true friendship—involves the involuntary responses of the heart just as much as it reflects the willed reasoning of the mind. But even more important than this critique of Locke's voluntarism is Emerson's questioning of the meaning of "free travel" as Locke deploys this concept in Section 119 of the *Second Treatise*.[20] As political philosophers such as Arendt have pointed out, viewed in historical terms, freedom of movement is the most elementary, necessary precondition for action. Arendt writes, "Of all the specific liberties which may come into our minds when we hear the word 'freedom,' freedom of movement is historically the oldest and also the most elementary. Being able to depart for where we will is the prototypical gesture of being free, as limitation of freedom of movement has from time immemorial been the precondition for enslavement. Freedom of movement is also the indispensible condition for action, and it is in action that men primarily experience freedom in the world."[21]

Taken together, Emerson's early writings on friendship constituted not just an innovative philosophical critique of liberal theories of consent and political obligation. The broader, cultural value of this theory of friendship was that it allowed him to construct a model of American national identity. The political community of friends Emerson imagines in these early writings is far more intimate and cohesive than any nation constituted by ties that are merely economic and contractual. Indeed, this startling discovery of the connection between, on the one hand, the philosophical question of obligation and, on the other, the largely cultural problem of imagining national identity ultimately results in a representation of group identity that is simultaneously global, infinitely permeable, and expansive (because any friendly person can join); and also exclusive and nationalist (because other individuals will be left out). Given the advent of civil war, the urgency of Emerson's nationalist project helps us to better understand why, as I will now show, Emerson eventually doubted the viability of friendship as a model of political obligation, turning instead to racialist discourse in the formulation of a collective identity for Americans.

When we look carefully at Emerson's various references to friendship, we can see that over the years he became more and more disillusioned with this concept as a useful vehicle for the expression of his utopianism. As early as 1835, he noted to himself, "Who is capable of manly friendship? Very few" (*JMN*, V, 38); two years later he wrote, "I was born a seeing eye not a helping hand. I can only comfort my friends by thought, and not by love or aid. But they naturally look for this other also, and thereby vitiate our relation, throughout" (*JMN*, V, 298). In 1839, he asked himself, "How can I hope for a friend to me who have never been one?" (*JMN*, VII, 204), and on October 26 of that same year, he observed, "Perhaps the true solution of this problem of spending a day well, is to be found for me and such as me in that social activity which I forbear. If I should (or say, *could*) set myself to the unhesitating mission of inviting all persons from house to house to come up into my way of thinking and seeing—boldly and lovingly affirming the peace which I find in my detached position and perfect reliance on the Universal Order . . . [,] that would be occupation, excitement, and the prolific occasion, no doubt, of antagonisms . . . , and friendships . . . —coincidences and collisions with the laws and the lawmakers, that would elicit deep traits of character in myself and in my fellows" (*JMN*, VII, 280). In a notebook dated from the late 1830s to early 1840s he wrote that "[f]riends are expedients like stoves" (*JMN*, XII, 321), and in 1842 he wrote, "You say perhaps Nature will yet give me the joy of friendship. But our pleasures are in some proportion to our forces. I have so little vital force that I could not stand the dissipation of a flowing and friendly life; I should die of consumption in three months. But now I husband all my strength in this bachelor life I lead, and no doubt shall be a well preserved old gentleman" (*JMN*, VII, 463). One year later he observed that "[i]t is a pathetic thing to meet a friend prepared to love you, to whom yet, from some inaptitude, you cannot communicate yourself with that grace and power which only love will allow. You wish to repay his goodness by showing him the dear relations that subsist between you and your chosen friends but you feel that he cannot conceive of you whom he knows so slow and cold, under these sweet and gentle aspects" (*JMN*, VIII, 365), and in 1846 he wrote that "[f]riends, pictures, books, lower duties, talents, flatteries, hopes, all are distractions which cause formidable oscillations in our giddy balloon, and seem to make a good poise and a straight course impossible" (*JMN*, IX, 366). That same year he privately observed that "[t]he lesson of life lately is a pretty rapid rotation of friends" (*JMN*, IX, 400), and two years later he noted that "I spoke of friendship, but my friends and I are fishes in their habit. As far as taking [Thoreau's] arm, I should as soon take the arm of an elm tree" (*JMN*, X, 343). Revising a note he made to himself in 1845,

Emerson wrote that "[m]uch of the time every man must be his own friend" (*JMN*, X, 387), and by 1850 he seemed to have disregarded the possibility of friendship altogether: "A man of 45 does not want to open new accounts of friendship," he noted in his journal. "He has said Kitty kitty long enough" (*JMN*, XI, 262).

The main point of this catalogue of quotations is simply to document Emerson's gradual disillusionment with friendship, both as a real-life possibility and as a utopian, nationalist ideal. This disillusionment with friendship makes an obvious, fundamental point about Emerson's nationalism that has never been shown in Emerson studies: namely, that only this abandonment of friendship as a model of political community can explain Emerson's increasing dependency on "race" as an expression of American national cohesiveness and distinctiveness.

Looked at from this sociohistorical standpoint, it is thus interesting (but not at all surprising) to find that the philosphical framework Emerson adduces in his early writings on friendship is essentially proto-racialist. This proto-racialism is visible as early as 1839, when in his journal Emerson pictured the intimacy of friendship in metaphorical terms as the admixture of blood. "Every friend whom not thy fantastic Will but the great and tender Heart in thee craveth, shall lock thee in his embrace," he writes, "and this, because the heart in thee is the Heart of all, not a valve, not a wall, not an intersection is there any where in nature,—but one blood rolls uninterruptedly an endless circulation through all men, as the water of the globe is all one sea, and truly seen its tide is one" (*JMN*, VII, 268). Two years later also pointed out this connection between friendship and metaphorically racial (or "native") affinity in "Spiritual Laws," when he briefly observed that "only that soul can be my friend which I encounter on the line of my own march, that soul to which I do not decline, and which does not decline to me, but, *native* of the same celestial latitude, repeats in its own all my experience" (*Essays*, 315; emphasis added).

The developing habit of association in Emerson's mind between friendship and race is even more explicit in writings that explore the claims of what he defines as "kindness." In Emerson's account, kindness is a political term that differs from the Lockean, liberal concept of political obligation in two main respects. First, it is important to note in connection with Emerson's emerging racialism that his utopian vision of kindness between friends was often expressed metaphorically in terms of racial homogeneity and unity. For Emerson, kindness is a crucial concept of obligation that systematically registers the subtle conceptual slippage between his idea of obligations associated with kindness between friends to political obligations that arise out of kinship as proto-racialist ideal. This interest in kindness as an exclusive, proto-racialist concept of political obligation is clearly put forward in "The Young American," a lecture read before the Mercantile Library Association in 1844. Although Emerson makes no mention of friendship, he does unequivocally promote the conceptual usefulness of kindness for the expression of his racial nationalism. Imagining a vigorous, racially cohesive political community of gentlemanly Young Americans, Emerson writes,

> Gentlemen, there is a sublime and friendly Destiny by which the human race is guided,—the race never dying, the individual never spared,—to results affecting masses and ages. It is not discovered in their calculated and voluntary activity, but in what befalls, with or without their design. . . . Remark the unceasing effort throughout nature at somewhat better than the actual creatures: *amelioration in nature*, which alone permits and authorizes amelioration in mankind. The population of the world is a conditional population; these are not the best, but the best that could live in the existing state of soils, gases, animals, and morals: the best that could *yet* live; there shall be a better, please God. This Genius, or Destiny, is of the sternest administration, though rumors exist of its secret tenderness. It may be styled a cruel kindness, serving the whole even to the ruin of the member; a terrible communist, reserving all profits to the community, without dividend to individuals. Its law is, you shall have everything as a member, nothing to yourself. (*Essays*, 217–218)

In addition to the slippage between racialism and kindness that we find in Emerson's writings is the fact of his own indecision regarding the voluntary or involuntary nature of obligations arising out of kindness between friends. The creative tension or contradiction between the voluntary and the involuntary implicit in Emerson's idea of kindness in friendship persists throughout his writings. In 1841, the same year that he published the essay "Friendship," Emerson distinguished between obligations owed to "new" friends that are voluntarily created and those associated with "natural" friends or related kin that are born into or found:[22]

> The new relations we form we are apt to prefer as *our own* ties, to those natural ones which they have supplanted. Yet how strict these are, we must learn later, when we recall our childhood and youth with vivid affection, and feel a poignant solitude even the the multitude of modern friends. . . . How our friendships . . . shame us now—they withdraw, they disappear, . . . — and our elder company, the dear children and grave relatives with whom we played and studied and repented,—they return and join hands again. I feel suddenly that my life is frivolous and public . . . ; I would fain quit my present companions . . . [and] bewail my innocency and recover it, and with it the power to commune again with these sharers of a more sacred idea. (*JMN*, VII, 444)

The paradoxical nature of obligations associated with kindness in friendship ultimately contributes to Emerson's critique of Lockean, liberal contractarianism. Earlier in this chapter we saw that that in his sermons Emerson used the concept of kindness to critique Locke's idea of rational, voluntary consent, and to support his own claims regarding the involuntary nature of Christian kindness to all our fellow men. In the sermon preached at the Boston Female Asylum, he makes a careful distinction between kindness we involuntarily owe to all our fellow men and another, special form of kindness or obligation we owe to our friends, obligations that we are in some sense at liberty to assume. But by the time he was writing his 1837 lecture "Society," Emerson had arrived at a new, different definition of obligations between friends that expresses an increasing emphasis on "kindness" as a proto-racialist concept. In this lecture, he argues that political obligations associated with kindness can bind together not simply an intimate circle of friends, but also casual acquaintances and neighborhoods, whole towns, countries, and even continents. The obligations that arise out of such kindness, in this account, are in every case involuntarily assumed. Just as he would later argue, in the published essay "Friendship," that the unspoken, involuntary acts and obligations of kindness extend to "the whole human family" (*Essays*, 341), so in "Society" he writes:

> The next society to marriage and the household is that of friendship, the league of kindness and congenial taste and temper from the most strict to the feeblest bond of acquaintance in all degrees of kindliness which make neighborhoods, towns, countries, continents of the globe interesting to each man by the names and social ties which draw his heart to them. . . . A great deal more is learned than is spoken in all conversation. The joy of kindness is here made known, the joy of love which admitteth of no excess. (*EL*, II, 103–104)

Later, in an 1849 lecture, "Private Life," Emerson once again modifies his position on the question of whether the obligations associated with kindness in friendship are voluntarily or involuntarily assumed. Here he insists instead that our friends should be a private matter of choice: "Nothing is more deeply punished than the neglect of the great affinities by which alone society should be formed and the foolish levity of choosing associates by others' eyes" (*EL*, III, 255).

The contradiction between voluntaristic rights discourse and the involuntary demands of racialism exhibited throughout Emerson's writings on political obligation and the model of individual and national identity he designates as "double-consciousness" will be taken up in the following chapter. For the moment, I will end with the simple observation that Emerson's theory of friendship as a form of political obligation is an important subject that has gone virtually unexamined by his critics, and that only one philosopher of friendship systematically explored the full significance of thinking about friendship for the developing expression of American nationalism.[23] I am thinking of the "Wednesday" section in Thoreau's *A Week on the Concord and Merrimack Rivers*, which Thoreau completed in 1847 and published two years later.[24] Viewed in connection with the tradition of politial writings on friendship, Thoreau's philosophy of friendship as obligation is distinctive insofar as he deploys such a concept of obligation in order to elaborate on Emerson's political critique and, in the end, to arrive at a cohesive theory of political identity that is both individual and collective or national.

For Thoreau, as for Emerson, friendship represents an effective vehicle for his imagination of political utopia in A Week:

> The State does not demand justice of its members, but thinks that it succeeds very well with the least degree of it, hardly more than rogues practice; and so do the neighborhood and the family. What is commonly called Friendship even is only a little more honor among rogues. But sometimes we are said to *love* another, that is, to stand in a true relation to him, so that we give the best to, and receive the best from, him. . . . There are passages of affection in our intercourse with mortal men and women, such as no prophecy had taught us to expect, which transcend our earthly life, and anticipate Heaven for us. What is this Love . . . that discovers a new world, fair and fresh and eternal, occupying the place of the old one, when to the common eye a dust has settled on the universe? (A Week, 218–219)

More specifically, as for Emerson, for Thoreau friendship represents possibilities for the characterization of an ideal relationship of political obligation, a system of higher rights and duties that marks the existence of a "pure and lofty society": "[Friendship] is not the highest sympathy merely," he insists, "but a pure and lofty society, a fragmentary and godlike intercourse of ancient date, still kept up at intervals, which, remembering itself, does not hesitate to disregard the humbler rights and duties of humanity" (A Week, 224).

In A Week, Thoreau stresses the involuntary nature of the act of assuming political obligations, and in this respect the critique of liberalism implicit in his model of friendship resembles the critique of liberalism set forth in Emerson's writings.

> The books for young people say a great deal about the *selection* of Friends; it is because they really have nothing to say about *Friends*. Friendship takes place between those who have an affinity for one another, and is a perfectly natural and inevitable result. No professions nor advances will avail. . . . It is a drama in which the parties have no part to act. We are all Mussulmen and fatalists in this respect. Impatient and uncertain lovers think that they must say or do something kind whenever they meet; they must never be cold. But they who are Friends do not do what they *think* they must, but what they *must*. (A Week, 219)

Thoreau's observation that "[w]e are all Mussulmen and fatalists" reflects the fact that in A Week his emphasis on the involuntary assumption of obligations leads him to imagine the ties of friendship in fated terms. "There is on the earth no institution which Friendship has established; it is not taught by any religion; no scripture contains its maxims. It has no temple, nor even a solitary column," he observes. "However, our fates at least are social. Our courses do not diverge; but as the web of destiny is woven it is fulled, and we are cast more and more into the centre. Men naturally, though feebly, seek this alliance, and their actions faintly fortell it" (A Week, 215).

Although Thoreau resembles Emerson in his emphasis on the involuntary, fated assumption of obligations in friendship, in A Week he carefully resists what I have identified as the incipient racialism of Emerson's writings on friendship. "For the most part we stupidly confound one man with another," Thoreau observes. "The dull distinguish only races or nations, or at most classes, but the wise man, individuals. To his Friend a man's peculiar character appears in every feature and in every action, and it is thus drawn out and improved by him" (A Week, 217). Later, he suggests that "[m]y Friend is not of some other race or family of men, but flesh of my flesh, bone of my bone. He is my real brother. I see his nature groping yonder so like mine. We do not live far apart. Have not the fates associated us in many ways?" (A Week, 231). The critique of Emerson's racialism in this passage is articulated as Thoreau's allusion to the Book of Genesis, the moment at which Eve has been given by God for the enjoyment of Adam (Genesis 2: 23). Like Emerson, Thoreau insists that friends represent a divine gift, and that as such friendship represents a critique of the liberal concept of private property rights: "The true and not despairing Friend will address his Friend in some such terms as these," he writes. "I never asked thy leave to let me love thee,—I have a right. I love thee not as something private and personal, which is your own, but as something universal and worthy of love, which I have found (A Week, 219). However, unlike Emerson, Thoreau claims that the existence of a fated kinship which friendship represents is proven not in terms of the mere structural similarity of bodies but rather in similar gaits of the soul or "groping natures."

Thoreau's critique of Emerson's racialism is also expressed in A Week as his resistance to the racialism implicit in Emerson's use of the word "kindness." "Friendship is not so kind as imagined," Thoreau argues, "it has not much human blood in it, but consists with a certain disregard for men and their erections, the Christian duties and humanities, while it purifies the air like electricity" (A Week, 224). Indeed, just as Emerson opens his discussion of political obligation in "Friendship" by referring to a form of kindness which extends to the whole human family, so Thoreau's discussion of friendship in A Week opens with his claim that

> [w]hile we float here, far from that tributary stream on whose banks our Friends and kindred dwell, our thoughts, like the stars, come out of their horizon still; for there circulates a finer blood than Lavoisier has discovered the laws of,—the blood, not of kindred merely, but of kindness, whose pulse still beats at any distance and forever.
>
> > True kindness is a pure divine affinity,
> > Not founded upon human consanguinity.
> > It is a spirit, not a blood relation,
> > Superior to family and station. (A Week, 211)

In contrast to Emerson, whose speculations about the involuntary assumption of obligations associated with kindness demonstrate the gradual but inevitable emergence of a racialist bias, Thoreau insists upon the difference between kindred and kindness, and argues in A Week that true kindness can never be founded upon the consanguinity associated with a scientific concept of race.

I have suggested that the critique of private property rights set forth in Emerson's writings on friendship functions to establish his claim to a divine right to property in his friend, and opens the possibility of Emerson's own act of limitless appropriation. In this respect, Emerson's model of friendship as political obligation forms as sound a conceptual basis for the imperialist act of expansion as it stands as an expression of his desire for a political community constituted by acts of friendship and love. By contrast, in A Week Thoreau makes explicit the imperialism which is only implicit in Emerson's writings on friendship:

> The Friend is some fair floating isle of palms eluding the mariner in Pacific seas. Many are the dangers to be encountered, equinoctial gales and coral reefs, ere he may sail before the constant trades. But who would not sail through mutiny and storm, even over Atlantic waves, to reach the fabulous retreating shores of some continent man? . . . Columbus has sailed westward of these isles by the mariner's compass, but neither he nor his successors have found them. We are no nearer than Plato was. The earnest seeker and hopeful discoverer of this New World always haunts the outskirts of his time, and walks through the densest crowd uninterrupted, and as it were in a straight line.
>
> > Sea and land are but his neighbors,
> > And companions in his labors,
> > Who on the ocean's verge and firm land's end
> > Doth long and truly seek his Friend. (A Week, 213–214)

Thoreau's most significant revision of Emerson's model of friendship as political obligation consists in his attempt to present explicitly and systematically the implications of this model for a theory of national identity. In many respects, the nation of friends Thoreau imagines in A Week is structurally analogous to the nation of disobedients he imagines in the essay "Resistance to Civil Government," published the same year as A Week. In "Resistance to Civil Government," Thoreau imagines an ideal political community or nation of disobedients that stands at once inside and outside of the state, and whose act of withdrawal is in fact compatible with the existence of the state. "I please myself with imagining a State at last which can afford to be just to all men, and to treat the individual with respect as a neighbor, which even would not think it inconsistent with its own repose, if a few were to live aloof from it, not meddling with it, nor embraced by it, who fulfilled all the duties of neighbors and fellow-men," he writes. "A State which bore this kind of fruit, and suffered it to drop off as fast as it ripened, would prepare the way for a still more perfect and glorious State, which also I have imagined, but not yet anywhere seen."[25] Thoreau conceives of this nation of disobedients as being infinitely expansive, because in theory any individual belongs who follows the coercive dictates of his or her conscience and involuntarily assumes the obligation to withdraw from America as an existing and unjust state. But the freer and disobedient nation Thoreau describes within the confines of his prison is a nation of one, because the political obligations or dicates of conscience he invokes represent both his personal opinion and a universal moral law. "I do not hesitate to say, that those who call themselves abolitionists should at once effectively withdraw their support, both in person and in property, from the government of Massachusetts, and not wait till they constitute a majority of one, before they suffer the right to prevail through them," he writes. "I think that it is enough if they have God on their side, without waiting for that other one. Moreover, any man more right than his neighbors, constitutes a majority of one already" (CD, 74).

Like the model of national identity Thoreau describes in "Resistance to Civil Government," the model of national identity or "pure and lofty society" he envisions in A Week is both infinitely expansive and contracts in size to the smallest possible nation of two:

> As for the number which this society admits, it is at any rate to be begun with one, the noblest and greatest that we know. Yet Friendship does not stand for numbers; the Friend does not count his Friends on his fingers; they are not numerable. The more there are included by this bond, if they are indeed included, the rarer and diviner the quality of love that binds them. I am ready to believe that as private and intimate a relation may exist by which three are embraced, as between two. Indeed, we cannot have too many friends; the virtue which we appreciate we to some extent appropriate, so that thus we are made at last more fit for every relation of life. A base Friendship is of a narrowing and exclusive tendency, but a noble one is not exclusive; its very superfluity and dispersed love is the humanity which sweetens society, and sympathizes with foreign nations, for though its foundations are private, it is, in effect, a public affair and a public advantage, and the Friend, more than the father of a family, deserves well of the state. (A Week, 225)

At the same time that he argues that this political community of friends stands aloof from what he identifies as the "large and respectable nation of Acquaintances," Thoreau imagines the possibility of appropration and inclusion of these acquaintances in the expanding nation of friends.

> This other word of entreaty and advice to the large and respectable nation of Acquaintances, beyond the mountains;—Greeting. My most serene and irresponsible neighbors, let us see that we have the whole advantage of each other; we will be useful, at least, if not admirable, to one another. I know that the mountains which separate us are high, and covered with perpetual snow, but despair not. Improve the serene winter weather to scale them. If need be, soften the rocks with vinegar. For here lie the verdant plains of Italy ready to receive you. Nor shall I be slow on my side to penetrate to your Provence. (A Week, 233)

Even "Strangers and Enemies" are incorporated into Thoreau's model nation of friends, bound by the friendly obligation Thoreau strategically undertakes in his essay, namely the obligation to serve them: "Ah, my dear Strangers and Enemies, I would not forget you," he insists. "I can well afford to welcome you. Let me subscribe myself Yours ever and truly,—your much obliged servant" (A Week, 234). The infinitely expansive model of national identity Thoreau imagines in A Week is articulated in the poem with which he concludes his discussion of friendship in the "Wednesday" section, a poem he addresses to "one and all," "Friends, Romans, Countrymen, and Lovers":

No warder at the gate
Can let the friendly in,
But, like the sun, o'er all
He will the castle win,
And shine along the wall. (A Week, 235)

I began this chapter with the suggestion that, for Emerson, friendship is associated with the existence and expression of deep religious feeling. The same holds true for Thoreau: in a passage that echoes Keats's "Ode to Autumn," Thoreau demonstrates that his faith in friendship is such that it enables him to confront lovingly the inevitable growth and decay of his world, and not avert his eyes.

As surely as the sunset in my latest November shall translate me to the ethereal world, and remind me of the ruddy morning of my youth as surely as the last strain of music which falls on my decaying ear shall make age to be forgotten, or, in short, the manifold influences of nature survive during the term of our natural life, so surely my Friend shall forever be my Friend, and reflect a ray of God to me, and time shall foster and adorn and consecrate our Friendship, no less than the ruins of temples. As I love nature, as I love singing birds, and gleaming stubble, and flowing rivers, and morning and evening, and summer and winter, I love thee, my Friend. (A Week, 232)

Thoreau insists that, as an expression of faith, the mutual, involuntary assumption of obligations between friends should always be tacit, a silent but eloquent act: "[Friendship] is a miracle which requires constant proofs," he writes. "It is an exercise of the purest imagination and the rarest faith. It says by a silent but eloquent behavior,—'I will be so related to thee as thou canst imagine; even so thou mayest believe. I will spend truth,—all my wealth on thee,'—and the Friend responds silently through his nature and life, and treats his Friend with the same divine courtesy. . . . The language of Friendship is not words, but meanings. It is an intelligence above language" (222). For Thoreau, faith is not a remembered assurance, but his profound enjoyment of knowledge that the mutual, unspoken, and daily recognition of friendship's obligations is the soundest proof that such obligations will inevitably endure.

SIX

The Claims of Double-Consciousness

Race, Nationalism, and the Problem of Political Obligation

T hus far we have seen that the logic and poetics of contradiction are
fundamental to Emerson's political critique and that the theory of ownership, identity, and association that develops involves Emerson's systematic merging of religious and political discourses. By Emerson's account,
the web of obligations drawing persons together in public space should not
only be described in traditionally political, liberal, contractarian terms. Rather,
he says that political obligation also involves demonstrated proofs of friendship—the barely visible (but nonetheless binding) commitments expressed
through bodily reflexes of eyes, hearts, and hands.[1]

Having underscored the importance of friendship in Emerson's critical
recuperation of democratic ideals, we need now to examine a sea change in
his thinking: Emerson's shift from a concept of obligation that is primarily
religious to one that is primarily racialist. The aim of this chapter is to show
that although Emerson initially referred to Locke's model of civil society in
order to speak about political community, by the early 1850s he had turned
instead to racialist premises as the basis for his nationalism.[2] Later works such
as *English Traits* (1856) and *Conduct of Life* (1860), in which Emerson is
obviously preoccupied with the problem of race, thus represent a clear continuity with the idea of personhood set forth in Emerson's writings even at
the very outset of his career.[3] This shift in Emerson's thinking about political
obligation leads him to invent a model of American identity that he designates
as "double-consciousness." In the essay "Fate," the description of double-
consciousness allows Emerson to negotiate between, on the one hand, his
belief in political obligations that result from Lockean, rational, voluntary acts

of consent and, on the other, the necessary claims of race—obligations that are to some extent involuntarily born into or found. The larger significance of Emersonian double-consciousness will be left for exploration in the concluding section of this book. There we shall see that Emerson's political critique is not only foundational to the development of American pragmatism and Du Bois's sociology but that it also contributed to the political thought of twentieth-century African-American philosophers such as Martin Luther King Jr. and Cornel West.

The sustained deliberation over the meaning of ownership undertaken in Emerson's early writings emerge as an important but previously neglected critique of liberal (and specifically Lockean) ideas about political representation, property, and personhood. At the same time he insists on the insufficiency of rights to represent the self—because, in his view, such a concept does not fit with a Christian belief in God as maker and owner of all persons and things— Emerson also insists on the necessity of ownership as a barrier to social injustice. At the same time that he rejects property rights as being central to the sophism of slavery, Emerson also argues for the conceptual necessity of the liberal idea of ownership. This recourse to contradiction in thinking about the self, as well as Emerson's dissatisfaction with the reductive popularization of rights discourse, are best understood in light of his broader cultural critique: namely, his attempt to sort out and confront the separate but related issues of slavery, power, and property in American culture.[4]

Although, as I argued in chapter 2, Emerson's interest in the meaning and political uses of rights discourse clearly has a direct bearing on the slavery debate, his interest in rights was also shared more generally by many nineteenth-century American legal theorists, who believed that understanding the significance of rights was fundamental to understanding the conceptual basis for liberal society as it was set forth in the United States Constitution. In his 1876 analysis of the political rights of citizenship, Theophilus Parsons observes that "[a] constitution is . . . the expression of the deliberate determination of the whole people, that the rights which it believes to lie at the foundation of all right, shall ever be preserved."[5] Almost twenty years earlier, in a treatise entitled *The American Citizen: His Rights and Duties, According to the Spirit of the Constitution of the United States*, John Hopkins argues that the study of rights was essential to the achievement of the liberal utopia celebrated in the Constitution:

> The hopes and best wishes of the masses are on our side, throughout all the civilized world; and the fears and interests of kings, nobles, and hereditary aristocrats are naturally and necessarily against us. They believe that the broken fragments of our grand confederation will cast aside the Utopian theory of equal rights, and assume the old, established, and only practicable form of monarchy. . . . For these reasons, I cannot but regard the position of the American citizen as pre-eminent in responsibility. . . . Every man,

therefore, who bears that title . . . should give himself thoughtfully and earnestly to the study of his RIGHTS AND DUTIES; in order that he may perform his share of the vast work which the nation is bound to accomplish, not only for itself, but for the world.[6]

Treatises elaborating on the formal, legal definition of rights proliferated at the end of the nineteenth century and included works such as George Smith's *The Law of Private Right* (1890), A. Jenkins Williard's *Examination of the Law of Personal Rights* (1882), and Oliver Barbour's *A Treatise on the Rights of Persons and the Rights of Property* (1890). However, in the first half of the nineteenth century, the attempt to construct a coherent theory of rights was already well underway. In his *Manual of Political Ethics*, published in Boston in 1838, Francis Lieber wrote:

> Man . . . is a being with free agency— . . . but as all his fellowmen with whom he lives in contact, are equally beings with free agency, . . . there results from it the necessity, founded in reason, i.e. the law, that the use of freedom by one rational being must not contradict or counteract the use of liberty by another rational being. The relation which exists between these rational beings, this demand of what is just made by each upon each, is the relation of *right*, and the society founded upon this basis . . . is the state.[7] (167)

American legal theorists speculated widely about the full range of rights protected by the Constitution—rights such as freedom of conscience, freedom of speech or opinion, the right to trial by jury and to form associations, and the right to sufferage. But none of these rights was considered to be as significant or as fundamental as the cherished right to property. In an 1832 study titled *The Rights of An American Citizen*, Benjamin Oliver insists that "every individual . . . has by nature, a right to appropriate to his or their use, so much land or territory, wherever it may be found not appropriated by others, as the individual . . . has occasion for . . . , by taking possession and keeping possession" (17). Almost a decade earlier, David McConaughy had observed in *The Nature and Origin of Civil Liberty* that property rights were central to the liberal theory of government because they formed the basis for the civil right to liberty. "Civil liberty includes personal freedom," he wrote. "Nothing can be considered more strictly our own property than our own persons. There is nothing to the government of which we have a more manifest right—nothing in the protection and free use of which we feel a deeper interest" (5). In 1839, James Stewart argued in *The Rights of Persons* that "[a] man's limbs . . . are . . . the gift of the wise Creator. . . . To these therefore he has a natural inherent right; and they cannot be wantonly destroyed or disabled without a manifest breach of civil liberty" (125).[8]

In contrast to the thoroughgoing examination of rights discourse undertaken by many of his contemporaries, the critique of Lockean liberalism embedded in Emerson's dual and contradictory position on the whole question of ownership is fundamental to his nationalist vision. For Emerson, Locke's vision of civil society as a community of autonomous, self-owning citizens who have been brought into association with one another by acts of rational, voluntary consent to social contract is not by any stretch of the imagination intimate or cohesive enough to represent America as a nation. As a result of this dissatisfaction with liberal contractarian definitions of the state, Emerson also refers to a scientific, Anglo-Saxonist, organicist, racialist discourse that affirms the existence of the intimate ties of race as shared descent, ties that represent obligations that are not at all assumed by volitional acts of consent but rather are born into or found as already existing. Earlier I suggested that Emerson's racialist vision of Columbus as a representative American self—a self whose divine mandate for imperialist expansion has been democratically extended to every man—is central to the expression of his nationalism. Even as early as 1836, in *Nature*, the contradiction between owning and not owning that lies at the heart of Emerson's political critique is articulated as a contradiction between a rights-based (or privately owned) and a racialist (or collectively owned) vision of the American self. As we shall see, the obvious, gross incompatibility between Emerson's recuperation of democratic ideals and his racism makes visible the imaginative pressures exerted by such a willed gesture of self-contradiction, a gesture that, as we have already seen, promotes dangerous exclusions from the public space of representation.

The contradiction between race and rights that is central to Emerson's representation of the self and nation is best understood in the context of a tradition of nineteenth-century American nationalist thought in which both racist dogma and democratic idealism were used to justify an aggressive policy of westward expansion. Many existing arguments in favor of expansion devolved upon the liberal conception of rights. As early as 1818, in a letter to Judge William Tudor, John Adams questions the validity of property rights as the conceptual basis for the Indians' claim to dominon in America. "If," he writes, "in search of our principles, we have not been able to investigate any moral, philosophical, or rational foundation for any claim of dominion or property in America . . . ; if the whole appears a mere usurpation of fiction, fancy, and superstition, what was the right to dominion or property in the native Indians?" Adams proceeds in his letter by arguing that even if the Indians do possess Lockian rights "to life, liberty and property," these cannot in any way be conceived of as the exclusive right to dominion:

> Shall we say that a few handfuls of scattering tribes of savages have a right of dominion and property over a quarter of this globe capable of nourishing hundreds of millions of happy human beings? Why had not Europeans a right to come and hunt and fish with them? Every Indian had a right to his wigwam, his armor, his utensils; when he had burned the woods about him, and planted his corn and beans, his squashes and pompions, all these were his undoubted right; but will you infer from this, that he had right of exclusive dominion and property over immense regions of uncultivated wilderness that

he never saw, that he might have the exclusive privilege of hunting and fishing in them, which he himself never expected or hoped to enjoy?[9]

By the 1840s, a popular and effective missionary rhetoric, which transformed the specific concern with property rights into a more general professed desire to further the spread of democracy, sanctioned the acquisition of a continental empire. In a letter on "The Texas Question" published in the *The Democratic Review* in 1844, one writer observes that Texas had in fact already been acquired from France in 1803 and was subsequently lost in the 1819 treaty with Spain:

> And who will say that the West shall remain dismembered and mutilated, and that the ancient boundaries of the republic shall never be restored? Who will desire to check the young eagle of America, now refixing her gaze upon our former limits, and repluming her pinions for her returning flight? . . . Who will oppose the reestablishment of our glorious constitution over the whole of the mighty valley which once was shielded by its benignant sway? . . . Our system of government is one which, rightly administered,—administered on the principles of the State-Rights theory—will bear indefinite extension; nor do we doubt but that in the fulness of time it is destined to embrace within its wide sweep every habitable square inch of the continent.[10]

That same year, an article that discussed Indian policy during the Monroe administration presented an argument for the removal of the Indians to an area west of the Mississippi in terms of the right to consent and to political sovereignty: "The most rational hope of success for this race, the only one which indeed appeared practical on a scale commensurate with the object, was to remove them, with their own consent, to a position entirely without the boundaries of the state jurisdictions, where they might assert their political sovereignty, and live and develope [sic] their true national character, under their own laws."[11]

Rights-based arguments promoting the spread of democratic ideals convinced many people in the United States of the overwhelming benefits of expansion. However, by the late 1820s, developments in racial science affirmed the doctrine of inequality between races, and in the 1830s and 1840s the popularity of racialist dogma created a new interest in national identity. Racist arguments markedly increased in popularity as the justification for expansion. A longing for racial homogeneity made many hesitant to confer full citizenship upon nonwhite residents of territories. In an article titled "Mexico" published in 1846, one writer insisted upon the subjection of inferior races. "*Race* is the key to much that seems obscure in the history of nations," he observed. "Throughout the world, the spectacle is everywhere the same, the whiter race ruling the less white, through all gradations of color, from the fairest European down to the darkest African. . . . In America, the aboriginal Red man and the imported Black man, are everywhere subject to the White man."[12]

Widely circulated publications such as *The Democratic Review* presented racist images of the Indians that contributed to the belief that the inherent inferiority of the race, not expansion, led inevitably to its extinction. "Doubtless the Indians have suffered in contact with us; but they have suffered, because of their own inherent vices of character and condition, such as their obstinate idleness and apathy, and their want of, and revulsion from all political institutions,—infinitely the rather than by any reason of any fault of ours," wrote one 1838 reviewer.[13] "Two types of human race, more fully and completely antagonistical, in all respects, never came in contact on the globe," another writer argued six years later. "If, therefore, the Red Race declined, and the white increased, it was because civilisation had more of the principles of endurance and progress than barbarism; . . . truth to error. Here lie the true secrets of the Red men's decline."[14] The popular perception of the Indians was that they were dangerously violent. "It is distinctive of the North American savages . . . to burn, destroy, and lay waste, in sheer vindictiveness, or wanton malice," one writer observes, "to slaughter women and children with unrelenting blood-thirstiness."[15] The close association of tribes such as the Mohawks with the British in times of war led many people to regard the occupation of such tribes on the frontier as a distinct threat to national boundaries. "Of course, the Mohawks gladly accepted permission to occupy a tract of country on the Grand River of Lake Erie," the same reviewer concludes, "ready to be again employed by England, when occasion should arrive, in savage inroads, against the frontier settlements of the United States" (125).

The various phases of Emerson's own speculations on the subject of race in his journals demonstrate the extent to which he was interested in current scientific theories and that he shared many of the racist perceptions of his time, even when such perceptions contradicted his belief in democratic first principles. "I believe that nobody now regards the maxim 'that all men are born equal,' as any thing more than a convenient hypothesis or an extravagant declamation," Emerson wrote in an 1822 journal entry. "For all the reverse is true,—that all men are born unequal in personal powers and in those essential circumstances, of time, parentage, country, fortune. The least knowledge of the natural history of man adds another important particular to these; namely, of what class of men he belongs to—European, Moor, Tartar, African? Because Nature has plainly assigned different degrees of intellect to these different races, and the barriers between are insurmountable." (JMN, II, 44). Like many of his contemporaries, Emerson speculated that inferior races which could not achieve national status would be exterminated. In 1838, he observed, "Each race of man resembles an apple or a pear, the Nubian, the Negro, the Tartar, the Greek, he vegetates, thrives, & multiplies, usurps all the soil & nutriment, & so kills the weaker races" (JMN, VII, 90). Two years later he would write that "[t]he negro must be very old & belongs, one would say, to the fossil formations. What right has he to be intruding into the late & civil daylight of this dynasty of the Caucasions & Saxons? It is plain that so inferior a race must perish shortly like the poor Indians" (*JMN*, VII, 393). In an 1854 journal entry, Emerson observed, "The Latin races are at last come to a stand, and are declining. Merry England and Saucy America striding far ahead. The dark man, the black man declines. The black man is courageous, but the white men are the children of God, said Plato. It will happen by and by, that the black man will only be destined for museums like the Dodo" (*JMN*, XIII, 286). And in a notebook used during the late 1830s, he observed that "it cannot be maintained by any candid person that the African race have ever occupied or do promise ever to occupy any very high place in the human family. Their present condition is the strongest proof that they cannot. The Irish cannot; the American Indian cannot; the Chinese cannot. Before the energy of the Caucasian race all other races have quailed and done obeisance" (*JMN*, XII, 152). In 1853, Emerson quoted Karl Marx as saying "[t]he classes and the races too weak to master the new conditions of life must give way" (*JMN*, VIII, 351), and five years later he argued that "[y]ou cannot preserve races beyond their term. St Michael pears have died out, and see what geology says to old strata. Tilobium is no more except in the embryonic forms of crab and lobster" (*JMN*, X, 357).

The sheer wealth of evidence that proves the fact of Emerson's racism is disturbing. However, we would miss the focus of this discussion—namely, the historical *function* of racism in Emerson's writings—were we simply to dismiss him for exhibiting the racist perceptions of his time. As we shall see, Emerson's racism is central to his vision of American nationality—a compelling, myopic vision that must be viewed in the context of a violent policy of westward expansion that prevailed in nineteenth-century America. In *Nature*, Emerson's unmistakable reference to the raciality of the American self allows him to situate that self at the brink of egocentric absolutism: at the same time he expresses a near disavowal of human society represented by ties to the liberal-democratic state in *Nature*, Emerson's racist imagination of the white, male body of Columbus is a framework for social cohesion. For Emerson, race functions to express both a threat to and an affirmation of social order.[16] Generally speaking, Emerson's racist vision of the representative self is essential for his articulation of a call to revolution—what Thoreau (and, much later, King) would designate as "civil disobedience."

Taken as a whole, Emerson's writings reveal a deep and longstanding interest in the Anglo-Saxons. As early as 1833, he copied in his journal a quotation from Sharon Turner's *History of the Anglo-Saxons*: "The infant state of this people when the Romans first observed them exhibited nothing from which human sagacity would have predicted greatness" (*JMN* IV, 416). In lectures such as "Genius of the Anglo-Saxon Race," delivered in 1843, Emerson demonstrates extensive knowledge of Anglo-Saxon history, and in an 1853 lecture titled "Anglo-Saxon," he cites Tacitus and makes explicit the connection between Anglo-Saxonism, and the fact of American expansion, which allows him to express American national unity as racial unity. "The *comitatus*, it appears from Tacitus, was the characteristic institution of the Saxon race," Emerson writes. "The . . . kindred of Alfred is the same. Each shall be responsible for the weal of the other. We will weave our repulsive Saxon individualism so close: oil and water shall mix that far. The Celt can run to battle under a king or captain: a knot of Saxons appoint a moderator and take the sense of the meeting, and the work is executed. This makes the aptitude of the Americans to annex Texas Mexico Louisiana California [Cuba Canada] that they can extemporise a government."[17] In the essay titled "Ability," published three years later in *English Traits* (1856), Emerson observes:

> The Saxon and the Northman are both Scandinavians. History does not allow us to fix the limits of the application of these names with any accuracy; but from the residence of a portion of these people in France, and from some effect of that powerful sail on their blood and manners, the Norman has come popularly to represent in England the aristocratic,—and the Saxon the democratic principle. And though, I doubt not, the nobles are of both tribes, and the workers of both, yet we are forced to use the names a little mythically, one to represent the worker, and the other the enjoyer. (806)

Not until *English Traits* does Emerson provide this gloss for the phrase "Saxon breasts," exploring racialist premises that form the basis for his concept of individual and national identity in "Self-Reliance," published fifteen years earlier.[18]

Emerson's rhetorical reference to "our Saxon breasts" is best understood in the context of a tradition of American nationalist thought that originated during the revolutionary era, when an elaborate mythology representing the ideal and free nature of Anglo-Saxon political institutions pervaded constitutional argument.[19] The colonists believed that the Anglo-Saxons were a successful branch of the Germanic peoples described by Tacitus. According to this myth, the golden age of Anglo-Saxon government was before the Norman Conquest, an event that initiated the erosion of English liberties. One radical pamphlet, by Allan Ramsay, titled the *Historical Essay on the English Constitution* (*1771*) and widely circulated in the United States praised Anglo-Saxon institutions in its discussion of the origin of the English constitution and describes Anglo-Saxon England as an ideal democratic community: "if ever God Almighty did concern himself about forming a government for mankind to live happily under, it was that which was established in England by our Saxon forefathers" (quoted in *RMD*, 17). Five years later, another pamphlet, titled *The Genuine Principles of the Ancient Saxon, or English Constitution*, summarized the arguments of the *Historical Essay* and argued that "this ancient and justly admired pattern, the old Saxon form of government, will be the best model, that human wisdom, improved by experience, has left them to copy" (quoted in *RMD*, 18). In his 1774 *Summary View of the Rights*

of British America,[20] Thomas Jefferson referred often to the history of the Saxons, arguing that the emigrants from England wielded the same rights to
possession as did "[o]ur Saxon ancestors" in "the earlier ages of the Saxon
settlement" during the ancient "introduction of the Feudal tenures into the
kingdom of England" (132). Although Jefferson insisted that "it is neither our
wish nor our interest to separate from [Great Britain]" (135), he also argued
that, as in the case of the ancient Saxons, the mother country could exert no
claim which justified taxation or unfair exclusion from the world market. Two
years later, in a letter to Edmund Pendleton, he wrote, "Are we not the better
for what we have hitherto abolished of the feudal system? Has not every
restitution of the antient Saxon laws had happy effects? Is it not better now
that we return at once into that happy system of our ancestors, the wisest and
most perfect ever yet devised by the wit of man, as it stood before the 8th
century?" (492).

Two competing concepts of the nation emerge in revolutionary writings.
One form of argument exhibits a theory of nationalism expressed in terms of
the state, an argument that invokes the Lockean right to revolution and to
breaking political ties with the government of Great Britain. Another form
of argument entails the appeal to Anglo-Saxonism, an appeal that constructs
a mythic, cohesive community of revolutionaries. The argument exhibited in
revolutionary pamphlets invoking the right to freedom and the pursuit of
happiness is by far the most familiar. However, most writers would not hesitate
in their reference to this Anglo-Saxon tradition, even though the assertion of
a collective Anglo-Saxon identity threatened individual autonomy. Indeed, in
1776 the problem of constructing and maintaining political community was
such that concepts of the public good and the will of the people often superseded the claims of individuals, whose rights were generally not conceived of
in modern terms.[21] In *Rights of Man*, Thomas Paine explicitly argues against
Burke's contention that rights reside in any single individual, citing the reverend Dr. Price as an authority: "Dr. Price does not say that the right to do
these things exists in this or that person, or in this or in that description of
persons," Paine observes, "but that it exists in the *whole*; that it is a right
resident in the nation."[22] Revolutionary writers such as Paine resisted the
concept of individual rights because they were confronted with Burke's contention that such rights were given up at the end of the 1688 Revolution by
persons now dead. "The method which Mr. Burke takes to prove that . . .
rights do not now exist in the nation . . . is of the same marvellous and mon-
strous kind with what he has already said," Paine writes, "for his arguments
are, that the persons, or the generation of persons, in whom they did exist,
are dead, and with them the right is dead also. To prove this, [Burke] quotes
a declaration made by parliament about a hundred years ago, to William and
Mary, in these words: 'The Lords Spiritual and Temporal, and Commons, do,
in the name of the people aforesaid,'—(meaning the people of England then
living)—'most humbly and faithfully *submit* themselves, their *heirs* and *poster-
ities*, for EVER' " (40).

Thus, at the same time that writers such as Paine defended the liberal structure of rights that was set in place during the American Revolution, they also justified the restriction of private interests and rights by celebrating the public welfare. At the heart of republican ideology lay a conception of the public good that entailed a clear delineation of national boundaries: "the people" referred to a unified, homogenous body. In this respect, the contradiction expressed in Emerson's writings between the suppression of difference and his promotion of the broadest possible rights and freedoms for the individual registers an important structural contradiction exhibited in the American tradition of revolutionary rhetoric. Emerson's Anglo-Saxonism, like that of revolutionary writers, simultaneously expresses withdrawal from the state and justifies the act of withdrawal by referring to an ancient tradition of political institutions embedded in an ideal and mythic past. But, unlike these eighteenth-century revolutionary theorists, Emerson's argument is developed in specifically nineteenth-century racialist terms. For Emerson, the invocation of ties to a mythic Anglo-Saxon past is also a reinforcement of racial ties to Great Britain. The nation of Americans is conceived of in Emerson's writings as being both racially distinct from and inextricably bound to Britain. On the one hand, Emerson repudiates the claims of racial affinity with Britain and invokes the liberal right to property and autonomy in "Self-Reliance." This persistent denial of kinship is figured as the act of shunning: "O father, O mother, O brother . . . I have lived with you after appearances hitherto," Emerson writes. "Henceforward I am truth's. . . . I shall endeavor to nourish my parents, to support my family, to be the chaste husband of one wife,—but these relations I must fill after a new and unprecedented way" (Essays, 273). On the other hand, in his essay Emerson also refers to and benefits from the fact of racial continuity between England and America. "If, therefore, a man claims to know and speak of God, and carries you backward to the phraseology of some old mouldered nation in another country, believe him not," he tells us. "Is the acorn better than the oak which is its fulness and completion? Is the parent better than the child into whom he has cast his ripened being?" (Essays, 270).

Emerson's deliberate reference to racialist discourse in his construction of American nationality is a strategy that distinguishes his nationalism as a critique of the tradition of liberal nationalism that culminated in the popular and influential nineteenth-century theory of nations set forth by John Stuart Mill. In Considerations on Representative Government published in 1860, Mill includes a brief but important chapter titled "Nationality as Connected With Representative Government." In this chapter, Mill argues that only the existence of what he calls a "feeling of nationality"—a feeling he claims is the "effect of race and descent," community of language or religion, geographical limits, or the possession of a shared national history—will allow for the proper functioning of representative government (CRG, 308). Generally speaking, Mill argues that the boundaries of the nation—boundaries determined by the limited extension of the "sentiment of nationality"—coincide with those of the organized government or *state*. "It is in general a necessary condition of free institutions that the boundaries of governments [i.e., the state] should coincide in the main with those of nationalities," he writes (CRG, 310). "Where the sentiment of nationality exists in any force, there is a *prima facie* case for uniting all the members of the nationality under the same government, and a government to themselves apart. This is merely saying that the question of government ought to be decided by the governed. . . . Among a people without fellow-feeling, especially if they read and speak different languages, the united public opinion necessary to the working of representative government can not exist" (CRG, 310).

Mill's definition of the word "nation," in which the bounds of nationhood coincide with those of the state, prevailed in the nineteenth century. The liberal concept of nationhood cast in such terms includes only those who bear the rights of citizenship: for Mill and other nineteenth-century liberal writers, the nation was conceived of as a collective and sovereign body of citizens whose capacity for political expression was manifested as their mutual act of constitution as a state. However, a pressing problem Mill hints at but does not explore in his discussion is the fact that the liberal-democratic model of the state—which is theoretically designed to include any equal and abstract subject who bears the rights of citizenship—is infinitely expansive. As such, this model of the state is at odds with a limited conception of nationhood constituted by racial ties that, as Mill argues, represent a "feeling of nationality," the combined effect of shared descent. Whereas the ideal democratic state conceived of in Lockean terms may be characterized as infinitely permeable and expansive, because in theory "Every Man" who is in possession of his own labor can join, Mill implicitly suggests that this model is necessary but insufficient to account for the existence of boundaries between nationalities that are racially distinctive. What Mill discloses (but fails to address directly) is the existence of a contradiction structuring his theory of nations: a contradiction between the limitless extension of rights associated with representative government, on the one hand, and on the other the undemocratic delineation of national boundaries as distinctly racial boundaries.

In nineteenth-century America, many political theorists who were engaged with the question of nationality were dissatisfied with the model of identity that resulted from the liberal framework. One such theorist was Elisha Mulford, who critiqued the liberal theory of nations in a treatise titled *The Nation: the Foundations of Civil Order and Political Life in the United States*, published in New York in 1870.[23] For Mulford, the liberal concept of nationhood was problematic because it was too atomistic. "They who exist in [the nation] are not held only by some external force, and are not bound only by some formal law," he writes. "The isolation of men presumes a conception which is inhuman, and it is not in its separation but in its relations that humanity is comprehended" (*Nation*, 5). In contrast to liberal theorists, Mulford argues that the ties of nationhood are born into or found, and are not made by rational, voluntary acts of consent. "The entrance to [the state] is not through a reflective process, nor by an act of individual volition," he insists. "It is not, in its normal course, out of a condition which is external that men enter the nation, but they are born in it" (*Nation*, 5). What Mulford suggests is that the liberal view that society originates in a contract cannot in any way account for the spiritual unity, and the involuntary devotion to duty, that characterizes his vision of the ideal nation. "The necessary being and end of the nation . . . cannot be brought within the scope of a contract," he writes. "A contract proceeds from and through a voluntary act. . . . But the process of justice, and the institution of rights . . . cannot be thus optional. . . . The contract furthermore cannot comprehend the spirit, the allegiance, the obedience to law, the apprehension of and devotion to public ends, which are integral in the state" (*Nation*, 47).

Despite the fact that Mulford works hard to construct a model of national identity that is more cohesive than the liberal model, he nonetheless refuses to accept the formulation of national unity as racial unity. Indeed, Mulford explicitly rejects Mill's description of "the sentiment of nationality" as the effect of shared descent, claiming that "[Mill's] analysis . . . offers no guide to the interpretation of history in the past or in the present age" (*Nation*, 410). For Mulford, the basis for national unity must be "moral," not racial. He argues,

> There may be in the physical distinction of races the elements of diversitude, and of an ampler and more opulent culture and character, and the physical laws and properties of races are to be studied and not to be disregarded. But to assert the identity of the nation with a race is to assume for it a physical foundation, and involves the denial of its moral unity and moral order. . . . It is the nation in its organic and moral unity, which acts as a power in history, and not a race in its special and separate physical character. (*Nation* 360–361, 362)

Mulford's emphasis on moral unity results in an infinitely expansive, Christian concept of ideal nationhood that embraces all of humanity: "As the nation is called to be a power in history, it is in the realization of its being the Christian nation," he insists. "The goal of history is in the fulfillment of the highest political ideal. It is . . . the end of the toil and conflict of humanity" (*Nation*, 368, 418). In this respect, Mulford's model of nationality is strikingly similar to the liberal model he purports to critique: like the infinitely expansive liberal concept of the nation, Mulford's Christian concept is problematic because does not allow for clear delineation of national boundaries.

Although theoretical discussions of "the nation" such as Mill's and Mulford's appeared relatively late in the nineteenth century, Emerson's writings show that by the 1830s he was already engaged in the project of imagining America as a nation. Like Mulford, Emerson critiques the liberal, atomistic view of the nation by affirming the existence of national ties that are born into or found, but, unlike Mulford, he expresses national identity in terms that are *both* racialist *and* liberal. For Emerson, the liberal theory of property rights that forms the basis for social order in the liberal-democratic state is conceptually limited because it does not demarcate national boundaries clearly enough. The infinite permeability attributed to the nation by writers such as Mill and Mulford fails to account for what makes America distinctively American in explicitly racial terms. Emerson's appeal to race demonstrates the degree to which the liberal construction of America as a *state* that embodies democratic ideals cannot account for a concept of America as a *nation*. In this respect, Emerson's writings expand upon possibilities that exist for the articulation of a liberal theory of nations.[24]

I have already tried to show that although Emerson's early writings emphasize the role of friendship and his critique of property rights in thinking about the self and civil society—that is, his recognition that neither the Christian ideal of friendship nor the democratic framework would provide him with a sound enough basis for his utopian vision of America as a nation—ultimately leads him in later writings to develop concepts of "kindness" and "race." In chapter 5, I noted that Emerson's habit of associating friendship and race is most explicit in exploration of the claims of kindness put forward in the address "The Young American." In this lecture, Emerson returns to a question he encountered in his celebrated "American Scholar" address delivered seven years earlier—namely, of how to define a distinctive race of Americans. Both "The Young American" and "The American Scholar" make the point that in order to fulfill the promise of their existence as a state, a promise of free and democratic institutions set forth in their Constitution, Americans must first imaginatively experience their unity as a "race." However, in these addresses Emerson presents radically different responses to the question of what "race" actually means. I have already argued that in "The Young American," Emerson refers to a concept of racial cohesion that is enforced by means of political obligations manifested in secret, tender acts of "cruel kindness." By contrast, as I now propose to show, in "The American Scholar" Emerson creates a nationalist model that describes racial unity in terms of cultural unity.

It was a commonplace in the nineteenth-century theory of nations that a nation could be defined either in terms of racial or cultural unity. Mill considered the existence of national history to be of primary importance in generating a feeling of nationality. However, he also noted that there were other significant factors such as "identity of race and descent" "and "community of language and community of religion" (CRG 308). In his 1835 study of English national character, Emerson emphasizes the cultural cohesiveness of the English, devoting considerable space to descriptions of the history of English literature. "This is distinctively English poetry," he tells us in "Permanent Traits of English National Genius." "It is unborrowed and native. . . . It is the poetry of a nation in which is much knowledge and much business so that their speculation and their fancy are filled with images from real nature and from useful Art. These are the verses of a people that require meat and not pap, to whom elegance is less native than truth and who demand their constitutional utility even in songs and ballads."[25] In "The American Scholar," delivered two years later, Emerson once again explores the relevance of cultural community to the theory of nations, this time in America. The now familiar call for a national literature in Emerson's address—his insistence that "[w]e have listened too long to the courtly muses of Europe"—expresses the nationalist premise that to be a nation America must have a shared and distinctive culture. For Emerson, a distinctive literary culture is essential to America's successful emergence as a nation, because poetry itself produces and registers the existence of political community.

The call for cultural unity in "The American Scholar" is striking insofar as, at key moments in Emerson's address, cultural unity is defined as a mark of racial unity that is itself indistinguishable from racial unity. The strategic conflation of race and culture, the definition of racial *as* cultural unity, allows Emerson to exhibit a concept of American national identity that is simultaneously affirmed and overturned in his address. The simultaneous affirmation and denial of America's distinctiveness as a nation occurs in Emerson's express hope for the unity of all American scholars under a single emblematic polestar: "Who can doubt, that poetry will revive and lead in a new age, as the star in the constellation Harp, which now flames in our zenith, astronomers announce, shall one day be the pole-star for a thousand years?" he asks (*Essays*, 53). On the one hand, Emerson suggests that the culture of American letters is specific to Americans, and America's national boundaries are represented as fixed. On the other hand, the culture of American letters is heralded in Emerson's address as representative of possibilities for reform and more perfect community that exist for Americans as representatives of the human race. The identification of race with culture allows Emerson in the same gesture to assert the existence of an exceptional nation of Americans marked by racial unity and to transcend racial and national boundaries by means of the infinite pervasiveness of the culture he describes.

The question of whether the polestar is a distinctively national emblem or an emblem that universally represents all men is central to the model of ideal nationhood Emerson describes in "The American Scholar." Emerson's reference to the limits imposed on the creative intellectual capacities of Americans, and to national boundaries, opens the conceptual possibility of surmounting those boundaries or limits. "A nation of men will for the first time exist, because each believes himself inspired by the Divine Soul which also inspires all men," he writes (*Essays*, 71). The nation described in Emerson's address is both limited and limitless; it is both the "true union" of a race of specifically American scholars and a union that includes "all men." The contradiction that structures Emerson's thinking about America as a nation may best be seen as a contradiction that structures Emerson's concept of the American scholar in his address. The tension or contradiction that characterizes the American scholar is a contradiction between national distinctiveness and a total lack of distinctiveness. On the one hand, Emerson describes the scholar

as an abstract, universal, and representative Man Thinking. "In this distribution of functions [in society], the scholar is delegated intellect," Emerson
writes. "In the right state, he is, *Man Thinking.* . . . In this view of him, as
Man Thinking, the theory of his office is contained. Him nature solicits with
all her placid, all her monitory pictures; him the past instructs; him the future
invites" (*Essays*, 54). On the other hand, in "The American Scholar" Emerson
makes clear reference to the specific conditions of his speech: his location at
Harvard, the function of his address as a Phi Beta Kappa oration, and the
identity of his audience are all factors that facilitate the construction of the
American scholar as a distinctive racial identity. "I ought not to delay longer
to add what I have to say, of nearer reference to the time and to this country,"
he tells us (*Essays*, 67). The model of the self Emerson constructs in "The
American Scholar" is not only a disembodied self, a univerally emblematic
Man Thinking, but also a new and distinctive kind or race of American Scholars whom he addresses and whose existence he thereby affirms.

The abstract representation of the scholar as Man Thinking leads Emerson in his address to argue for the identity and equality of all individuals. "Is
not, indeed, every man a student, and do not all things exist for the student's
behoof?" he asks (*Essays*, 54). The act of political association according to
this model of the self implies that national boundaries are permeable and
infinitely expansive: America, in these terms, includes all those who think.
Emerson speaks in his address of the "conversion of the world," an idea of
America expresses the persistent transcendence of national boundaries, a
world community that lives under a single polestar. "It is one central fire,
which, flaming now out of the lips of Etna, lightens the capes of Sicily,"
Emerson writes, "and, now out of the throat of Vesuvius, illuminates the
towers and vineyards of Naples. It is one light which beams out of a thousand
stars. It is one soul which animates all men" (*Essays*, 67). At the same time
that Emerson imagines the act of political association by scholars defined as
all Men Thinking, he also alludes to a condition of racial unity that exists for
American scholars, "born in . . . the age of Revolution" (*Essays*, 68): in these
terms, the imagination of national identity is inextricably bound up with the
construction of the American scholar as a distinctive racial identity. "Mr.
President and Gentlemen, this confidence in the unsearched might of man
belongs, by all motives, by all prophecy, by all preparation, to the American
Scholar," Emerson concludes (*Essays*, 70). Almost a decade after the 1837
address, Emerson expressed a concern with racial identity in terms similar to
those presented in "The American Scholar." "The puny race of Scholars in
this country have no counsel to give, and are not felt," he observed in his
journal. "In England, it is not so" (*JMN*, VII, 37).

In "The American Scholar," Emerson constructs a model of American
nationality that provides for all the cohesiveness, homogeneity, and distinctiveness of "race," but also preserves the equality and individual autonomy
implicit in the liberal concept of "rights." Emerson's insistence upon the emblematic and representative attributes of the American Scholar, a gesture that

paradoxically contributes to the powerful assertion of national distinctiveness in his address, makes sense when we consider the aversion to nationality that Emerson repeatedly expresses in his journals. In 1851, he observed, "Nationality is babyishness for the most part" (JMN, XI, 399), and two years later he noted, "Puerile to insist on nationalities over the edge of individualities. Yet there is use in brag" (JMN, XIII, 12). In 1862, he insisted that "English nationality is very babyish, and most exhibitions of nationality are babyish" (JMN, XV, 174). And in *English Traits*, published almost two decades after "The American Scholar," the idea of the scholar as an abstract and representative Man Thinking reemerges in the essay titled "Cockayne," which includes a brief meditation on the problem of national identity. "Coarse local distinctions, as those of nation, province, or town, are useful in the absence of real ones," Emerson writes, "but we must not insist on these accidental lines. Individual traits are always triumphing over national ones. There is no fence in metaphysics discriminating Greek, or English, or Spanish science. Aesop, and Montaigne, Cervantes, and Saadi are men of the world; and to wave our own flag at the dinner table or in the University, is to carry the boisterous dulness of a fire-club into a polite circle" (*ET*, 849).

Emerson's appeal in "Cockayne" to the identity of all scholars as "men of the world" amounts to a disavowal of racial nationalism. However, elsewhere in *English Traits* Emerson reasserts a belief in the racial distinctiveness of Americans. For example, confronted with the fact of British university life in "Universities," he compares the native capacities of British and American scholars, writing,

> The diet and rough exercise secure a certain amount of old Norse power. A fop will fight, and, in exigent circumstances, will play the manly part. In seeing these youths, I believed I saw already an advantage in vigor and color and general habit, over their contemporaries in the American colleges. No doubt much of the power and brilliancy of the reading-men is merely constitutional or hygienic. With a hardier habit and resolute gymnastics, with five miles more walking, or five ounces less eating, or with a saddle and gallop of twenty miles a day, with skating and rowing-matches, the American would arrive at as robust exegesis, and cheery and hilarious tone. I should readily concede these advantages, which it would be easy to acquire, if I did not find also that they read better than we, and write better. (*ET*, 881)

The act of comparing English and American scholars reflects Emerson's long-standing fascination with respect to America's racial and thus national identity. "In America I grieve to miss the strong black blood of the English race," Emerson would write in 1844. "Ours is a pale, diluted stream. What a company of brilliant young persons I have seen with so much expectation! The sort is very good, but none is good enough of his sort. Every one an imperfect specimen; respectable, not valid" (JMN, VI, 501).

Just as in "The American Scholar" Emerson imagines the scholar as being both racially distinctive and a universally representative man of the world, so in *English Traits* he offers up a concept of his own identity that is structured on a strikingly similar contradiction: for Emerson, England is both a racial Other and a familiar, known, internalized cultural resource. Even as he represents himself as distinctively American, outside the bounds of the culture he observes, Emerson carefully marks aspects of English culture as his own. In the essay "Stonehenge," for example, he writes, "we walked in and out, and took again and again a fresh look at the uncanny stones. The old sphinx put our petty difference of nationality out of sight. To these conscious stones we two pilgrims were like known and near. We could equally revere their old British meaning" (*ET*, 918). Emerson's flexibility of stance with respect to the English results from a lifetime of engaged reflection upon the meaning of race, a concept that shapes his understanding of national identity. It is to the development of this race concept that I now turn our attention.

A coherent theory of race appears in Emerson's writings as early as 1836, when in a journal entry he identified various racial and national traits as ideal possibilities toward which all persons may aspire:

> Whilst thus I use the Universal Humanity, I see plainly the fact that there is no progress to the race, that the progress is one of individuals. One element is predominant in one; another is carried to perfection in the next; Art in the Greek; power in the Roman; piety in the Hebrew; letters in the Old English; commerce in the late English; Empire in Austria; erudition in Germany; free institutions in America. But in turn the whole man is brought to light. . . . It is like the revolution of the globe in the ecliptic: each part is brought in turn under the more direct beams of the sun to be illuminated and warmed, and to each a summer in turn arrives. (*JMN*, IV, 158–159)

Just as in this 1836 journal entry Emerson arrives at a formulation for "race" that would ground and facilitate his description of an ideal representative self, so in the lecture "Permanent Traits of English National Genius," delivered a year earlier, he presents a framework for thinking about race that would ultimately contribute to his subsequent development of a racialist concept of national identity in *English Traits*. Here, as in *English Traits*, Emerson underscores the importance of racial ties that bind America to England. And here, as in the later writings, Emerson's explicitly stated concern regarding the racial origins of the English is expressed in terms that show his preoccupation with America's racial origins. "The inhabitants of the United States especially of the Northern portion are descended from the people of England and have inherited the traits of their national character," he notes. "It has been thought by some observers acquainted with the character of both nations that the American character is only the English character exaggerated; that as some plants which grow in the temperate zone only one or two feet high in the torrid zone are found to attain four or six feet, so the features of the English genius both good and bad, have, in the greater freedom of our institutions, become more prominent. Are they lovers of freedom? We more; Are they lovers of commerce? We more. Are they lovers of utility? We more"

("Permanent Traits," 1). During the course of his argument concerning En-glish national genius, Emerson points out a connection between racial origin and the existence of a stable and enduring national character. "It ought to be written in a settled conviction that no event is casual or solitary," he observes, "that all events proceed inevitably from peculiar qualities of the national char-acter which are permanent or every slowly modified from age to age" ("Per-manent Traits," 2). Expanding on this point, Emerson explicitly cites Tacitus's writings in order to authorize his own claims regarding the racial origins of the English. "The traits of national character are almost as permanent as the grander natural forms of a country, the mountains, rivers and plains. Amid all the multitude of causes that have operated for centuries to alter their laws, manners, customs, the English of the present day bear deeply engraven on their character the marks by which their ancestors are described by Caesar and Tacitus 1800 years ago: 'that they were blue-eyed men, lovers of liberty, yielding more to authority than to command, and respecting the female sex' " ("Permanent Traits," 3).

Taken together, this emphasis Emerson places on biological descent, as well as the natural (and even botanical) metaphors he deploys in his com-parison of English and American national character, suggest that his race concept is fundamentally biological. Strangely enough, however, his writings on the subject show that he often questioned the validity and usefulness of such a biological race concept in his developing theory of nationality. "I be-lieve, that races, as Celtic, Norman, Saxon, must be used hypothetically or temporarily, as we do by the Linnaean classification, for convenience simply, and not as true and ultimate," he wrote in an 1854 journal entry. "For, oth-erwise, we are perpetually confounded by finding the best settled traits of one race, claimed by some more acute or ingenious partisan as precisely charac-teristic of the other and antagonistic. It is with national traits as with virus of cholera or plague in the atmosphere, it eludes chemical analysis, and the air of the plague hospital is not to be discriminated by any known test from the air of Mont Blanc" (JMN, XIII, 288). In a gesture that is typical of much of his description of race, Emerson resorts to a concrete, biological metaphor—in this case, the cholera virus—in order to express the elusiveness of the concept and its very lack of concreteness.

Just as in his early writings Emerson simultaneously upholds and re-nounces the democratic ideal of ownership, so in later writings such as English Traits the concept of race that emerges is one that exhibits a contradictory structure. On the one hand, Emerson discloses what he insists is the "ideal or metaphysical necessity" of race. "An ingenious anatomist has written a book to prove that races are imperishable, but nations are pliant political construc-tions, easily changed or destroyed," he writes. "But this writer did not found his assumed races on any necessary law, disclosing their ideal or metaphysical necessity" (ET, 790). On the other hand, Emerson's repudiation of the popular biological meaning of the word "race" only serves to demonstrate the inex-tricability of race and physical attributes. "We anticipate in the doctrine of race something like that law of physiology, that, whatever bone, muscle, or essential organ is found in one healthy individual, the same part or organ may be found in or near the same place in its cogener; and we look to find in the son every mental and moral property that existed in the ancestor," he writes. "In race, it is not the broad shoulders, or litheness, or stature that gives advantage, but a symmetry that reaches as far as to the wit" (*ET*, 791). What Emerson suggests is that the marks of race, even those which extend to "wit," can be conceived of only in bodily terms. "All the admirable expedients or means hit upon in England, must be looked at as growths or irresistible offshoots of the expanding mind of the race," he writes in the essay "Ability." "A man of that brain thinks and acts thus; and his neighbor, being afflicted with the same kind of brain, though he is rich, and called a baron, or a duke, thinks the same thing, and is ready to allow the justice of the thought and act in his retainer or tenant, though sorely against his baronial or ducal will. . . . Is it their luck, or is it in the chambers of their brain,—it is their commercial advantage, that whatever light appears in better method or happy invention, breaks out *in their race*. They are a family to which a destiny attaches" (*ET*, 808, 816). For Emerson, wit and luck may be just as readily characterized as racial attributes as the chambers of the brain. In *English Traits*, the concept of race represents an "ideal necessity" and may not be confined to reductive biological categories, but the model of national identity that Emerson constructs is never completely dissociated from the notion of family destiny and ties to kin that are born into or found. "Every nation has yielded some good wit, if, as has chanced to many tribes, only one," he observes in "Ability." "But the intellectual organization of the English admits a communicableness of knowledge and ideas among them all. An electric touch by any of their national ideas, melts them into one family, and brings the hoards of power which their individuality is always hiving, into use and play for all. Is it the smallness of the country, or is it the pride and affection of race,—they have solidarity, or responsibleness, and trust in each other" (*ET*, 819).

Emerson's writings on the subject of race reflect his extensive knowledge of various racialist treatises that were widely circulated throughout the nineteenth century, ranging from what were then considered serious scientific studies to sensational, amateur endeavors. He often alludes to the racial theories of Tacitus and Linnaeus, and he was deeply affected by his reading in 1845 of Robert Chambers's *Vestiges of Creation*, a work that set forth the general principle of ameliorative evolution. Emerson was also aware of the debate over the polygenetic origins of races, and makes repeated references to phrenology, a practice whose popularity continued well into the nineteenth century and that led many to believe in the inequality of races. In *English Traits*, Emerson explicitly mentions the influential race theorist Johann Friedrich Blumenbach, who relied on Linnaeus's taxonomic system in a 1775 study titled *On the Natural Variety of Races*.[26] Comparing various attributes such as skin color and hair, skull, and facial characteristics, Blumenbach theorized that there were five races: Caucasian, Mongolian, American, Ethiopian, and Malay. Indeed, Blumenbach invented the term "Caucasian," which he derived from the name of the mountain upon which Noah's Ark came to rest after the flood. "I have taken the name of this variety from Mount Caucasus," he wrote, "both because of its neighborhood, and especially its southern slope, produces the most beautiful race of men." (269). For Blumenbach, the Caucasian not only represented the most beautiful of races, it was also the standard from which which all inferior races deviated: "For in the first place, that stock displays . . . the most beautiful form, of the skull, from which, as a mean and primeval type, the others diverge by most easy gradations on both sides to the ultimate extremes (that is, on the one side the Mongolian, on the other the Ethiopian). Besides, it is white in colour, which we may fairly assume to have been the primitive colour of mankind, since, as we have shown above . . . , it is very easy for that to degenerate into brown, but very much more difficult for dark to become white, when the secretion and precipitation of this carbonaceous pigment . . . has deeply struck root" (269).

Two other popular racial theorists whom Emerson mentions in *English Traits* are Charles Pickering and Robert Knox. In his *Races of Man*, published in Boston in 1848, Pickering argued that there were eleven existing races, which he identified by traits such as gradation of color and geographical distribution. In his sensational treatise titled *The Races of Men: A Philosophical Enquiry into the Influence of Race over the Destinies of Nations*[27] Knox dismissed Blumenbach's earlier study as leading to no results and investigating no causes. Knox argued for the existence of numerous unmixable races, none of which could live in all climates. "The races of men as they now exist on the globe constitute a fact which cannot be overlooked," he writes. "I . . . am prepared to assert that race is everything in human history" (13, 14). For Knox, race was of supreme importance in the history of nations, and racial traits such as the Saxon's self-dependence superseded feelings of nationality. "In spite of the lesson taught the Saxon race by the United States of America, a lesson without parallel in the world, the Norman government of England persists in the same colonial policity which caused her the loss of America," he writes. "Nothing can teach certain men. The promoters fancy that they can alter human nature; the Saxon nature: that *British feelings or nationality* is to prevail over the eternal qualities of race" (315).

Emerson's confrontation with theories of racial science in *English Traits* results in an unmistakable and consistent pattern of contradiction: at the same time that he upholds the scientific concept of race as a fixed category of biological descent, a category that "works imortally to keep its own," he also systematically undermines and questions the fundamental validity of such a concept. "But whilst race works immortally to keep its own, it is resisted by other forces," he writes in the essay "Race" (*ET*, 792). "These limitations of the formidable doctrine of race suggest others which threaten to undermine it, as not sufficiently based. The fixity or incontrovertibleness of races as we see them, is a weak argument for the eternity of these frail boundaries" (*ET*, 793). Later in the same essay, Emerson remarks, "The English composite character betrays a mixed origin. Every thing English is a fusion of distant and antagonistic elements. . . . Neither do this people appear to be of one stem; but collectively a better race than any from which they are derived. Nor is it easy to trace it home to its original seats. Who can call by right names what races are in Britain? Who can trace them historically?" (*ET*, 794).

Thus, just as in his early writings on the subject of ownership Emerson's recourse to the rhetoric of contradiction is central to the expression of his political critique, so his efforts to articulate a logic of contradiction within "race" should be regarded as fundamentally strategic. At the same time that his obvious dissatisfaction with the limits of the scientific concept gives him room to speculate about the existence of a more broadly conceived "anthology of temperaments," the indisputable fixity he attributes to English national character also guarantees the conceptual coherence of the theory of nations he arrives at in *English Traits*. "In the impossibility of arriving at satisfaction on the historical question of race, and,—come of whatever disreputable ancestry,—the indisputable Englishman before me, himself very well marked, and nowhere else to be found,—I fancied I could leave quite aside the choice of a tribe as his lineal progenitors," Emerson observes. "On the whole, it is not so much a history of one or of certain tribes of Saxons, Jutes, or Frisians, coming from one place, and genetically identical, as it is an anthology of temperaments out of them all" (*ET*, 794).

In *English Traits*, Emerson relies on the biological significance of race when he affirms the superiority of the Saxons in his account of British national destiny and expanding world dominance. For example, in the essay "Land," the myth of national origins he constructs is explicitly framed as a history of racial origins, biologically conceived. Conflating popular earlier mythic representations of racial origin and contemporary nineteenth-century scientific racial theory, Emerson describes Nature as holding counsel with herself and saying, "My Romans are gone. To build my new empire, I will choose a rude race, all masculine, with brutish strength. I will not grudge a competition of the roughest males. . . . For I have work that requires the best will and sinew. Sharp and temperate northern breezes shall blow, to keep that will alive and alert" (*ET*, 788). "The spawning force of the race has sufficed to the colonization of great parts of the world," he observes in "Race." "They have great assimilating force, since they are imitated by their foreign subjects; and they are still aggressive and propagandist, enlarging the dominion of their arts and liberty. . . . It is race, is it not? that puts the hundred millions of India under the dominion of a remote island in the north of Europe" (*ET*, 791, 792). In "Character," Emerson argues that "it is in the deep traits of race that the fortunes of nations are written, and however derived, whether a happier tribe or mixture of tribes, the air, or what circumstance, that mixed for them the golden mean of temperament,—here exists the best stock in the world . . . ; a race to which their fortunes flow, as if they alone had the elastic organization at once fine and robust enough for dominion; as if the burly inexpressive, now mute and cotumacious, now fierce and sharp-tongued dragon, which once made the island light with his fiery breath, had bequeathed his ferocity to his conqueror" (ET, 840). "But who would see the uncoiling of that tremendous spring," he concludes in the essay "Result," "the explosion of their well-husbanded forces, must follow the swarms which pouring out now for two hundred years from the British islands, have sailed, and rode, and traded, and planted, through all climates, mainly following the belt of empire, the temperate zones, carrying the Saxon seed. . . . —acquiring under some skies a more electric energy than the native air allows,—to the conquest of the globe" (ET, 931). Although he does not always describe the fact of British dominion in such positive terms—for example, he speaks in the essay "Cockayne" of the "insular limitation" that imposes unacceptable constraints on English foreign policy and causes the Englishman to "force his island by-laws down the throat of great countries . . . and trample down all nationalities with his taxed boots" (ET, 846)—the racial nationalism that is evident even in Emerson's earliest writings finds expression as the celebration of British imperialism in *English Traits*.

Even a cursory reading of Emerson's *Conduct of Life* suggests that in 1860 he was far less concerned with the creation of a theory of nations than he was when he wrote *English Traits*.[28] This is ironic when we consider that *Conduct of Life* was published in the same month South Carolina seceded, an event that marked the destruction of the Union and the onset of civil war. *Conduct of Life* was written during a tense, unsettled period in American history, a period of massive social change that signalled a crisis in the cultural formation of American national identity. Thus it makes sense that, although Emerson repeatedly dismissed the concept of nationality as being "babyish" and "puerile" in the 1850s, by 1863 this attitude had dramatically changed. "We are coming, thanks to the war, to a nationality," he wrote. "It has created patriotism. We regarded our country as we do the world. It had no enemy and we should as soon have thought of vaunting the atmosphere or the sea, but let the comet or the moon or Mercury or Mars come down on us, we should get out our buffers and electricities and stand for the Earth with fury against all comers" (JMN, XV, 326). Indeed, only a year after the publication of *Conduct of Life*, Emerson delivered a lecture titled "American Nationality" that reveals his deep interest in the subject of American nationalism. In this lecture, he insists upon the enduring stability of national identity in America, even at a time in which that identity was in clearest danger of being called into question. "What an instant union is operated in our wide and various population!" Emerson writes. "Things have taken proportions. Nothing is as it was. Nobody suspected our people of such love of country. We have often fancied that our country was too large to permit any strong nationality. Patriotism could not expand to take in a geography so vast."[29]

Although Emerson does not explicitly confront the problem of American nationalism in *Conduct of Life*, the imaginative crisis he experiences in the representation of national identity is vividly revealed in a remarkable passage from the essay "Fate." "I seemed, in the height of a tempest, to see men overboard struggling in the waves, and driven about here and there," Emerson writes. "They glanced intelligently at each other, but 'twas little they could do for one another; twas much if each could keep afloat alone. Well, they had a right to their eye-beams, and all the rest was Fate" (CL, 951–952). The image of men struggling in the waves and powerless to help one another, each having a right only to his eye-beams and nothing else, conveys in deeply personal terms Emerson's sense of the insufficiency of the liberal discourse of rights to represent a model of identity that is both individual and national. The tortured abstraction of Emerson's argument in *Conduct of Life* shows the extent of his unwillingness or inability to speak publicly about his sense of the crisis brought on by slavery and the advent of war. However, Emerson's persistent attempt to grapple with the contradictory claims of rights and race arguably culminates in a theory of national identity, which he sets forth in *Conduct of Life*. Despite the aversion to history Emerson exhibits in *Conduct of Life*, the contradictory model of the self he constructs is one that has applicability to a theory of national identity, and expresses an unmistakable continuity of thought even with his earliest writings.

Given what we already know about Emerson's thinking on the subject, the racial doctrine put forward in *Conduct of Life* should by now be, in many respects, familiar. Just as in *English Traits* Emerson speculates that the natural history of nations depicts their inevitable rise and fall, observing, "As we find stumps of vast trees in our exhausted soils . . . so history reckons epochs in which the intellect of famed races became effete" (ET, 898), so in *Conduct of Life* he refers to the life-cycle of nations and the inevitable existence of racial inequality, of "effete races . . . [that] must be reckoned calculable parts of the system of the world" (CL, 951). "The face of the planet cools and dries," he writes, "the races meliorate, and man is born. But when a race has lived its term, it comes no more again" (CL, 949). As in his earlier writings, in "Fate" Emerson is explicit about the undeniable link between racial origin and national destiny.

> We know in history what weight belongs to race. We see the English, French, and Germans planting themselves on every shore and market of America and Australia, and monopolizing the commerce of these countries. We like the nervous and victorious habit of our own branch of the family. We follow the step of the Jew, of the Indian, of the Negro. . . . See the shades of the picture. The German and the Irish millions, like the Negro, have a great deal of guano in their destiny. They are ferried over the Atlantic, and carted over America, to ditch and to drudge, to make corn cheap, and then to lie down prematurely to make a spot of green grass on the prairie. (CL, 950)

More specifically, the central issue Emerson addresses in "Fate" is expressed in terms of what should by now be a familiar contradiction between, on the one hand, the claims represented by the existence of liberal, political rights and, on the other hand, the constraints imposed on human life by natural and fateful phenomena that are manifested, in part, as racial traits. Indeed, in "Fate," Emerson argues that it is his primary task as a writer to express the effect of these contradictory forces, which are democratic first principles and a doctrine of race that (as we have seen) he formulated in his journal as early as 1822. "If we must accept Fate, we are not less compelled to affirm liberty, the significance of the individual, the grandeur of duty, the power of character," he wrote nearly four decades later. "This is true, and that other is true. But our geometry cannot span these extreme points and reconcile them. What to do? By obeying each thought frankly, by harping, or, if you will, pounding on each string, we learn at last its power. By the same obedience to other thoughts, we learn theirs, and then comes some reasonable hope of harmonizing them. We are sure, that, though we know not how, necessity does comport with liberty, the individual with the world, my polarity with the spirit of the times" (CL, 943). In "Fate," contradiction is central to a model of the self Emerson explicitly casts as a "stupendous antagonism," the juxtaposition of body and spirit, of necessity and liberty, of racial attributes and the abstract possession of rights:

> Man is not order of nature, sack and sack, belly and members, link in a chain, nor any ignominious baggage, but a stupendous antagonism, a dragging together of poles of the Universe. He betrays his relation to what is below him,—thick-skulled, small-brained, fishy, quadrumanous,—quadruped ill-disguised, hardly escaped into biped, and has paid for the new powers by loss of some of the old ones. But the lightning which explodes and fashions planets, maker of planets and granite, rock-ledges, peat-bog, forest, sea and shore; and, on the other part, thought, the spirit which composes and decomposes nature,—here they are, side by side, god and devil, mind and matter, king and conspirator, belt and spasm, riding peacefully together in the eye and brain of every man. (CL, 953)

What Emerson argues in this passage, and in his essay as a whole, is that expressive possibilities are created only in the poetic act of accepting and exploring the contradiction between rights and race that structures this model of the self. "It was a poetic attempt to lift this mountain of Fate, to reconcile this despotism of race with liberty, which led the Hindoos to say, 'Fate is nothing but the deeds committed in a prior state of existence'" (CL, 948), he writes. "To hazard the contradiction,—freedom is necessary" (CL, 953).

If Emerson's methodical, radical resistance to conceptual limitations of any kind in imagining the American self and nation ultimately leads him to vacillate between rights and race as competing but equally necessary poles of thought, this dissatisfaction with Lockean rights discourse is also reinforced in later writings by his description of national expansion as an ongoing process of racial hybridization. Whereas in early texts such as "The American Scholar"

Emerson describes the process of expansion, in recognizably Lockean terms, as the "conversion of the world" to democratic principles, in his account of national expansion in *English Traits* and *Conduct of Life* he justifies the expansion of national boundaries in terms that are far more explicitly racial than they are liberal. In *English Traits*, Emerson describes a process of racial hybridization that threatens the clear demarcation of boundaries between races. In the essay "Race," he observes:

> The low organizations are simplest; a mere mouth, a jelly, or a straight worm. As the scale mounts, the organizations become complex. We are piqued with pure descent, but nature loves innoculation. A child blends in his face the faces of both parents, and some feature from every ancestor whose face hangs on the wall. The best nations are those most widely related; and navigation, as effecting a world-wide mixture, is the most potent advancer of nations. ... Though we flatter the self-love of men and nations by the legend of pure races, all our experience is of the gradation and resolution of races, and strange resemblances meet us everywhere," he observes. "It need not puzzle us that Malay and Papuan, Celt and Roman, Saxon and Tartar should mix, when we see the rudiments of tiger and baboon in our human form, and know that the barriers of races are not so firm, but that some spray sprinkles us from antediluvian seas." (*ET*, 793)

Emerson's interest in the connection between racial hybridization and national identity emerges as early as 1823, when he noted in his journal that "[a] nation, like a tree, does not thrive well till it is engraffed with a foreign stock" (*JMN*, I, 304). He refers to a similar process again twelve years later when he asks himself, "What of these atrocious ancestors of Englishmen, the Briton, Saxon, Northman, Berserkir? Is it not needful to make a strong nation that there should be strong wild will? If a man degenerates in goodness he must be grafted again from the wild stock" (*JMN*, III, 562, 1835). In his journals Emerson often describes hybridization as a process that is both natural and beautiful: in 1846, he wrote, "The whole art of Nature is in these juxtapositions of diverse qualities to make a lucky combination, as green and gold, dry oak leaves and snow, enhance each other, and make a delicious mixture to the eye" (*JMN*, VII, 214), and one year later, he observed, "Nature loves crosses, as inoculations of barbarous races prove. ... Where two shadows cross, the darkness thickens: where two lights cross, the light glows" (Porte, *Emerson in His Journals*, 369). Like other racial theorists, Emerson thought that at some time all nations would experience a natural and inevitable lapse from power. However, in *English Traits* he expresses a belief that at least for the present the process of hybridization was creating a beautiful new race of Americans. In 1845, he wrote:

> Man is the most composite of all creatures. Well, as in the old burning of the Temple at Corinth, by the melting and admixture of silver and gold and other metals a new compound more precious than any, called the Corinthian brass, was formed; so, in this continent,—asylum of all nations,—the energy

of Irish, Germans, Swedes, Poles, and Cossacks, and all the European tribes,—of the Africans, and of the Polynesians,—will construct a new race, a new religion, a new state, a new literature, which will be as vigorous as the new Europe which came out of the smelting-pot of the Dark Ages, or that which earlier emerged from the Pelasgic and Etruscan barbarism. *La Nature aime les croisements.*" (JMN, VII, 115–116)[30]

In some respects, Emerson's emphasis on racial hybridization in the unfolding of national destiny resembles the nationalism of John Stuart Mill in his essay on representative government.

> Experience proves that it is possible for one nationality to merge and be absorbed in another; and when it was originally an inferior and more backward portion of the human race, the absorption is greatly to its advantage. Whatever really tends to the admixture of nationalities, and the blending of their attributes and peculiarities in a common union, is a benefit to the human race. Not by extinguishing types, of which, in these cases, sufficient examples are sure to remain, but by softening their extreme forms, and filling up the intervals between them. The united people, like a crossed breed of animals (but in a still higher degree, because the influences in operation are moral as well as physicial), inherits the special aptitudes and excellencies of all its progenitors, protected by the admixture from being exaggerated in to the neighboring vices. (CRG, 315)

Both Emerson and Mill ease the tension between racial specificity and the abstract, liberal conception of the representative self and uphold the possibility of a nation that is both racially distinctive and democratic by referring to the fact of hybridization. However, unlike Mill, in his defense of the imperial act of expansion Emerson vacillates between the strictly biological process of racial hybridization and the act of cultural assimilation. Just as in "The American Scholar" Emerson conflates racial unity and cultural unity in his construction of national identity, so in *English Traits* the absorptive act of assimilation is described in both racial and cultural terms. "More intellectual than other races, when they live with other races, [the English] do not take their language, but bestow their own," he writes. "They subsidize other nations, and are not subsidized. They proselyte, and are not proselyted. They assimilate other races to themselves, and are not assimilated. The English did not calculate the conquest of the Indies. It fell to their character. So they administer in different parts of the world, the codes of every empire and race" (ET, 841). The popular biological meaning of the word "race" forms the conceptual basis for Emerson's account of cultural assimilation, because the natural superiority of English character justifies the act of assimilation as Emerson describes this act in *English Traits*.

Following this line of argument, it makes sense that in *Conduct of Life* Emerson represents expansion as being both democratic and the result of racial hybridization, a process that demonstrates the divine mandate to dominion possessed by an imperial Saxon race. "But every jet of chaos which threatens to exterminate us, is convertible by intellect into a wholesome force," Emerson writes. "Cold and sea will train an imperial Saxon race, which nature cannot bear to lose, and, after cooping it up for a thousand years in yonder England, gives a hundred Englands, a hundred Mexicos. All the bloods it shall absorb and domineer: and more than Mexicos,—the secrets of water and steam, the spasms of electricity, the ductility of metals, the chariot of the air, the ruddered balloon are awaiting you" (CL, 958). In this passage, the capacity for conquest and dominion Emerson celebrates in English Traits is a racial attribute that he appropriates as his own. Just as we saw in Nature that the figure of Columbus represents a model of the self that is simultaneously representative or rights-bearing and explicitly racial, so in this passage the pronoun "you" invokes a representative subject that is also the product of an inevitable process of hybridization and absorption into the Saxon race. The model of the self Emerson creates in this passage is cast in terms that simultaneously demonstrate the universal applicability of democratic ideals and justify American exceptionalism in distinctly racial nationalist terms.

In chapter 2, I argued that the critique of Lockean property rights undertaken in Emerson's early writings signals his engagement with the problem of slavery in America. Although in English Traits Emerson does on occasion criticize what he regards as an excessive love of wealth in English society, in which "[h]igh stone fences, and padlocked garden-gates announce the absolute will of the owner to be alone" (ET, 856), his discussion of property is relatively shallow in comparison with the intensity and clear focus exhibited in the earlier phase of his intellectual development.[31] Viewed in light of Emerson's early engagement with property rights, it is striking (if not surprising) that in the essay "Fate" Emerson turns instead to what he regards as an even higher, more fundamental right to individual liberty.[32] Although Emerson implicitly critiques the Lockean notion of property rights when he asserts the fundamental unity of all minds in "Fate," arguing that "[o]ur thought . . . is not mine or thine, but the will of all mind" (CL, 956), his concern with property and argument against slavery is, in Conduct of Life, ultimately addressed in terms of the much broader cultural issues of race and national identity. Even though Emerson's silence regarding the pressing issue of slavery in Conduct of Life is a source of dissatisfaction for many readers, we should note that in the essay "Fate" he does confront the important question of positionality and the particular, racial conditions of his own speech with considerable directness. He writes, "Who likes to believe that he has hidden in his skull, spine, and pelvis, all the vices of a Saxon or Celtic race," he writes, "which will be sure to pull him down,—with what grandeur of hope and resolve he is fired,—into a selfish, huckstering, servile, dodging animal?" (CL, 960).[33] In "Fate," the contradiction between rights and race has obvious applicability to a theory of national identity.

Generally speaking, the function of race in Emerson's writings is to express a concept of the nation that is both myopic and innovative. It is myopic, as I have argued, insofar as it must be viewed in the context of a violent policy of westward expansion that prevailed in nineteenth-century America. Viewed historically, it is also innovative, because Emerson's critique of liberalism and theory of nationalism introduces "race" as a category into the field of liberal nationalist thought. Indeed, in this respect Emerson's expression of a theory of American nationalism is a crucial gesture that opens the possibility for critique and the production of other specifically African-American forms of nationalism in which race plays a central role. The impact of Emerson's thinking about identity on Du Bois and King will be taken up at length in the next part of this book. However, before concluding this part, I will briefly mention the significance of Emerson's thinking about race and nationalism for his theory of political obligation, a theory that represents an important resource for Du Bois's self-contradictory model of African-American identity as double-consciousness.

In "Fate," Emerson explicitly defines the self in terms of "double-consciousness":

> One key, one solution to the mysteries of human conditions, one solution to the old knots of fate, freedom, and foreknowledge, exists, the propounding, namely, of the double consciousness. A man must ride alternately on the horses of his private and public nature. . . . To offset the drag of temperament and race, which pulls down, learn this lesson, namely, that by the cunning co-presence of two elements, which is throughout nature, whatever lames or paralyzes you, draws in with it the divinity, in some form, to repay. (CL, 966, 967)

What is important to note is that as a model of political identity structured on the contradictory claims of rights and race, "double-consciousness" also expresses the creative tension between voluntary and involuntary aspects of political obligation.

Perhaps the most beautiful instance of Emerson's rendering of political identity as double-consciousness occurs in the 1844 essay "Experience." At one point in his argument, Emerson pictures his idea of what it means to be "American" as an illuminating, near-religious experience of conversion cast in personal terms. The conversion to raised double-consciousness is imagined by Emerson as a state of near speechlessness, a stuttering state that registers his own, newly acquired insight into a shocking existential truth. For Emerson, America actually *is* the discovery of his own brilliant and deliberate performance of self-contradiction, a discovery that in turn opens onto an infinite series of brilliant, endlessly novel expressive possibilities. In Emerson's sense, America is a "new and excellent region of life" or "realm of thought" (*Essays*, 484, 485)—a social utopia that has been *both* socially contracted *and* revealed or given to him by God. In contrast to pragmatists such as William James, who contend that identity is socially constructed, Emerson's writings disclose a self-contradictory model of American identity that is not only rights-based, a self described in democratic terms as something *made* and owned, but one that is also defined as an irreducibly racial self, constituted by ties of community and obligation that are born into or *found* as already existing.[34]

> When I converse with a profound mind, or at any time being alone I have good thoughts, I do not at once arrive at satisfactions, as when, being thirsty, I drink water, or go to the fire, being cold: no! but I am at first apprised of my vicinity to a new and excellent region of life. . . . *I do not make it; I arrive there, and behold what was there already. I make! O no!* I clap my hands in infantine joy and amazement before the first opening to me of this august magnificence. . . . And what a future it opens! I feel a new heart beating with the love of a new beauty. I am ready to die out of nature and be born again into this new yet unapproachable America I have found in the West. (*Essays*, 485; emphasis added)[35]

The special applicability of double-consciousness to Emerson's theory of political obligation is visible as early as 1842, in a lecture titled "The Transcendentalist" read at the Masonic Temple in Boston. In this lecture, Emerson uses the concept of double-consciousness to express a state of simultaneous withdrawal from and participation in the public realm. The self he describes is possessed of attributes that are simultaneously public and private. At one point, Emerson describes a momentary glimpse into a "different faith" that causes certain persons to withdraw from society. By Emerson's account, the experience is one that constitutes an involuntarily assumed obligation to withdraw from the state.

> But, to come a little closer to the secret of these persons, we must say, that to them it seems a very easy matter to answer the objections of the world, but not so easy to dispose of the doubts and objections that occur to themselves. . . . When I asked them concerning their private experience, they answered somewhat in this wise: It is not to be denied that there must be some wide difference between my faith and other faith; and mine is a certain brief experience, which surprised me in the highway or in the market, in some place, at some time,—whether in the body or out of the body, God knoweth,—and made me aware that I had played the fool with fools all this time, but that law existed for me and for all; that to me belonged trust, a child's trust and obedience, and the worship of ideas, and I should never be fool more. Well in the space of an hour, probably, I was let down from this height; I was at my old tricks, the selfish member of a selfish society.
>
> These two states of thought diverge at every moment, and stand in wild contrast. To him who looks at his life from these moments of illumination, it will seem that he skulks and plays a mean, shiftless, and subaltern part in the world. . . . The worst feature of this double-consciousness is, that the two lives, of the understanding and of the soul, which we lead, really show very little relation to each other, never meet and measure each other: one prevails now, all buzz and din; and the other prevails then, all infinitude and paradise; and, with the progress of life, the two discover no greater disposition to reconcile themselves. (*Essays*, 205–206)

In this earliest formulation, then, Emerson is arguing that "double-consciousness" simultaneously represents a person's involuntary assumption of the obligation to disobey or withdraw from the state, and requires that person's participation as a trickster in the selfish, public world of politics.

By far the most striking difference between Emerson's early characterization of political identity as double-consciousness in "The Transcendentalist" and the meaning he arrives at in "Fate" is that in "Fate" double-consciousness reflects the racialist bias of all his later writings. Whereas in 1842 Emerson suggested that the individual involuntarily assumes an obligation to withdraw from society because he experiences a "different faith" from those around him, eighteen years later he would justify the involuntarily assumed obligation to withdraw from the state in explicitly racialist terms.

Although rights and race represent contradictory views of the self and nation, the two concepts are not at cross-purposes in Emerson's writings. Neither rights nor race alone is sufficient to represent Emersonian double-consciousness, and the two concepts gain justification and force by the fact of their juxtaposition. In the next and final part of this book, I will show that this incessant elaboration upon this condition of double-consciousness in Emerson's writings—his affirmation of ties that are simultaneously racial and rights-based—profoundly influenced W. E. B. Du Bois's critique of the mainstream tradition in American nationalism, a tradition in which the social significance of "race" has too often been overlooked in the compromised extension of rights.

PART III

Protest

SEVEN

W. E. B. Du Bois
and the Critique of
Liberal Nationalism

In recent years, there has been a growing awareness of "race" as a modern category of social recognition and self-representation. Various meanings have been assigned to the term "race" in contemporary analyses, each of which implies a particular set of social commitments.[1] Taken as a whole, the writings of W. E. B. Du Bois constitute a lengthy, engaged, and public confrontation with the terms set forth in the contemporary critical debate about race. As a practitioner of William James's pragmatic method, Du Bois did not simply advocate the truth of a particular concept of race. Rather, his contribution consists in his consideration of the question of the *difference it practically makes* to say that a particular concept of race is or is not true. Reading Du Bois, we may trace the practical consequences of embracing the truth of the biological concept of race—for Du Bois, the meaning of "race" has been shaped by the history and possibilities of its use.

In Part II, I explored the significance of Emerson's critique of Lockean contractarianism for the expression of his nationalism. The model of political obligation as "double-consciousness" Emerson arrives at in his later writings is, I argued, the result of his lifelong researches into the meaning of the representative American self. The self Emerson describes in his writings is not only privately made and owned, it is also defined by political obligations that are, like the collective ties of race, born into or found as (always) already existing. At the same time he embraces the popular premises of liberal contractarianism, Emerson also resists these conceptual limitations and extends monarchical rights and obligations to every representative American. By Emerson's account, such universally extended monarchical rights and duties are not, strictly speaking, democratic, because they are divinely mandated and thus are not at all assumed by volitional, rational acts of consent.

With this brief synopsis of Emerson's political critique in mind, we may now begin to trace out some of the major implications of Emerson's ideas about ownership, obligation, and nationalism for the development of twenti-eth-century African-American political philosophies up through the writings of Martin Luther King Jr. and Cornel West. The aim of the present chapter is to show the connection between Emersonian "double-consciousness" and W. E. B. Du Bois's critique and inheritance of that term. Du Bois's funda-mental insight was that he deployed Emerson's simultaneous invocation of rights and race for the purposes of conceptualizing black American identity. Just as, in "Fate," Emerson characterizes and specifically elaborates upon "dou-ble-consciousness" as a central contradiction between rights and race that structures his thinking about the self, so Du Bois's critique of the liberal theory of nations entails a conception of the African-American Self as "double-consciousness" and presents a model of ideal nationhood that mandates the coexistence of rights and race as contradictory but equally necessary rhetorics of political representation. Like Emerson, Du Bois simultaneously invokes the liberal discourse of rights to represent the ideal self as an equal political par-ticipant in the American polis, *and* resists these conceptual parameters by having recourse to racialism as an available nineteenth-century discourse on obligation. The consistent pattern of contradiction in Du Bois's writings rep-resents his methodical, radical resistance to conceptual limitations that inhere in both liberal and racialist models of national identity. The significance of this contradiction is implicit but not directly stated in Du Bois's early works, such as his 1897 pamphlet titled *The Conservation of Races*. It is not until *The Souls of Black Folk*, published six years later, that Du Bois explicitly constructs his model of the African-American self and nation as a veiled state of "double-consciousness," a model inflected by the contradictory claims of rights and race as competing, mutually effacing discourses on national identity.

Du Bois's development of this simple, central contradiction between rights and race culminates in the nationalist rhetoric he uses in *Dusk of Dawn*, subtitled *An Autobiography of a Race Concept*. Here, Du Bois observes that "[t]he concept of race has so changed and presented so much of contradiction that as I face Africa I ask myself: what is it between us that constitutes a tie which I can feel better than I can explain?"[2] By Du Bois's account, the evo-lution of his race concept is such that, by 1940, the meaning of "race" is *both* biological *and* represented in terms of rights discourse that contradicts scien-tific descriptions of racial identity. In a clear affirmation of biologism, Du Bois insists, "My tie to Africa is strong. On this vast continent were born and lived a large portion of my direct ancestors going back a thousand years or more. The mark of their heritage is upon me in color and hair" (*DD*, 117). But in a self-conscious, self-contradictory gesture that is central to his whole political critique, Du Bois also transcends and works against this biologism by also referring to the liberal, rights-based description of personhood. "The actual ties of heritage between the individuals of this group, vary with the ancestors that they have in common and many others," he observes. "But the physical bond is least and the badge of color relatively unimportant save as a badge; the real essence of this kinship is its social heritage of slavery; the discrimination and insult; and this heritage binds not simply the children of Africa, but extends through yellow Asia and into the South Seas. It is this unity that draws me to Africa" (*DD*, 117).

The broader, cultural significance of Du Bois's racialism is that it generates a coherent oppositional identity for African Americans and expresses withdrawal from America as an existing and unjust state. But in this passage, as in all his later writings, Du Bois also discloses an infinitely capacious meaning for "race" that includes any person who has suffered a deprivation of rights. The concept of nationhood associated with this latter definition of race is infinitely expansive and signals the dissolution of national identity. By describing "race" in terms of rights, by defining "race" both as shared descent and as a heritage of violated rights, Du Bois produces an innovative and self-contradictory race concept that not only binds the children of Africa but also extends through yellow Asia and into the South Seas.

The unresolved tension between biological and sociohistorical meanings for race in Du Bois's writings has been clearly demarcated in Anthony Appiah's work titled *In My Father's House: Africa and the Philosophy of Culture*. In this attempt to situate Du Bois's conceptualization of philosophical categories within the exigencies of culture, Appiah suggests that in early writings such as *The Conservation of Races*, Du Bois's primary aim is not, as Du Bois explicitly claims it is, "the transcendence of the nineteenth-century scientific conception of race . . . [,] but rather, . . . a revaluation of the Negro race in the face of the sciences of racial inferiority."[3] And with regard to later writings such as *Dusk of Dawn*, Appiah insists that "Du Bois was unable to escape the notion of race he explicitly rejected" (*In My Father's House*, 46); that this biological notion was never transcended but only "buried" below the surface of Du Bois's sweeping claims for the enduring sociohistorical ties of common history that bind him to Africa (*In My Father's House*, 41). For Appiah, it is precisely this failure on Du Bois's part to transcend biological descent as a culturally unmediated tie to Africa that accounts for Du Bois's inability to identify "an African residue to take hold of and rejoice in, a subtle connection mediated not by genetics but by intentions, by meaning" (*In My Father's House*, 41–42). What this lack of conceptual resources leads to in Du Bois's writings is a definition of Pan-African identity that is so broad as to be, in Appiah's view, incoherent. "If what Du Bois has in common with Africa is a history of 'discrimination and insult,' then this binds him, on his own account, to 'yellow Asia and . . . the South Seas' also. How can something he shares with the whole nonwhite world bind him to part of it? Once we interrogate the argument here, a further suspicion arises that the claim to this bond is based on a hyperbolic reading of the facts" (*In My Father's House*, 42).

My concern with the theoretical significance and historical function of contradiction in Du Bois's writings is not meant to deny the force of Appiah's claim that Du Bois's rights rhetoric obscures crucial particularities of cultural difference—the fact that, as Appiah aptly reminds us, Du Bois's experience of discrimination differs from that of people in colonized West Africa and in Asia or other parts of the world (*In My Father's House*, 42). Rather, I wish to point out what is at stake in Du Bois's refusal to disavow either the claims of race or those of rights, and that this balancing act—Du Bois's attempt to stand forever poised between the poles of contradiction—is a deliberate gesture of critique and not a conceptual limitation, as Appiah suggests.[4] By showing that Du Bois's mediation between "rights-talk" and racial discourse allows him to acknowledge the dangers and oppositional possibilities of each and, in particular, by arguing that the pattern of contradiction in Du Bois's writings represents a critical recuperation of Emerson's thinking about identity, I hope to contribute to the work of situating Du Bois's theoretical engagement with rights and race within a larger cultural domain.

The significance of "double-consciousness" as a critique of available, nineteenth-century liberal and racialist discourses on identity has on occasion been referred to in various philosophical and literary debates, but has never been established in a concrete analysis of texts. In a footnote to his discussion of the process of naming in African-American literature, Kimberly Benston has written that " '[d]ouble-consciousness' was, of course, a favorite expression of Emerson's, and . . . Du Bois no doubt learned of 'double-consciousness' as a general philosophical coinage from his quasi-Emersonian mentor at Harvard, William James."[5] More important is the fact that, as Cornel West points out in *The American Evasion of Philosophy*, there exists a relationship between Emersonian and Du Boisian forms of double-consciousness, insofar as "Emerson grappled with the 'double-consciousness of being an American, or having a European culture in an un-European environment."[6]

There is textual evidence that Emerson's writings represent a considerable resource for the development of Du Bois's political philosophy. For example, Du Bois's corpus of writings is full of references to Emerson's poetry: "The Rhodora" appears as part of his 1896 address on "The Art and Art Galleries of Modern Europe" delivered at Wilberforce University; in September 1961, "Sacrifice" is used in a speech delivered at a banquet in honor of Henry Winston; and Du Bois habitually drew on selected passages from Emerson's writings as epigraphs for *The Horizon: A Journal of the Color Line*.[7] References to Emerson are included in Du Bois's 1921 essay titled "The Contribution of the Negro to American Life and Culture," published in *The Pacific Review*, and in "The Negro as a National Asset," published in *The Homiletic Review*

two years later.[8] Indeed, Du Bois himself was regarded by many of his contemporaries as a literary successor to Emerson: in an October 15, 1937, letter
to Du Bois, Harrison J. Pinkett wrote, "Your contribution has been very great
. . . , greater than that of any American writer. Emerson, of course, gave us
some standing among men of letters in the older states, but your writing has
taught a whole nation the lesson of intellectual equality among men."[9]

Viewed in the context of his writings as a whole, Du Bois's fleeting references to Emerson seem relatively few and far between. But given what we
already know about Emerson's political critique—namely, his sustained meditation on the meaning of ownership and on the obligation to reform, and his
critique of the contractarian ideal of "consent" that is purely rational and
voluntary—Du Bois's engagement with Emerson at these moments appears all
the more compelling. We saw in chapter 1, for example, that Emerson's concept of "the representative" enacts a critique of self-ownership as a cherished
first premise of liberal democracy, because the proper role of representative
men is to dismantle boundaries between persons and to found what Emerson
envisions as an intimate "union of all minds" and "commonwealth of souls"
(RM, 631). In "Does Education Pay?", an 1891 address on the importance of
education and self-culture delivered before the National Colored League of
Boston, Du Bois alluded to Emerson's critique of property rights in order to
exhort his audience to strive for self-cultivation and thus to inherit a commonwealth of accumulated knowledge. For Du Bois, as for Emerson, the right
to inherit such a cultural legacy devolves upon the notion of "representativeness"—the fact that this "living bequest of . . . human souls" comes from "men
who have had the same thoughts." Reciting one of Emerson's famous "Mottoes
to 'History' "—a poem that specifically alludes to the critique of ownership
put forward by Emerson in Representative Men—Du Bois argues that

> we have, by tradition, by Art, and by Literature, the great heritage of the
> age, the great conglomerate which we call knowledge; the accumulated ex-
> perience of millions of human beings like you is yours: men who have had
> the same thoughts, have striven under the same difficulties—laughed in your
> joy, and sorrowed in your sorrow. All this the living bequest of a million
> human souls is the property of you, the children of the Nineteenth Century,
> if you choose to take it. There is none so humble but can say with Emerson:
>
> "I am the owner of the sphere
> Of the seven stars and solar year;
> Of Caesar's hand, and Plato's brain,
> Of Lord Christ's Heart and Shakespeare's strain."[10]

Elsewhere in his lecture, Du Bois elaborates on another aspect of Emerson's political critique discussed in chapter 3: namely, the ethical demand for
reform. Following Emerson, Du Bois unfolds a vision of liberal education that
demonstrates a close, necessary connection between the process of self-
cultivation or "self-culture," the fundamental right of access to a larger, cultural commonwealth, and the obligation to perform inward acts of

self-transformation as a means of social reform. "You only realize the possibilities of the world in which you live in such a degree as you have liberally educated yourselves either in the high school or college, or in the long, careful, and diligent self-culture" (DEP, 6), he writes. By calling on Emerson's philosophy of obligation as a conceptual resource, Du Bois successfully casts the "moral duty" to see a theatrical production of Shakespeare's *Hamlet* as a personal duty to reform that has larger social and political significance. Du Bois concludes with a stanza from Emerson's "Voluntaries":

> So tonight the great warm bursting heart of the mother of God is calling us to be men in the race that needs us, in the world that awaits us. Will you do it? Can you do it?
>
> > *"So near is the grandeur to our dust,*
> > *So near is God to man;*
> > *When duty whispers low thou must,*
> > *The youth replies—I can." (DEP, 18)*

Du Bois's engagement with Emerson's writings on the ethical demand for self-cultivation as an act of social reform—and, in particular, his interest in Emerson's critique of the Lockean, liberal notion that "consent" to participation in society should always be a rational, voluntary act—is evident in another address on the importance of intellectual culture he delivered nine years later, to a meeting of African-American teachers in Athens, Georgia. In this address, Du Bois alludes to the same stanza from Emerson's "Voluntaries." For Du Bois, as for Emerson, the obligation to perform the personal act of self-cultivation as a means of improving society as a whole cannot be assumed by an act of consent that is rational and purely "voluntary." Rather, the duty to self-culture is best expressed in the striking juxtaposition of phrases: "I can" and "you must."

> The truly educated man is he who has learned in school how to study and in life what to study. . . . And this he can do—in spite of sordid surroundings in the absence of all incitements to self-culture, in spite of the demands of home and school and work, he can—you can leave time for self-cultivation and self-development—for the realization of some of the high ideals of your youth—you can do it because others have done it and above all because you must: "So near is grandeur to our dust. . . ."[11]

At this point, we can see that Du Bois was deeply engaged with Emerson's political thought. In addition to my claims about the overall importance of Du Bois's explicit references to Emerson, however, I will also go even further, and suggest that Alexander Crummell and Booker T. Washington—two nineteenth-century African-American political philosophers to whom Du Bois devotes a chapter each in *The Souls of Black Folk*—were influences that shaped Du Bois's critique of Emerson. The critique of liberal nationalism undertaken by Crummell in his Liberian nationalist sermons represents a revision and appropriation of the American tradition in Protestant election sermons that culminated, in the first half of the nineteenth century, in the writings of American intellectuals such as William Ellery Channing. Drawing on Crummell as a scholarly resource, Du Bois was granted even broader access to the mainstream tradition in American sermonic rhetoric. And drawing on insights from Washington's critique of popular Emersonianism in *Up From Slavery*, Du Bois was able to develop a radically new political critique that underscored the importance of rights and race as facets of Black American identity. In order to understand this larger philosophical and cultural development, we need now to consider the respective contributions of Crummell and Washington in more detail.

The nineteenth century has long been regarded by historians as a critical period in the formation and flourishing of American discourses on identity including, of course, the emergence of American black nationalisms.[12] One mid-nineteenth-century writer who has often been described as influential in the development of black nationlist ideology is Alexander Crummell. Born free in New York on March 3, 1819, Crummell was active in black community efforts and abolitionist activities in the early 1800s. From 1836 to 1839, he attended the Oneida Institute, founded by the radical abolitionist and Presbyterian minister Beriah Green, who encouraged Crummell to enter into holy orders. Crummell was raised to the order of priesthood in 1844. In the 1850s, a period that represented the high point of American black nationalism, Crummell became a missionary to Liberia.

Although, unlike Emerson, Crummell's nationalist vision reflects his revaluation of the status assigned to the Negro race in the context of the scientific doctrine of racial inequality,[13] his political philosophy is fundamentally similar to Emerson's critique of Lockean liberalism and model of American national identity in that, like Emerson, Crummell structures his theory of nations on a central contradiction between claims embedded in liberal and racialist discourses. Like Emerson's nationalism in "The American Scholar," Crummell's nationalist rhetoric has the curious effect of simultaneously affirming and erasing national identity. For example, in his 1855 address "The Duty of a Rising Christian State" (FOA, 58–73), delivered before the Common Council and citizens of Monrovia at the festival of Liberian National Independence, Crummell's vision of Liberian nationality is dual and contradictory. At the same time he specifically delineates and names Liberia's "new-born nationality,"[14] Crummell also appeals to Christian ideals that work against the cherished premises of nineteenth-century racialism by emphasizing the "mutual dependence of the different families of men" and "the obligation of all states and commonwealths and empires to contribute to human well-being and the progress of nations" (FOA, 59). "And so there is no isolation," he writes, "no absolute disseverance of individual nations; for blood and lineage, and ancient manners, and religion, and letters, all tend to combine nationalities and link them in indissoluble bonds, despite all the lapses of time" (FOA, 64).

Like Emerson's imagining of America as a nation in "The American Scholar," Crummell's model of national identity is characterized by boundaries that are both fixed and infinitely expansive. For Crummell, the ideal concept of a nation that is also a rising Christian state entails obligations to the human race that threaten national identity and lead to the infinite expansion of boundaries. "We are but a small nation, as yet hardly productive, certainly not self-supporting; but we have nationality, and also the duties and responsibilities which are of twin birth with it," Crummell writes. "Our nationality is to be carefully guarded and cherished as a most precious jewel; but the obligations which are connected with it are of equal worth, and demand equal interest, and earnest zeal, for their preservation. I have already shown the obligations of nations to contribute to the world's well-being. As an humble member of the great sisterhood of nations, this obligation rests upon us" (FOA, 73). The national distinctiveness and infinite expansiveness of a rising state that Crummell describes as being *both* Liberian *and* Christian in his address recall Emerson's description of both the racial distinctiveness and the representative quality he attributes to the nation of American Scholars. While in "Hope for Africa" Crummell assigns a divine destiny to the Negro race, in "The Duty of a Rising Christian State" he affirms the existence of universal moral obligations and presents a concept of the human race that contradicts his division of humanity into distinct races. "A nation is but a section of the great commonwealth of humanity, a phase of the common type of being, and no more" he writes (FOA, 60). "The race, in the aggregate, is to go forward and upward" (FOA, 63).

The central tension between boundedness and boundlessness in Crummell's nationalist rhetoric is, by Crummell's own admission, instrumental to a broader critique of laissez-faire individualism that is registered on a national level as the promotion of a national self-interest. Throughout his writings, Crummell expresses a faith in the beneficial influence of commerce on a rising Christian state: like many liberal thinkers who accepted Adam Smith's classical theory of economy, Crummell believed that economic development was essential to the anticolonial expression of national independence and provided a necessary boost to national identity. "The primary ends of civil government are the conservation of men's lives, bodies, and goods," he writes (FOA, 65). "A non-commercial spirit and practice has always stifled the life of nations, or laid them low in ruins. In the history of the 'Decline and Fall' of nations, this will yet be shown to have been one of the most potent agencies of national decay" (FOA, 69–70).

Paradoxically, however, at the same time Crummell articulates this belief that commerce is essential to the creation of the independent nation, he also argues that to the extent that commerce "binds men and nations to each other," its development ultimately results in the erasure of national identity. "We can easily see what a civilizer is commerce; how it binds men and nations to each other; how it promotes good-will, and builds up sterling charact he writes. "And the consideration of this topic serves to show how, by the order of nature and the will of God, nations are bound to contribute to the well-being and civilization of the great family of man" (FOA, 72). In this respect, Crummell's theory of nationalism reflects a problematic that is typical of the nationalist writings of many nineteenth-century liberals who also accepted the arguments of classical political economy. In his monumental *Inquiry into the Nature and Causes of the Wealth of Nations* published in 1776, Adam Smith demonstrated that individual self-interest would function as by the operation of an invisible hand to promote the "public interest." "Every individual necessarily labours to render the annual revenue of the society as great as he can," Smith writes. "He generally, indeed, neither intends to promote the public interest, nor knows how much he is promoting it. By preferring the support of domestic to that of foreign industry, he intends only his own security; and by directing that industry in such a manner as its produce may be of the greatest value, he intends only his own gain, and he is in this, as in many other cases, led by an invisible hand to promote an end which was no part of his intention."[15] Crummell's position regarding the tenets of Smith's laissez-faire capitalism is thus, characteristically, twofold and contradictory.[16] At the same time that he argues for the benefits of commerce as a boost to national identity, he also warns that the primary ends of government should be Christian and moral, not economic. "The primary ends of civil government are the conservation of men's lives, bodies, and goods," he writes. "But there are also remote and ultimate ends, which pertain to Morals, Duty, Obligations, and Justice" (FOA, 65). The conflation of individual and public interest in Smith's writings is articulated by liberal thinkers such as Crummell as the conflation of national interests.

In his attempt to show that the primary ends of the state should be moral and not economic, Crummell participates in an American sermonic tradition—specifically, a proto-nationalist Protestant tradition in what have been generically designated "election" sermons that culminated in the sermons of William Ellery Channing. The writers in this tradition all regard liberal principles as insufficient to express their concept of more perfect political community, but paradoxically regard the liberal idea of the state as a necessary barrier to social injustice that cannot be discarded. In "Duty of a Rising Christian State," Crummell explicitly quotes a claim put forward by Channing in an election sermon preached in Boston on May 26, 1830, that "[t]he moral principle is the life of communities" (quoted in FOA, 65). Like Crummell, in this sermon Channing affirms both liberal and Christian ideals. "I fear, that various causes are acting powerfully among ourselves . . . and madden that enslaving and degrading principle, the passion for property," Channing writes. "Think not that I would disparage commerce, industry, internal improvements, mechanical invention, political economy, and peace. Think not that I would disparage commerce, mechanical skill, and especially pacific connexions among states. But there is danger that these blessings may by perversion

love of lucre. . . . The chief ties that hold men together in
not self-interest, or compacts, or positive institutions, or
ivisible, refined, spiritual ties, bonds of the mind and heart"
23, 32). The moral and religious critique of liberal ideals
hanning also involves his consideration of the role of con-
olitical life of nations, a philosophical problematic that, in
Crummell's political critique and theory of obligation. For
Crummell, as iv. Channing and later Thoreau, liberal concepts such as property right, contract and consent are necessary but insufficient to account for
the full spectrum of Christian, moral obligations that the bonds of political
community should properly entail.[17]

In an 1897 lecture titled "The Conservation of Races" delivered before
the American Negro Academy, which had been founded that same year by
Alexander Crummell, Du Bois asked, "What is the real meaning of race; what
has, in the past, been the law of race development, and what lessons has the
past history of race development to teach the rising Negro people?"[18] Du Bois's
subtle phrasing of this question marks a significant break from Crummell's
earlier nationalism: Du Bois's reference to "the rising Negro people" stands in
opposition to the conception of a "rising Christian State" that was so central
to Crummell's nationalist writings. Like Crummell, who expressed a deep faith
in the God-given gifts of nature and Divine Destiny assigned to his race, Du
Bois's expression of nationalist ideals in "The Conservation of Races" reflects
his revaluation of the status assigned to the Negro race. "Manifestly some of
the great races of today—particularly the Negro race—have not as yet given
to civilization the full spiritual message which they are capable of giving," Du
Bois writes (CR, 78). However, while Crummell emphasized the infinite expansiveness of a rising Christian state, in 1897 Du Bois emphasized the fixed
and distinctive racial boundaries that define the "rising Negro people" whom
he addresses and whose existence he thereby affirms.

In "The Conservation of Races," Du Bois repeatedly insists upon the
viability of a scientific race concept defined as shared biological descent. He
mentions the work of racial scientists such as Huxley, Raetzel, and Blumenbach, observing that "[t]he final word of science, so far, is that we have at
least two, perhaps three, great families of human beings—the whites and Negroes, possibly the yellow race" (CR, 75). While the exact number of existing
races is unclear, Du Bois insists that the profound influence of the scientific
race concept on the course of human history means that "[i]n our calmer
moments we must acknowledge that human beings are divided into races. . . .
We find upon the world's stage today eight distinctly differentiated races, in
the sense in which history tells us that the word must be used" (CR 73, 76).
The role of such a concept in Du Bois's theory of nationalism is to express a
model of African-American identity that stands in opposition to America as
an existing unjust state. Defining race as shared descent, Du Bois calls into
existence "a peculiar people," a "mighty nation" that coheres by virtue of
maternal ties that are irreducibly biological: "No people that laughs at itself,

and ridicules itself, and wishes to God it was anything but itself ever wrote its name in history," he writes. "It *must* be inspired with the Divine faith of our black mothers, that out of the blood and dust of battle will march a victorious host, a mighty nation, a peculiar people, to speak to the nations of earth a Divine truth that shall make them free" (CR, 81–82).

Earlier, I showed that in "The American Scholar" Emerson relies on the idea of a universally inspiring "Divine Soul" to establish his claims regarding the infinite permeability and inclusiveness of American nationality while at the same time failing to examine the race- and gender-based exclusions built into that concept of nationality. As Emerson sees it, a nation of American men will for the first time exist, because each man believes himself to be inspired by the Divine Soul that also inspires all men (*Essays*, 71). Here we can see that Du Bois's invocation of the "Divine faith of our black mothers" represents a critique of Emerson's nationalism in two major respects. First, in contrast to the universalism implicit in the Emersonian notion of the "Divine Soul," which works against the stability and coherence of national boundaries, Du Bois's appeal to the "Divine faith of our black mothers" results in a distinctive racial nationalist concept of identity for African Americans and as such expresses a revolutionary act of withdrawal from the state.[19] Second, unlike Emerson's reference to the "Divine Soul," Du Bois's reference to the "Divine faith of our black mothers" clearly underscores Du Bois's profound awareness of the necessary role of black women—both as historical participants and as rhetorically effective symbols—in the process of shaping a cohesive group identity for African Americans.[20]

The significance of Emerson's influence on Du Bois's thinking about race and liberal nationalism takes on a more pressing relevance when we consider the fact that, like Emerson, in "The Conservation of Races" Du Bois invokes race ideals in order to articulate a broader critique of liberal contractarianism; for Du Bois, as for Emerson, "race" represents a model of political identity and obligation that works against the insufficiencies of the liberal discourse of rights. In "The Conservation of Races," Du Bois shows that obligations arising out of racial ties that are born into or found are qualitatively different from obligations arising out of voluntary, rational acts of consent and that mark the constitution of the liberal-democratic state. "What, then, is a race?" Du Bois asks. "It is a vast family of human beings, generally of common blood and language, always of common history, traditions and impulses, who are *both voluntarily and involuntarily* striving together for the accomplishment of certain more or less vividly conceived ideals of life" (CR, 75–76; emphasis added). For Du Bois, race ideals stand in opposition to other, specifically liberal national ideals. "Turning to real history," he continues, "there can be no doubt, first, as to the widespread, nay, universal, prevalence of the race idea, the race spirit, the race ideal.... We who have been reared and trained under the individualistic philosophy of the Declaration of Independence and the laisser-faire [sic] philosophy of Adam Smith, are loath to see and loath to acknowledge this patent fact of human history" (CR, 76).

But in sharp contrast to Emerson, whose racialism affirms the supremacy of Anglo-Saxons and functions as a governing principle of American national cohesion and social order, Du Bois's racialism represents a revaluation of the status of the Negro race in light of the doctrine of inferiority, and functions to express his vision of a collective, distinctive identity for "eight million people of Negro blood in the United States of America" that forms an un-assimilated and internally unified whole:

> The advance guard of the Negro people—the eight million people of Negro blood in the United States of America—must soon come to realize that if they are to take their just place in the van of Pan-Negroism, then their destiny as a race is *not* absorption by the white Americans.

> And such a people must be united; not merely united for the organized theft of political spoils, not united to disgrace religion with whoremongers and ward-heelers; not united merely to protest and pass resolutions, but united to stop the ravages of consumption among the Negro people, united to keep black boys from loafing . . . ; and united in serious organizations, to determine by careful conference and thoughtful interchange of opinion the broad lines and policy and action for the American Negro. This is the reason for being which the American Negro Academy has. It aims at once to be the epitome and expression of the intellect of the black-blooded people of America, the exponent of the race ideals of one of the world's great races. (CR, 79, 81–82)

Du Bois's affirmation of racial unity is so repetitive as to be almost jarring. Indeed, the very persistence of that affirmation suggests the existence of a threat to racial unity. What Du Bois's rhetorical strategy in "The Conservation of Races" discloses is that the coherence of racial ties are threatened by con-tradictory claims that arise out of a concept of national identity for blacks as Americans. Race ideals are contradicted by liberal as national ideals that Du Bois manages simultaneously to retain and discard in his address. This con-tradictory stance with respect to liberalism is clearly articulated as the con-tradiction between mutually effacing and competing models of national identity inherent in the concept of "The American Negro"—a concept Du Bois works to construct in this passage, and in his address as a whole. In crucial respects, Du Bois's rhetorical construction of "The American Negro" is reminiscent of Emerson's construction of "The American Scholar" sixty years earlier. For Emerson, the word "American" is a mark of racial distinc-tiveness, while the word "scholar" refers to a representative, abstract, and universal "Man Thinking." For Du Bois, the word "American" has a dual and contradictory function. At the same time that the word "American" is asso-ciated with a liberal, rights-based model of identity that contradicts and thus poses a sustained and internal threat to racial unity that is invoked by the word "Negro," it also has a powerful national specificity, and functions to delineate boundaries and to further distinguish the group of revolutionaries in

Du Bois's address. Viewed in these terms, the word "Ameri
works against Du Bois's racial nationalism and also promc

As a critique of existing, nineteenth-century liberal dis
the concept of "the nation" Du Bois establishes in "Th
Races" is innovative in two respects. First, by insisting upc
effect of race ideals that are distinct from what he calls "p
democratic ideals Du Bois expands upon possibilities that
pression of a liberal theory of nations and constructs a der
national identity that is also marked by the coexistence of ..v..se racial nationalisms. "If . . . there is substantial agreement in laws, language and religion," he observes, "if there is a satisfactory adjustment of economic life, then
there is no reason why, in the same country and on the same street, two or
three great national ideals might not thrive and develop, that men of different
races might not strive together for their race ideals as well, perhaps even
better, than in isolation" (CR, 80).

Second, Du Bois's nationalist rhetoric represents a critique of American
liberal nationalist thought because, although he deploys the colonialist and
expansionist rhetoric associated with American imperialism, he does not call
for the constitution of a new state to demonstrate the fact of its realization.
"We are Americans," he insists, "not only by birth and by citizenship, but by
our political ideals, our language, our religion. Farther than that, our Ameri-
canism does not go. At that point, we are Negroes, members of a vast historic
race that from the very dawn of creation has slept, but half awakening in the
dark forests of its African fatherland. We are the first fruits of this new nation,
the harbinger of that black tomorrow which is yet destined to soften the
whiteness of the Teutonic today" (CR, 81).

In this passage Du Bois's invocation of an "African Fatherland" functions
rhetorically to establish a framework for racial cohesion, but he does not in
any way rely on the possibility of acquiring it as a newfound territory. Although Du Bois's interest in Africa as the actual site for the building of a new
nation and his emigration to Ghana in 1961 are of primary significance in
any assessment of his life and writings as a whole, the fact of Du Bois's emi-
grationism should be carefully distinguished from the project he conceives of
in his early writings: namely, the development of a nationalist theory and
rhetoric that he uses to construct a coherent model of African-American as
American identity.[21]

Shortly after his publication of "The Conservation of Races" and well
before his publication of Dusk of Dawn, Du Bois developed and explored "double-consciousness," a concept of political obligation that registers his critique
of liberal nationalism and stands as his best known contribution to the field
of African-American studies. He writes:

> The Negro is a sort of seventh son, born with a veil, and gifted with second-
> sight in this American world,—a world which yields him no true self-

consciousness, but only lets him see himself through the revelation of the other world. It is a peculiar sensation, this double-consciousness, this sense of always looking at one's self through the eyes of others, of measuring one's soul by the tape of a world that looks on in amused contempt and pity. One ever feels his twoness,—an American, a Negro; two souls, two thoughts, two unreconciled strivings; two warring ideals in one dark body, whose dogged strength alone keeps it from being torn asunder.[22]

At the same time that the black nation Du Bois imagines behind the Veil is marked by racial unity—and, as such, stands in a dissenting position of withdrawal from the United States—he also envisions this nation as a political entity that is possessed of rights and receives all the benefits of American citizenship. The boundaries that enclose this black nation, and which Du Bois purports to sketch in *The Souls of Black Folk*, are thus both impermeable and infinitely permeable. Du Bois represents the contradiction between rights and race that structures his imagination of a black nation as the act of lifting the Veil, an act that simultaneously constitutes and threatens the dissolution of the nation he describes and to which he himself belongs. "Leaving, then, the white world, I have stepped within the Veil, raising it that you may view faintly its deeper recesses,—the meaning of its religion, the passion of its human sorrow, and the struggle of its greater souls," Du Bois writes. "And . . . need I add that I who speak here am bone of the bone and flesh of the flesh of them that live within the Veil?" (*Souls*, 209).[23]

Du Bois's engagement with the whole problematic of double-consciousness calls our attention to a second major intellectual resource that, in addition to Crummell's philosophical writings, contributed to his developing critique of Emerson: namely, Booker T. Washington's *Up from Slavery*.[24] Viewed in the context of Emerson's writings on culture or self-cultivation and social reform, the famous disagreement between Washington and Du Bois regarding the best means of accomplishing the task of racial uplift devolves upon their different interpretations of Emerson's dualistic notion of "culture" put forward in the essay "Self-Reliance."[25] As we saw in chapter 4, the concept of "culture" explored in Emerson's writings refers to *both* an inner process of spiritual unfolding (or intellectual self-cultivation) *and* agricultural labor. Thus, in their ongoing debate over the problem of reform, Washington and Du Bois were simply emphasizing different sides of the same Emersonian coin.[26]

Although, like Du Bois, Washington does not cite Emerson very often in his writings, we know that he was a careful reader of Emerson. References to Emerson in Washington's speeches and letters emphasize Emerson's commitment to self-discovery and self-reliance.[27] Indeed, Washington's faith in Emersonian aphorisms was such that he even organized an Emerson Club at Tuskegee Institute, which met each Tuesday for the purpose of reading sentences that would provide lessons in self-improvement.[28]

Reading *Up from Slavery*, we can see that Washington's involvement in the world of public affairs best explains his interest in showing the accessibility of philosophical ideas and thus their applicability in working for social change. By Washington's own admission, the model of the African-American self he constructs in *Up from Slavery* represents a critique of nine-teenth-century popular Emersonianism best seen in the widely read, "pull yourself up by the bootstraps," Horatio Alger stories of success in America. Washington recalls:

> In those days, and later as a young man, I used to try to picture in my imagination the feelings and ambitions of a white boy with absolutely no limit placed upon his aspirations and activities. I used to envy the white boy who had no obstacles placed in the way of his becoming a Congressman, Governor, Bishop, or President by reason of the accident of his birth or race. I used to picture the way that I would act under such circumstances; how I would begin at the bottom and keep rising until I reached the highest round of success.
>
> In later years, I confess that I do not envy the white boy as I once did. I have learned the success is measured not so much by the position that one has reached in life as by the obstacles which he has overcome while trying to succeed. (*Up from Slavery*, 50)

Washington's interest in and critique of Emerson makes even more sense when we consider the obvious applicability of Emerson's philosophy to Washington's political project. If Emerson's critique of rights discourse and argument against slavery might have been too scholarly or esoteric for the general public to grasp in their entirety,[29] concepts such as "self-reliance" were obviously available for popularization to black activists such as Washington who were interested in promoting actual social change and racial uplift during the Reconstruction era.

It should thus come as no surprise to us that Washington's critique and inheritance of Emerson's philosophy is central to the political philosophy he espouses in *Up from Slavery* and, even more important, that this critique explicitly hinges on Washington's strategic recasting of Emersonian "self-reliance."

> From the very beginning, at Tuskegee, I was determined to have the students do not only the agricultural and domestic work, but to have them erect their own buildings. My plan was to have them, while performing this service, taught the latest and best methods of labour, so that the school would not only get the benefit of their efforts, but the students themselves would be taught to see not only utility in labour, but beauty and dignity, would be taught, in fact, how to lift labour up from mere drudgery and toil, and would learn to love work for its own sake. My plan was not to teach them to work in the old way but to show them how to make the forces of nature—air, water, steam, electricity, horse-power—assist them in their labour.
>
> At first many advised against the experiment of having the buildings erected by the labour of the students, but I was determined to stick to it. I told those who doubted the wisdom of the plan that I knew that our first buildings would not be so comfortable or so complete in their finish as build-

ings erected by the experienced hands of outside workmen, but that in the teaching of civilization, self-help, and *self-reliance*, the erection of the buildings by the students themselves would more than compensate for any lack of comfort or fine finish. (*Up from Slavery*, 108; emphasis added)

Washington's critique of Emerson's philosophy has two main facets. First, unlike Emerson's concept of self-reliance—a concept that, as we have seen, expresses a personal solution to the question of social reform by *equating* public action with social or privately meditative acts of philosophical critique and poetic making—Washington's concept of self-reliant personhood as revolutionary action is unequivocally visible and public. In Washington's sense, self-reliance involves the self-conscious enlistment of natural and technological forces in order to contribute to human progress, progress he defines in strictly industrial terms. Second, it follows from this that, unlike Emerson's relatively abstract, philosphical affirmation of inner development as self-reliant personhood, Washington's vision of African-American self-reliance is expressed in terms of the built environment. Whereas Emerson emblematizes self-reliance abstractly by drawing on the masonic and religious iconography of the upright column, Washington says that, for black Americans, self-reliant uprightness actually *is* a building erected by and for black Americans.

Washington's cultural critique of popular Emersonian individualism devolves upon actual buildings as a model of group identity for African-Americans that also stands as an affirmative monument to the usefulness and possible concretization of Emersonian ideals. On a symbolic level, the message of these buildings is, paradoxically, one that is both profoundly pessimistic and profoundly optimistic and life-affirming. At the same time that they register in symbolic (and, indeed, in powerfully concrete) terms the tragedy of Reconstruction, because they stand as a monument, not a testament, to what America might have been, Washington's buildings also represent a philosophy that is pragmatic and forward-looking. We might say that Washington's most famous philosophical thought was about the importance of building schools.

Most important of all, Washington's philosophy of the built environment represents a deliberate recasting of the contradiction between rights discourse and racialism that structures Emersonian double-consciousness. Instead of explicitly invoking rights, Washington instead discusses buildings as the concretization of abstract labor. On the one hand, buildings perfectly express Washington's aspirations to democracy and the pragmatic project of assimilation because they fit perfectly into the landscape and show self-evident progress toward equal access to benefits of citizenship such as education. On the other hand, Washington affirms the premises of racialism by insisting that the building be a "black" building—a building built by and for blacks. Later, in *Up from Slavery*, this critique of the Emersonian self culminates in Washington's construction of an entirely new, processual model of political identity. Double-consciousness, as Washington imagines it, is best seen and understood as the laborious process required to overcome obstacles (which he identifies with blackness), as well as the achievement of having overcome obstacles (which he assigns to whiteness). He observes:

> Looked at from this standpoint I almost reach the conclusion that often the Negro boy's birth and connection with an unpopular race is an advantage, so far as real life is concerned. With few exceptions, the Negro youth must work harder and must perform his task better than a white youth in order to secure recognition. But out of the hard and unusual struggle which he is compelled to pass, he gets a strength, a confidence, that one misses whose pathway is comparatively smooth by reason of birth and race.
>
> From any point of view, I had rather be what I am, a member of the Negro race, than be able to claim membership with the most favoured of any other race. (*Up from Slavery*, 50)

I began this chapter with the suggestion that Du Bois's most fundamental philosophical insight was that he recognized the uses and limits of Emerson's political critique—in particular, Emerson's simultaneous invocation of liberal and racialist discourses—for his conceptualization of black American identity as double-consciousness. I would like in closing to point to a further development, which shows that the critique of Emerson undertaken by Du Bois is formally, both by necessity and design, a democratic and collaborative process, a project to which any individual may contribute and for the completion of which no individual will receive full credit.

In the next, concluding chapter of this book, I will argue for the significance of Martin Luther King Jr.'s and Cornel West's respective critiques of Emerson's philosophy—and their insistence on reconceptualizing American political philosophy as a public, disobedient, necessary response to social crisis. The last point I want to make in this chapter is that the significance of King's thinking about double-consciousness is that he weaves together two separate strands in the tradition of African-American political philosophy. In *Where Do We Go from Here: Chaos or Community*, first published in 1967, in an important chapter, "The Dilemma of Negro Americans" King brilliantly merges both Du Bois's dialectical concept and Washington's processual concept of black identity as double-consciousness. King quotes at length the key passage of Du Bois's *Dusk of Dawn* in which Du Bois describes himself as looking out from a dark cave, speaking to the world outside, "showing them how these entombed souls are hindered in their natural movement, expression, and development; and how their loosening from prison would be . . . aid to all the world."[30] Later, however, King deliberately recasts Du Bois's metaphor for double-consciousness in Washington's terms—a gesture that simultaneously underwrites his own inheritance of African-American political philosophy and establishes his mandate for articulating a call to political action: "For his own inner health and outer functioning, the Negro is called upon to be as resourceful, as productive and responsible as those who have not known such oppression and exploitation," he writes. "He who starts behind in a race must forever remain behind or run faster than the man in front. . . . With a dynamic will, we must transform our minus into a plus, and move on aggressively through the storms of injustice . . . toward the beaconing lights of fulfillment" (*Where Do We Go from Here*, 120). The distinctive metaphor of the race King invents to represent the state of double-consciousness is one that conveys Washington's, as well as his own, unequivocal belief that the experience of African-American identity is inextricably bound up with public, visible, disobedent activity as a means of demanding change in American society.[31]

EIGHT

Martin Luther King Jr.

Publicity, Disobedience, and the
Revitalization of American
Democratic Culture

On Forty-seventh Street, on the south side of Chicago, there is a large graffiti mural that depicts an undulating series of sea-green waves. Below this striking image are spray-painted letters that spell out the following words, attributed to Emerson: OUR GREATEST GLORY CONSISTS NOT IN EVER FALLING BUT IN RISING EVERYTIME WE FALL [sic].[1] The graffiti serves as a reminder of the various ways language performs the cultural work of inventing and perpetuating values—values to which we, in turn, find ourselves deeply and naturally committed. The creation of the graffiti mural— the spray-painting of Emerson's words and name on the wall—is a form of cultural practice that also points out the uses of philosophy as a response (however meaningful or thoughtless that response might be) to social crisis. Taken in its literally concrete context, the graffitied epigram establishes a cohesive group identity for individuals involved in an ongoing struggle for social justice—a collectivity or "we" whose glory consists in rising every time it falls.

The significance of Emerson's contribution to the revitalization of American political culture and the expression of political thought both during and after the civil rights movement becomes more apparent when we recall that Martin Luther King Jr. repeatedly and explicitly referred to Emerson in his speeches, lectures, and sermons. For example, in a classic sermon delivered at the Ebenezer Baptist Church in Atlanta collected in the volume titled *Strength to Love*, King—in an attempt to exhort his listeners to harness and master their fears of what they might encounter in their fight for civil rights—quotes Emerson's observation that "[h]e has not learned the lesson of life who does not every day surmount a fear."² And in "Facing the Challenge of a New Age," a 1956 address before the First Annual Institute on Non-Violence and Social Change in Montgomery, Alabama, King quotes Emerson's aphorism that "[i]f a man can write a better book, or preach a better sermon, or make a better mousetrap than his neighbor, even if he builds his house in the woods the world will make a beaten path to his door." Glossing Emerson, he reminds his congregation that "[a] . . . challenge that the new age brings to each of us is that of achieving excellency in our various fields of endeavor. In the new age many doors will be opening for us that were not opened in the past, and the great challenge which we confront is to be prepared to enter these doors as they open. . . . We must set out to do a good job, irrespective of race, and do it so well that nobody could do it better" (*Strength to Love*, 70).

King's creative interpretation of Emerson registers an acute awareness of the necessary contingencies of his own time and place: what he discloses in this passage is the important connection between striving for excellence in any creative endeavor and establishing rights of citizenship. This insistence that excellence in the act of invention—whether this act is one of preaching, building, or making a mousetrap—opens doors onto political life bears a striking resemblance to Hannah Arendt's account of the public, political space of the Greek *polis*. King's reading of Emerson makes explicit his own claim that excellence is assigned to what Arendt describes in *The Human Condition* as "the public realm": "Every activity performed in public," Arendt argues, "can attain an excellence never matched in privacy; for excellence, by definition, the presence of others is always required, and this presence needs the formality of the public."³ But whereas Arendt fails to clarify the exclusions built into this concept of publicity when she recounts the loss of the public realm for modernity, King's words and the situation of their utterance demonstrate the extent to which, for African Americans during the sixties, striving for excellence and thus a stalwart belief in publicness were necessary because they represented a crucial means of attaining civil rights. As Seyla Benhabib has observed, "The struggle over what gets included in the public agenda is itself a struggle for justice and freedom."⁴ Excellence, when performed in public, is a visible marker of civility that facilitates access to the benefits of citizenship.

King's recourse to Emerson's aphorism to designate a means of crossing the threshold onto the freedoms of public life appears an even more accurate and compelling response to Emerson's philosophy when we consider this 1855 journal entry, which forms the basis for Emerson's aphorism published sixteen years later:

> I trust a good deal to common fame, as we all must. If a man has good corn, or wood, or boards, or pigs, to sell, or can make better chairs or knives or crucibles or church-organs than anybody else, you will find a broad hard beaten road to his house, though it be in the woods. And if a man knows the law, people find it out, though he live in a pine shanty, & resort to him. And if a man can pipe or sing . . . ; or can liberate or intoxicate all people who hear him with delicious songs & verses; 'tis certain that the secret can-

not be kept: the first witness tells it to a second, and men go by fives & tens & fifties to his door.

Well, it is still so with a thinker. If he proposes to show me any high secret, if he profess to have found the profoundly secret pass that leads from Fate to Freedom, all good heads & all mankind aspiringly & religiously wish to know it, and, though it sorely & unusually taxes their poor brain, they find out at last whether they have made the transit, or no. If they have, they will know it; and his fame will surely be bruited abroad. If they come away unsatisfied, though it be easy to impute it (even in their belief) to their dulness in not being able to keep step with his snow-shoes on the icy mountain paths—I suspect it is because the transit has not been made. 'Tis like that crooked hollow log through which the farmer's pig found access to the field; the farmer moved the log so that the pig in returning to the hold, & passing through, found himself to his astonishment still on the outside of the field. . . .

Whatever transcendent abilities Fichte, Kant, Schelling, & Hegel have shown, I think they lack the confirmation of having given piggy a transit to the field. . . . If they had made the transit, common fame would have found it out. So I abide by my rule of not reading the book, until I hear of it through the newspapers.[5]

The passage expresses Emerson's hopes for the comprehensibility and public appeal of philosophy and invites us to explore the complex imbrication of philosophy and culture. Despite his ambivalent affection and disdain for "common" readers who, like the farmer's pig, are trying to find the secret pass in his text that leads from Fate to Freedom, Emerson also values the accessibility and currency of philosophy, believing that philosophy, like fame, should be heard of in newspapers and otherwise bruited abroad.

Writing in 1968, the year of King's assassination, in the wake of student uprisings and urban rioting in Newark and Detroit, the philosopher Stanley Cavell posed the question of publicity as a question of philosophy's audience and performance, observing that "[t]he question of philosophy's audience is born with philosophy itself. . . . No man is in any better position for knowing it than any other man—unless *wanting* to know is a special position. Then what makes it relevant to know, worth knowing? . . . The effort is irrelevant and worthless until it becomes necessary to you to know such things. There is the audience of philosophy; but there also, while it lasts, is its performance."[6] Emerson's practices as a lecturer, even more than his stated interest in philosophy heard about in newspapers, show his preoccupation with the phenomenon of fame and the public performance of philosophy.[7] Taken together, the graffiti, the sermon, and the journal entry provide us with an occasion to consider the relationship of Emerson's ideas to social action—what some might regard as the responsibilities of philosophy to culture—and suggest just how wide the audience for philosophy can be.

We know that in addition to reading Emerson, King also referred to Thoreau's philosophy throughout his writings.[8] In *Stride toward Freedom*, a widely circulated text that eventually became a handbook for the civil rights movement, King traced the following relationship between his role as an activist in the 1955 Montgomery bus boycott and his first exposure to Thoreau's philosophy of civil disobedience:

> As I thought further I came to see that what we were really doing was withdrawing our cooperation from an evil system, rather than merely withdrawing our economic support from the bus company. The bus company, being an external expression of the system, would naturally suffer, but the basic aim was to refuse to cooperate with evil. At this point I began to think about Thoreau's *Essay on Civil Disobedience*. I remembered how, as a college student, I had been moved when I first read this work. I became convinced that what we were preparing to do in Montgomery was related to what Thoreau had expressed. We were simply saying to the white community, "We can no longer lend our cooperation to an evil system."
>
> Something began to say to me, "He who passively accepts evil is as much involved in it as he who helps to perpetrate it. He who accepts evil without protesting against it is really cooperating with it." When oppressed people willingly accept their oppression they only serve to give the oppressor a convenient justification for his acts. Often the oppressor goes along unaware of the evil involved in his oppression so long as the oppressed accepts it. So in order to be true to one's conscience and true to God, a righteous man has no alternative but to refuse to cooperate with an evil system. This I felt was the nature of our action. From this moment on I conceived of our movement as an act of massive noncooperation. From then on I rarely used the word "boycott." (*TH*, 429)

For King, the experience of wanting to know and the necessity of knowing philosophy, as well as his performance of it, are shaped by his commitments to public life. The aspect of King's political philosophy that will be the primary focus for this analysis is his work on the nature of political obligation and his performance of civil disobedience in the public realm. In *The Human Condition*, Arendt describes the public realm of politics as the space of visibility. She writes, "Everything that appears in public can be seen and heard by everybody and has the widest possible publicity. For us, appearance—something that is being seen and heard by others as well as by ourselves—constitutes reality" (50). Although, as we shall see, both Emerson and Thoreau are concerned with the problem of political obligation, and although Thoreau's critique of Emerson points up the importance of visible, symbolic action as a means of publicizing the claims of conscience, King's demand for racial equality is distinctive in that his performance of philosophy involves a commitment to a scale of publicity and visibility that involves life-threatening bodily risks. In particular, King's attempt to put the philosophical ideals of civil disobedience into practice depended for its success on his high visibility as a media star firmly ensconced in a national symbology, constructed and manipulated in innumerable newspaper and televised images, radio appearances, and cover treatment by advertiser-financed illustrated magazines.[9] The necessity of this immense media publicity and high visibility associated with King's performance of philosophy and the significance of this visibility for his extension of critical political publics during the sixties,[10] distinguish King's response to the tradition in American political thought represented by the writings of Emerson and Thoreau. It is part of the work of this chapter to consider the nature of this response, thereby making the exigencies and consequences of King's critique of the Emersonian tradition comprehensible to a wider audience of readers and critics.[11]

Of the many recent critical commentaries written about Emerson, two philosophical responses have a direct bearing on this discussion of King's political thought and help to elucidate the tense, necessary embrace of philosophy and politics in King's writings. The first is "Finding as Founding: Taking Steps in Emerson's 'Experience,' " the final lecture in Stanley Cavell's 1989 Carpenter Lecture series, collected in the volume *This New yet Unapproachable America*.[12] The second is Cornel West's *The American Evasion of Philosophy*, also published in 1989.[13] Both Cavell and West show a preoccupation with the meaning of "Americanness": for Cavell, the attempt to characterize Emerson's inheritance of philosophy as being "not only for himself but for America" (*New yet Unapproachable*, 83), provides a suitable occasion to ask whether the edifice of Western philosophy has an "American inflection" (*New yet Unapproachable*, 109), and, for West, the project of locating Emerson within the genealogy of pragmatism involves serious inquiry into "the American heritage" (*American Evasion*, 4) and the possibility of there being an "indigenous mode of thought" (*American Evasion*, 5) in America. Both Cavell and West offer readings of Emerson that reflect their respective projects and stated prospects for philosophy. Cavell's observation that Emerson's inheritance is figured as "conversion" (or "transfiguration" or "reattachment") of philosophical terms supports his claim that Emerson underwrites the defense of proceeding in philosophy from ordinary language; the fact that, as Cavell has stated elsewhere, Emerson "returns" words to "the life of language, to language transfigured, as an eventual everyday."[14] And West's insistence that Emerson contributes to the pragmatic reconception of philosophy as social and cultural criticism supports West's conception of an "Emersonian culture of creative democracy" (*American Evasion*, 235) that underlies his defense of prophetic pragmatism as "a practice that has some potency and effect or makes a difference in the world" (*American Evasion*, 232).

But Cavell's and West's philosophical responses to Emerson differ radically in their approach to the problem of publicity and the relationship between philosophy and politics. For example, Cavell's insistence that the inheritance of philosophy enacted as Emerson's rebirth or conversion to America is "his way of founding a nation, writing its constitution, constituting its citizens" (*New yet Unapproachable*, 93) prompts Cavell, at the very margins of his own text, to take up philosophically the question of "the public." Exploring the problem of whether philosophizing is, or ought to be, also something done to the world, Cavell maintains that the question "Can mere philosophy *do* anything?" (*New yet Unapproachable*, 94) should always remain a question for philosophy. On this point, Cavell aligns himself with Emerson, whom he regards as being at odds with Dewey's pragmatism: "For Emerson," Cavell writes, "putting the philosophical intellect into practice remains a question for philosophy. For a thinker such as John Dewey it becomes, as I might put it, merely a problem" (*New yet Unapproachable*, 95).[15] Indeed, Cavell practices his own stated methodological preference when, a few pages later, he poses a provocative, rhetorical question concerning the publicness of Emerson's writing, a question that invites but does not require the reader's connecting leap between Emerson's power to demand social transformation and the public realm in which such demands are ultimately effected:

> The most renowned phrase for what I was calling the power of passiveness—a power to demand the change of the world as a whole, Emerson sometimes calls it revolution, sometimes conversion—is what Thoreau will call civil disobedience. This phrase notes the register of lasting as it appears in a public crisis, call it a tyranny of the majority. Emerson may seem to confine himself on the whole to the lasting's appearance not at the public end of crisis but at the private end, call this the tyranny of thinking. Yet he says that he would write on the lintels of the door-post (in 'Self-Reliance'). Perhaps he is now writing so. Is that a public place? (*New yet Unapproachable*, 115)

Following his own dictum that the problem of the public—that is, philosophy's audience or capacity to make a difference in the world—should appear as an enduring, provocative question for philosophy, Cavell asks here whether philosophy is visibly performed or invisibly pondered; whether self-reliance is a "revolution" against the tyranny of public opinion or of mind. Such questions point to the significance of, but do not directly clarify, the meaning of "the public" as a conceptual resource.

Whereas Cavell's method of provocative questioning broaches the topic of philosophy's relationship to political culture, in *The American Evasion of Philosophy*, West unequivocally advocates philosophy's entry into public life for explicitly moral and political purposes—as "a form of cultural criticism in which the meaning of America is put forward by intellectuals in response to distinct social crises . . . [;] a continuous cultural commentary or set of interpretations that attempt to explain America to itself at a particular historical moment" (*American Evasion*, 5). Indeed, throughout *The American Evasion of Philosophy*, West's writing is clearly motivated by, and derives much of its justification and force from, a capacious conception of what he identifies in *Race Matters* as "the public square"[16]—a place not only for rational deliberation but also for expressing love; a realm that includes not only philosophers, but also extends to gay, feminist, working class, Chicano, black, Asian-American, and third world collectivities, all working together in service of "the public interest."

The political substance of the American evasion of philosophy is that what was the prerogative of philosophers, i.e., rational deliberation, is now that of the people—the populace deliberating is creative democracy in the making. Needless to say, this view is not a license for eliminating or opposing all professional elites, but it does hold them to account. Similarly, it is citizenry in action, with its civil consciousness molded by participation in public-interest-centered and individual-rights-regarding democracy. (*American Evasion*, 213)

West's fundamental difference with Cavell in visualizing the relationship between philosophy and the public realm is reflected in West's interpretation of Emerson's philosophy as having important consequences for the emergence of Dewey's pragmatism. According to Dewey, the public (as distinguished from the social) consists of all persons who have been indirectly affected by various consequences that follow from the fact of associated behavior. This public extends to all those affected who require systematic care by the state.[17] Unlike much of West's later work, which is devoted to elaborating on the idea of publicity entailed by prophetic pragmatism,[18] *The American Evasion of Philosophy* does not explore the similarities and differences between, on the one hand, West's own concept of publicity that undergirds his prophetic pragmatism and role as an organic intellectual, and, on the other, Dewey's vision of "a discursive and dialogical space wherein various 'publics' can find common ground" (*American Evasion*, 105). Nonetheless, West's commitment to his idea of "the public"—to knowing more about the connection between thought and action, and what he clearly regards as the necessary alignment of philosophical ambition with felt responses to the political world—is registered in his dissatisfaction with Emerson's doctrine of "self-reliance" as a program for social change. Unlike Cavell, West does not read Emerson's essay as prompting even the question of publicity. He writes, "Emerson's nonconformist conception of self-reliance resists mere ideological support of capitalist development. Yet his viewpoint also provides very little substantive opposition to it" (*American Evasion*, 21). And: "Emerson is not a social revolutionary because 'he believes he is already on the right track and moving toward an excellent destiny.' Moral transgression essentially consists for Emerson in the exercise of personal conscience against custom, law, and tradition. It rests upon a deep distrust of the masses, a profound disenchantment with the dirty affairs of politics and a fervent defense of individual liberties" (*American Evasion*, 17).

That "Self-Reliance" should emerge as a key text eliciting such philosophical deliberation over the meaning of the public is understandable when we consider that this essay stands as Emerson's best known contribution to a nineteenth-century tradition of liberal discourse that represents public opinion as a coercive force. At the same time that the proliferation of American publics during the nineteenth century created new political possibilities for individuals, particularly women, who had previously been excluded from such institutional sites,[19] philosophical inquiry into the subject tended to demote and finally to denounce the insidious powers of what John Stuart Mill describes in *On Liberty* as the "yoke of opinion,"[20] and Alexis de Tocqueville once called the "mistress of the world."[21]

In his celebrated diatribe against public opinion, Mill is less at pains to describe, as Tocqueville does, the etiology, actual operation, and effects of public opinion[22] than he is to attack and undermine its formidable power to impose serious, undemocratic constraints upon individual liberty. "It is easy," he writes, "for anyone to imagine an ideal public which leaves the freedom and choice of individuals in all uncertain matters undisturbed and only requires them to abstain from modes of conduct which universal experience has condemned. But where has there been seen a public which set any such limit to its censorship? . . . In its interferences with personal conduct it is seldom thinking of anything but the enormity of acting or feeling differently from itself" (*On Liberty*, 82). For Mill, the only time when public opinion may be properly used to coerce any member of a civilized community is when such coercion prevents harm to others.

What Mill stresses above all else in his discussion of publicity is the necessity and importance of addressing the public, the making of private arguments and opinions public: "The liberty of expressing and publishing opinions [is] . . . almost of as much importance as the liberty of thought itself and . . . is practically inseparable from it" (*On Liberty*, 11–12). A few pages later, he insists that "the peculiar evil of silencing the expression of an opinion is that it is robbing the human race, posterity as well as the existing generation—those who dissent from the opinion, still more than those who hold it" (*On Liberty*, 16). And finally, he observes that conformity to public opinion by even the brightest of individuals ruins society's chances for self-improvement because all possibilities of intellectual development and fearless innovation have been effectively done away with:

> A state of things in which a large portion of the most active and inquiring intellects find it advisable to keep the general principles and grounds of their convictions within their own breasts, and attempt, in what they address to the public, to fit as much as they can of their own conclusions to premises which they have internally renounced, cannot send forth the open, fearless characters and logical, consistent intellects who once adorned the thinking world. The sort of men who can be looked for under it are either mere conformers to commonplace, or timeservers for truth, whose arguments on all great subjects are meant for their hearers, and are not those which have convinced themselves. (*On Liberty*, 31–32)

Like Mill's *On Liberty*, Emerson's writings exhibit a profound ambivalence toward the public: for Emerson, as for other liberal philosophers, public opinion is both burdensome and conceptually indispensable in thinking about democracy.[23] Although, as we have seen, Emerson values the fame-making attributes of mass circulation newspapers as vehicles for philosophy, in "Self-Reliance" he contemptuously describes "the sour faces of the multitude, [which] like their sweet faces, have no deep cause, but are put on and off as the wind blows and a newspaper directs."[24] Like Mill, Emerson deplores the extent to which newspapers have become shapers of public opinion that do away with any capacity for thought that might exist among the masses.[25] And like Mill, Emerson believes that custom and public opinion work against the nurturing of precious individuality; that, as Emerson famously puts it, "It is easy in the world to live after the world's opinion; it is easy in solitude to live after our own; but the man is he who in the midst of the crowd keeps with perfect sweetness the independence of solitude" (*Essays*, 263).

In contrast to Mill, however, Emerson does not emphasize the importance of public address and of making private, original views public. Rather than defending the freedom of public, published expression, in "Self-Reliance" Emerson insists that the rigidity and impediments associated with public opinion will be effectively undone once it has been rightly conceived of as mirroring private conviction. Paradoxically, at the same time that Emerson's claim that what is privately true holds true for all men encourages freedoms of expression, it also obviates what Mill regards as the urgent necessity of free, public speaking. By Emerson's account the liberties of public expression Mill would fight for eighteen years later are there for the taking but altogether unnecessary, because of this striking and inexplicable but inevitable convergence of public and private. He writes, "Speak your latent conviction, and it shall be the universal sense; for the inmost in due time becomes the outmost,—and our first thought is rendered back to us by the trumpets of the Last Judgment" *Essays*, 259).

The curious enfolding of the vocabulary of the public into the private that takes place over the course of Emerson's essay is nowhere more in evidence than in this reference to the publicness once only borne by the person of the monarch or feudal lord, now available to every man:

> In history, our imagination plays us false. Kingdom and lordship, power and estate, are a gaudier vocabulary than private John and Edward in a small house and a common day's work; but the things of life are the same to both. . . . Why all this deference to Alfred, and Scanderbeg, and Gustavus? Suppose they were virtuous; did they wear out virtue? As great a stake depends on our private act to-day, as followed their public and renowned steps. When private men shall act with original views, the lustre will be transferred from the actions of kings to those of gentlemen.
>
> The world has been instructed by its kings, who have so magnetized the eyes of nations. It has been taught by this colossal symbol, the mutual reverence that is due from man to man. The joyful loyalty with which men have everywhere suffered the king, the noble, or the great proprietor to walk among them by a law of his own, make his own scale of men and things, and reverse theirs, pay for benefits not with money but with honor, and

represent the law in his person, was the hieroglyphic by which they obscurely signified their consciousness of their own right and comeliness, the right of every man. (*Essays*, 268)

As Habermas points out, the phenomenon of "representative publicness" that was the ground of manorial authority in feudal society of the High Middle Ages was inseparable from the lord's presence and the visibility of his physical attributes—his insignia, dress, demeanor, and rhetoric—all of which contributed to the endowment of what Habermas describes as his powerful "aura" (*Structural Transformation*, 7).[26] In "Self-Reliance," the primary features of this publicness inherent in the vocabulary of kingdom and lordship have been fundamentally altered. In Habermas's account, the king's representative publicity was such that it effectively barred private people from stepping into the public sphere—during the Middle Ages in Europe, he claims, there existed no legal status that could define such a capacity for translation into the public (*Structural Transformation*, 5). By contrast, Emerson's description of the publicity involved in his notion of "the representative" renders the experience of publicity—the enjoyment of personal magnetism, the reverence and loyalty of fellow men, and the prerogative to live "by a law of his own"—as a right that is democratically extended to "every man."

Setting aside for a moment the unacknowledged exclusions built into Emerson's concept of representative publicity, at first glance Emerson appears to be promoting something like universal access to publicity. But in fact he is simply *equating* the private with the public. He tells us that as great a stake depends on private acts as public ones, and thus what is called for is not entry into the public realm but rather a universal assertion of the right to act *as private men* with original views.[27] The modern, legal vocabulary of public representation—the language of acts, rights, and laws—has been saturated in this passage with personal, common-sense or everyday meanings. The effects of such an altered vocabulary are dual and contradictory. At the same time that Emerson encourages an original first step onto the path leading to public life, he also presents a barrier to publicity and obviates the need for public action because, by his account, no distinct public realm exists beyond the intimate confines of the private.[28] Thus he is able to insist, with stunning self-assurance, that the truest form of participation in public life is a vanishing from that life; that publicity is best accomplished by sitting at home. "All concentrates," he writes. "[L]et us not rove; let us sit at home with the cause. Let us stun and astonish the intruding rabble of men and books and institutions, by a simple declaration of the divine fact. Bid the invaders take the shoes from off their feet, for God is here within. Let our simplicity judge them, and our docility to our own law demonstrate the poverty of nature and fortune beside our native riches" (*Essays*, 272).

This same unclarity as to the significance of the public recurs in Emerson's reference to the visibility of the body. Whereas previously we saw that Emerson strategically blurs the distinction between the public and the private, in "Self-Reliance" we are also left with a question as to whether the body is public or social. For example, when Emerson complains about the conformity that characterizes various "communities of opinion"—describing the uniformity of faces and bodies, "the gentlest asinine expression" that is "the prison-uniform of the party to which we adhere"—he does not indicate whether these parties function as actual political entities or as social clubs (*Essays*, 264). Indeed, the sociality and not the publicity of the body seems to be at issue when Emerson describes the physical experience (and not the visible appearance) of what he calls " 'the foolish face of praise,' the forced smile which we put on in company where we do not feel at ease in answer to conversation which does not interest us. Thus muscles, not spontaneously moved, but moved by a low usurping wilfulness, grow tight about the outline of the face with the most disagreeable sensation" (*Essays*, 264).

Emerson's imagining of the public in "Self-Reliance"—his simultaneous invitation and denial of access to a world beyond domestic life—calls our attention back to the fact, and consequences, of the central issue raised both by West's criticism of Emerson's essay as providing little substantive opposition to social injustice and by Cavell's question regarding the lintel's publicity : namely, whether the liminal act of writing philosophy is, or ought to be, defined as public action. The debate over whether Emerson's doctrine of "self-reliance" is or is not revolutionary, over whether and how philosophy may be said to shape or revitalize political culture, takes on an even more pressing relevance to King's political philosophy when we consider the fact that King's sermon "Transformed Nonconformist," published in his widely circulated collection *Strength to Love*, does in many respects reflect Emerson's ideas and exhortations to nonconformity.[29] Indeed, King structures the sermon around what might be seen as the most famous and quotable of aphorisms in "Self-Reliance": "Whoso would be a man must be a nonconformist" (*Strength to Love*, 12). Unlike Emerson, who simultaneously precludes and facilitates access to the public realm, King unequivocally promotes political action by deploying Emerson's famous mandate for nonconformity to communicate King's own vision of the social crisis brought about by the deadening conformity of racism. He observes:

> Many people fear nothing more terribly than to take a position which stands out sharply and clearly from the prevailing opinion. The tendency of most is to adopt a view that is so ambiguous that it will include everything and so popular that it will include everybody. . . . Not a few men, who cherish lofty and noble ideals, hide them under a bushel for fear of being called different. Many sincere white people in the South privately oppose segregation and discrimination, but they are apprehensive lest they be publicly condemned. . . . How *few* people have the audacity to express publicly their convictions, and how *many* have allowed themselves to be "astronomically intimidated"! (*Strength to Love*, 10)

Emerson's own formulations of the doctrine notwithstanding, self-reliance, as presented in King's strategic interpretation, implies some public mode of speech or action that also resists conformity by unveiling the unique distinctness of individuals. In King's terms, self-reliance as public action promises to bring about a direct confrontation with the dominant culture that results in "true brotherhood, true integration, true person-to-person relationships" ("Love, Law and Civil Disobedience," *TH*, 51), in a public realm in which individuals appear to each other not as physical objects, but in all their personal dignity and worth.

The critique of Emerson embedded in King's sermon—a rhetorical performance that evidently worked to perpetuate "self-reliance" as important cultural value promoting entry into the public realm during the struggle for black liberation[30]—is in many respects similar to the critique set forth in Thoreau's "Resistance to Civil Government," a work published eight years after "Self-Reliance" and which was foundational to King's developing theory of political obligation and symbolic action. In *This New yet Unapproachable America*, Cavell acknowledges Thoreau as "Emerson's purest interpreter, no one more accurate, no one else so exclusive" (84). In Thoreau's treatise on civil disobedience, the line of this inheritance is clearly etched. Like Emerson and other nineteenth-century liberal philosophers, Thoreau attempts to work against the stultifying claims of public opinion. But unlike Mill, who argues that private opinion should be freely made public, and unlike Emerson, who insists that private opinion will, in the end, be universally affirmed in public, Thoreau's writing is directed against the expression of *any* opinions whatsoever, when such opinions take the place of public, political action. Again and again in his essay, Thoreau refers to the urgent necessity of what he calls "doing": "There are thousands who are in opinion opposed to slavery and to the war, who yet in effect do nothing to put an end to them; who, esteeming themselves children of Washington and Franklin, sit down with their hands in their pockets, and say that they know not what to do, and do nothing."[31] "How can a man be satisfied to entertain an opinion merely, and enjoy *it*?" he asks. Even voting is not tantamount to doing, because, as Thoreau puts it, "[e]ven voting *for the right is doing* nothing for it. It is only expressing to men feebly your desire that it should prevail" ("Resistance," 139).

For Thoreau, the problem with Emerson's idea of self-reliance as a strategy for resistance is that, like any mere expression of opinion, self-reliance does not stake the character of the individual; instead, it contributes to the illusion that living expediently in the world is in fact doing something for it. He observes:

> The American has dwindled into an Odd Fellow, one who may be known by his development of his organ of gregariousness, and a manifest lack of intellect and cheerful self-reliance; whose first and chief concern, on coming into the world, is to see that alms-houses are in good repair; and, before yet he has lawfully donned the virile garb, to collect a fund for the support of

the widows and orphans that may be; who, in short, ventures to live only by the aid of the mutual insurance company, which promised to bury him decently." ("Resistance," 140)

Thoreau's dissatisfaction with the inadequacies of self-reliance to effect real changes in society results in his articulation of what he identifies as a "revolutionary" concept of performance as public action. He writes, "Action from principle,—the perception and the performance of right,—changes things and relations; it is essentially revolutionary, and does not consist wholly with any thing which was" ("Resistance," 142).

Thoreau's emphasis on public performativity represents a critique of Emerson in two major respects. First, unlike Emerson's "Self-Reliance," in which the term "conscience" is conspicuously absent, Thoreau's account of performance as disobedient, symbolic action—namely, his refusal to pay his poll tax and subsequent night in jail—underscores the claims of conscience by stressing the importance of making these claims visible to the public eye.[32] Thoreau argues that only when these powerful claims of conscience, as opposed to mere opinion, have been made public, can there be any possibility of forming a collective identity, a corporation or "nation" of disobedients. In such a revolutionary situation of visibility and publicity, he contends, the claims of conscience are *both* privately experienced *and* shared in public: "It is truly enough said, that a corporation has no conscience; but a corporation of conscientious men is a corporation *with* a conscience" ("Resistance," 136). Second, whereas Emerson's descriptions of the body in "Self-Reliance" blur the distinction between the public and the social, Thoreau presents the performance of symbolic action as an innovative, visible vocabulary of the body that publicizes the claims of conscience.

Although Thoreau's emphasis on symbolic action marks a significant departure from Emerson's "cheerful" self-reliance, his model of disobedience still relies for much of its effectiveness on Emerson's conception of "the representative man." For Thoreau, as for Emerson, the concept of representativeness dismantles individual boundaries and paves the way for universal identification or "diffusion of spirit" between persons: as Emerson put it in his 1850 essay "Uses of Great Men," "all touch by their summits. . . . Thought and feeling, that break out there, cannot be impounded by any fence of personality. This is the key to the power of the greatest men,—their spirit diffuses itself" (RM, 631). Thoreau's promotion of himself as a civil disobedient entails this "representative" status, a status that by definition involves free access to the public realm. Thoreau's capacity to speak on behalf of slaves—his moral universalism—and thus his claim to identify and merge his own conscience with the conscience of an imagined disobedient collectivity derive much of their justification and force from the "representative" whiteness and maleness of his body. Paradoxically, the fact of this physical inconspicuousness—in combination with Thoreau's genius—grants him formidable powers of visibility, audibility, and thus publicity in his expression of dissatisfaction with the state.

In her critique of Thoreau's essay set forth in *Crises of the Republic*, Arendt denies Thoreau the public status of a civil disobedient because, she argues, his claims of conscience are inherently unpolitical, and as such can never be made public. According to Arendt, "[conscience] is not primarily interested in the world where the wrong is committed or the consequences that the wrong will have for the future course in the world . . . because it trembles for the individual self and its integrity."[33] Indeed, she continues, once conscientious objection has been made public, it represents one, indistinguishable opinion in a marketplace of public opinion in which only large numbers of coinciding consciences will have any political significance. What Arendt insists is that conscience, like philosophy, must first be heard of in newspapers as public opinion in order to have any realizable effect:

> No doubt . . . conscientious objection can become politically significant when a number of consciences happen to coincide, and the conscientious objectors decide to enter the market place and make their voices heard in public. But then we are no longer dealing with individuals, or with a phenomenon whose criteria can be derived from . . . Thoreau. What had been decided in *foro conscientiae* has now become part of public opinion, and although this particular group of civil disobedients may still claim the initial validation—their consciences—they actually rely no longer on themselves alone. In the market place, the fate of conscience is not much different from the fate of the philosopher's truth: it becomes an opinion, indistinguishable from other opinions. And the strength of opinion does not depend on conscience, but on the number of those with whom it is associated. (*Crises*, 67–68)

Arendt's dismissal of Thoreau's premise that the private claims of conscience can be exhibited in public also dismantles his contention that civil disobedients should band together and form a visible, public collectivity or corporation that simultaneously recognizes its individual, conscientious members and represents, as Thoreau puts it, a corporation *with* a conscience. Moreover, Arendt's insistence that civil disobedients are organized in accordance with the principle of voluntary association denies the force of Thoreau's attempt to present the appeal to conscience, and the intimate ties of shared conscience, as a means of resisting the purely volitional, rational, contractual assumption of obligations that are fundamental to Arendt's specific engagement with liberal political philosophy.

Arendt's myopia regarding matters of race and the significance of civil disobedience—the pressing need to believe in the public visibility and efficacy of conscience—for African Americans in the struggle for racial justice during the sixties has been duly noted by her critics. In a salient critique of Arendt's striking inability to distinguish between publicity and sociality in the question of racial justice, Seyla Benhabib has drawn on the example of Arendt's confusion over the problem of school desegregation in Little Rock, Arkansas:

> Arendt likened the demands of the black parents, upheld by the U.S. Supreme Court, to have their children admitted into previously all-white

schools to the desire of the social parvenue to gain recognition in a society that did not care to admit her. This time around Arendt failed to make the final distinction and confused an issue of public justice, equality of educational access, with an issue of social preference, who my friends are or whom I invite to dinner. ("Models of Public Space," 79)

But in spite of this serious conceptual limitation, Arendt's commentary on Thoreau does illuminate two significant difficulties faced by King and other civil disobedients that Thoreau himself does not address. First, that civil disobedience depends for its success upon the responsive performances of others—people who witness, listen, and believe; who confer visibility and publicity on the inner, whispered voice of conscience, thereby making it real. What Thoreau does not emphasize, and King's work on disobedience makes clear, is the fact that the body of the civil disobedient is offered in the hope that witnesses will regard it as authenticating the claims of conscience.[34] As various commentators have pointed out, King's public discourse relies for much of its effectiveness on an embodied, sermonic, rhetorical dimension that authorizes and enacts the claims of his conscience and philosophy of beloved community.[35] In "The Time for Freedom Has Come," King praised the commitment of black youth to the cause for freedom and their persistent exercise of rights by remarking that "[t]hey have offered their energies, their bodies to effect this result" (TH, 165). In "A Gift of Love," King recalls how in the summer of 1966, during the Freedom March through Mississippi, young gang members who engaged in nonviolent direct action "were to be called upon to protect women and children on the march, with no other weapons than their own bodies" (TH, 63). And in his famous 1963 "Letter from Birmingham City Jail," King defended his use of direct nonviolent action as a strategy "whereby we would present our very bodies as a means of laying our case before the conscience of the local and national community" (TH, 291). Taken as a whole, King's writings and life's work disclose his belief that only such a visible, bodily performance should authorize and make real his claims in creating access to public life. As one of King's recent commentators has observed, "King was a master of political theater."[36]

A second difficulty follows from this reliance on the body; namely, that for King and other African Americans, disobedient entry into the public realm is complicated by racial visibility and the phenomenology of the gaze.[37] We have seen that the whiteness and maleness of Thoreau's "representative" body grants him access to formidable powers of publicity in his expression of dissatisfaction with the state, and that for Thoreau the appeal to conscience derives much of its effectiveness from the fact that it has been enacted in his political capacity as a taxpaying citizen. In Civil Rights and the Idea of Freedom, Richard King has observed that "as a representative man, King's public words and actions revealed something essential about himself and about the movement generally":[38] like Thoreau, King's success as a civil disobedient requires that he assume a "representative" status, speaking and acting on behalf of the

oppressed, exhibiting his own exemplary conduct to organize and inspire commitment and disobedient political action on the part of thousands of men,
women, and children involved in the black freedom struggle.[39] But in contrast
to Thoreau's deft, easy assumption of a representative status, King's performance as a civil disobedient and thus his aspiration to Emersonian representativeness involves a dangerous and even life-threatening situation of racial
visibility that has, historically speaking, denied black Americans access to
citizenship and resulted in a pernicious condition of political invisibility in
the public realm.

King's own account of his philosophy of direct nonviolent action shows
the extent to which he was influenced by Thoreau's vocabulary and theoretical
framework for thinking about civil disobedience and political obligation. Like
Thoreau, King's model of civil disobedience represents a critique of liberal
ideals that is itself an expression of his faith in those ideals: "And I submit,"
he writes in "Love, Law, and Civil Disobedience," "that the individual who
disobeys the law, whose conscience tells him it is unjust and who is willing
to accept the penalty by staying in jail until that law is altered, is expressing
at the moment the very highest respect for law" (*TH*, 49). And, like Thoreau,
King's critique of liberal democracy and the limits of contractarianism centers
on his broadening of our conception of political obligation to include both
those which are "enforceable" or legislated and those which are "unenforceable," such as the moral obligation to refuse to cooperate with evil. In a 1962
speech titled "The Ethical Demands of Integration," King argues that such
moral, unenforceable political obligations are met "by one's commitment to
an inner law, written on the heart" (*TH*, 123). Just as in "Resistance to Civil
Government" Thoreau calls attention to the efficacy and force of conscience
as a source of political obligations that may not be assumed by acts of consent
that are wholly volitional and rational, so King's writings emphasize obligations that resist the Lockean, liberal notion that political community is constituted by contract and consent. But whereas Thoreau's essay makes visible
the obligations associated with his individual act of conscience, King's writings
explore the political ties that arise out of the disobedient's capacity to love.

The centrality of love to King's conception of disobedience registers a
crucial difference between, on the one hand, the ties of loving obligation that
bind together King's idea of a beloved community, and, on the other, the
coincidence of consciences that is the governing principle for group cohesion
in Thoreau's model of disobedience: as one commentator has noted, "King's
conception of the nature and power of love is probably his greatest singular
contribution to . . . American social philosophy."[40] By King's own account, the
love ethic reflected in his vision of a "beloved community" as the aftermath
of resistance was fundamental to the acts of disobedience promulgated by the
student movement.[41] "Now when the students talk about love," he observes,
"certainly they are not talking about emotional bosh, they are not talking
about merely a sentimental outpouring; they're talking about something much
deeper . . ." ("Love, Law, and Civil Disobedience," *TH*, 46). And: "To retal-

iate with hate and bitterness would do nothing but intensify the hate in the world. Along the way of life, someone must have sense enough and morality enough to cut off the chain of hate. This can be done only by projecting the ethics of love to the center of our lives" ("Nonviolence and Racial Justice," *TH*, 8).

The critique of liberal ideals undertaken in King's writings was central to his ongoing attempt to bring together a biracial coalition demanding civil rights and basic structural changes within American society. His death was a devastating loss to the cause for racial freedom in this country, one which threatened the cohesiveness and thus the political efficacy of further reform movements. But in the United States, at least, the consequences of King's philosophy remain, and have shaped some of our most cherished theoretical premises in the current debate over the uses and justification of defensive violence, on the one hand, and on the other hand a desire to believe in the political efficacy of civil disobedience and love. As Cornel West put it in 1990,

> King believed in the fundamental trustworthiness of human existence, that creation was essentially good and only existentially evil. . . . This trust presupposes that the unearned suffering of *agapic* nonviolent resisters can educate, transform, and even convert one's opponents. . . . And if one concludes that no such development is possible—that the adversary not only has no moral sense or conscience but, in addition, no longer even has the *capacity* to develop one—then we are forced to admit that we are doomed to an unending cycle of violence and oppression, that human history is the slaughterhouse that Hegel said it was, with the old victims of violence soon to become the new perpetrators of violence. That's the nightmare that hangs in King's closet.[42]

King's performance and critique of American philosophy not only broadens our theoretical vocabulary for describing publicity and political obligation; it also forms the basis for an innovative, ongoing critique undertaken in literatures of protest written in the wake of sixties activism. Many of the doubts and hopes raised by King's philosophy—his abiding faith in the political efficacy of civil disobedience and love—have, in turn, led to a reassessment and response on the part of African-American poets and novelists interested in developing what might be called, for lack of a better term, a poetics of disobedience. This poetics—which clearly exhibits the impact of King's involvement in the civil rights movement and critique of the American political tradition—is one that explores the limits and expressive possibilities of King's philosophical framework and allows each writer to grapple with the conceptual premises of disobedience and arrive at a unique formulation of prospects for entry into the public realm. Examples range from Toni Cade Bambara's *The Salt Eaters*, which examines tensions within black activist groups during the Carter administration and elaborates on the trauma, and need for healing, experienced by black women as a result of their entry into public life[43] to the novel *Beloved*, in which Toni Morrison's portrait of Baby Suggs may be read as a celebration and critique of King's vision of beloved community—his emphasis on the importance of love in working against nihilism and contributing to a sense of agency and hope among oppressed people.[44] Even nationalist poems by Amiri Baraka and Nikki Giovanni assert a distinctive black identity and cultural formation only insofar as they confront the rhetorical problem of constructing a "representative," public position from which to articulate a disobedient call to revolution—a poetic project that reflects the legacy of King's work on disobedience and critique of American philosophy.[45] And Alice Walker's novel *Meridian* examines both the uses and the inadequacies of King's philosophy by detailing moral contradictions and conflicting allegiances involved in either the commitment to love as a force for social change or the decision to kill for the Revolution.[46] I want to conclude by briefly elaborating on Walker's example, because it offers a direct clarification of what I am identifying as one major consequence of King's response to the American philosophical tradition, namely, the critique of King's framework registered as a persistent engagement with the vocabulary of rights and an innovative poetics of disobedience developed in works by contemporary African-American authors and poets.

In a series of essays and addresses collected in the volume *In Search of Our Mothers' Gardens*, Walker assesses King's impact as a leader in the black community as well as his significance for Walker's own development as a writer. What is particularly striking about Walker's analysis is the extent to which she dwells on the fact of King's visibility and publicity. For example, in a 1967 essay titled "The Civil Rights Movement: What Good Was It?" she recalls that the first time she ever saw King was when his arrest was shown on a television news broadcast: "Six years ago," she recalls "after half-heartedly watching my mother's soap operas and wondering whether there wasn't something more to be asked of life, the Civil Rights Movement came into my life. Like a good omen for the future, the face of Dr. Martin Luther King, Jr., was the first black face I saw on our new television screen. And, as in a fairy tale, my soul was stirred by the meaning for me of his mission . . . and I fell in love with the sober and determined face of the Movement."[47] And in "Choice: A Tribute to Martin Luther King, Jr.," an address delivered five years later, she deliberately underscores the fact of King's overwhelming publicity and life-threatening visibility—attributes that, as we have seen, were essential to the success of his ongoing attempt to practice the ideals of his revolutionary philosophy.

> The public acts of Dr. King you know. They are visible all around you. His voice you would recognize sooner than any other voice you have heard this century—this in spite of the fact that certain municipal libraries, like the one in downtown Jackson, do not carry recordings of his speeches, and the librarians chuckle cruelly when asked why they do not.
>
> You know, if you have read his books, that his is a complex and revolutionary philosophy that few people are capable of understanding fully or

have the patience to embody in themselves. Which is our weakness, which is our loss.[48]

As in many of her essays, in the novel *Meridian*, which was published almost a decade after King's assassination, Walker reveals that the pressing question of identity devolves upon her coming to terms with King's death and her assessment of the civil rights movement's political ideals and goals. From the novel's opening scene, which takes place in the southern town of Chicokema, we are presented with the vestiges of sixties activism: Truman Held, a former activist, arrives at the public square in his green Volvo and notices that although the streets are lined with people, no one is saying anything. He tries to find out what is going on from an old black man with a broom and learns that a nonviolent protest is being staged because black children in the community have not been allowed to see a circus exhibit except on a designated day:

> "Well," said the sweeper, giving Truman a guarded look as he clutched his broom, supporting himself on it, "some of the children wanted to get in to see the dead lady, you know, the mummy woman, in the trailer over there, and our day for seeing her ain't till Thursday."
> "*Your* day?"
> "That's what I said."
> "But the Civil Rights Movement changed all that!"
> "I seen rights come and I seen 'em go," said the sweeper sullenly, as if daring Truman to disagree. (*Meridian*, 19)

The effect of our being inundated with these details is to raise the question of whether, in fact, anything has changed as a result of King's eloquent call for direct nonviolent action: in *Meridian*, Walker reflects upon the Movement's impact on subsequent attempts to enact the assertion of political identity—both individual and collective—through acts of civil disobedience. The pivotal moment in this opening scene occurs as Truman watches Meridian, standing in the public square, staring down a tank painted red, white, and blue and decorated with ribbons, a tank that, we are told, was bought by white townspeople

> during the sixties when [they] felt under attack from "outside agitators"—those members of the black community who thought equal rights for all should extend to blacks.

> Meridian did not look to the right or to the left. . . . As she drew nearer the tank, it seemed to grow larger and whiter than ever and she seemed smaller and blacker than ever. And then, when she reached the tank she stepped lightly, deliberately, right in front of it, rapped smartly on its carapace—as if knocking on a door—then raised her arm again. The children pressed onward, through the ranks of the arrayed riflemen up to the circus car door. The silence, as Meridian kicked open the door, exploded in a mass exhalation

of breaths, and the men who were in the tank crawled sheepishly out again to stare.

"God!" said Truman without thinking. "How can you not love somebody like that!"

"Because she thinks *she's* God," said the sweeper, "or else she just ain't all there. I think she ain't all there, myself." (*Meridian*, 21–22)

As an imaginative exploration of the radical potentiality and applicability of King's theoretical framework, and as a report of the possibilities that now exist for oppositional politics in the United States, *Meridian* presents us with what at first appears to be a bleak and startling ambiguity: as a symbol of dissent, Meridian is either someone whom we thoughtlessly worship, as does Truman; or she is someone whom we dismiss, as does the old sweeper, as harboring grandiose and insane delusions about herself and utopian prospects for political community in America.

Walker's acute awareness of the inadequacy of the symbol-making process to enact real changes in society and in the way people see the world is evident in her description of the circus exhibit in the public square that is the focus for Meridian's act of disobedience. The circus wagon, we are told, contains the mummified body of a woman who was killed by her husband, Henry, for the crime of adultery. The uncontrollable darkening of the mummy's skin— the irrepressible question of whether the body on display is in fact the body of a black woman—calls our attention to the significance of the "representative" body in the performance of disobedience. Although, like King, Walker is acutely aware that Meridian's entry into the public realm is necessarily complicated by the fact of her racial visibility, Walker's critique of King's model of civil disobedience inheres in her vivid detailing of the complications that *both* race *and* gender present for the construction of Meridian as a "representative" American Self, a Self whose representative qualities would—as we have seen in the cases of Emerson, Thoreau, and King—have otherwise contributed to the formation of political community and established a mandate for a call to collective action.

There is clearly a world of difference between Walker's recorded response to King as a representative civil disobedient—a man whose life, by her own description, "seeming bigger and more miraculous than the man himself, because of all he had done and suffered, offered a pattern of strength and sincerity I felt I could trust" (*In Search of Our Mothers' Gardens*, 124)—and Truman's response to Meridian's act of disobedience as Walker depicts it in her novel. This crucial difference demonstrates Walker's recognition of the political necessity but also the insufficiency of Emersonian "representativeness" as a rhetorical position from which to articulate Meridian's demand for social change. Meridian's invisibility and lack of access to the public realm, her incapacity to deploy a symbolic vocabulary of the body that publicizes the claims of conscience and promotes real changes in society, all reflect Walker's concern over the fact that, in the wake of the 1960s, symbolic action has increasingly resulted in a disobedient's loss of control over the production of meaning. On a public level, this has meant that the sym-bology of disobedience has been dismissed or emptied of its radical significance and appropriated for the promotion of dominant cultural norms. On a private or individual level, Meridian's attempt to inherit King's philosophy—to find a proper mode of public action and a standard of revolutionary conduct she can live by—is made even more difficult by Truman's jaded, willful ignorance:

> "Then you think revolution, like everything else in America was re-duced to a fad?" [asked Meridian.]
>
> "Of course," said Truman. "The leaders were killed, the restless young were bought off with anti-poverty jobs, and the clothing styles of the poor were copied by Seventh Avenue. . . ."
>
> "But don't you think the basic questions raised by King and Malcolm and the rest still exist? Don't you think people, somewhere deep inside, are still attempting to deal with them?"
>
> "No," said Truman.
>
> "Is there no place in a revolution for a person who *cannot* kill?" asked Meridian, obviously not believing him.
>
> "Why do you drive yourself crazy over these questions?" asked Truman, leaning over her. "When the time comes, trust yourself to do the right thing."
>
> "The 'right thing?' Or merely the thing that will save my life?"
>
> "Don't nitpick." (*Meridian*, 189)

At the end of *Meridian*, Walker presents us with an image of Truman's own symbolic act that expresses his sympathetic comprehension of Meridian's, and thus King's, life's work: Truman climbs into Meridian's sleeping bag and puts her cap on his head. But this is a questionably disobedient gesture at best—and the urgent but as yet uncertain matter of precisely what effective civil resistance should look like and how we can know when we are, in fact, *doing the right thing* is left open for future examination.

Epilogue

In a poem called "The Question of Loyalty," Mitsuye Yamada describes the terrible self-doubt faced by a Japanese immigrant when she was required to forswear allegiance to the Japanese emperor. Yamada's words convey the fear of self-annihilation raised by the problem of divided loyalties, the conflicting claims of double-consciousness experienced by all Japanese-Americans who were interned in the World War II concentration camps.

> *If I sign this*
> *What will I be?*
> *I am doubly loyal*
> *to my American children*
> *also to my own people.*
> *How can double mean nothing?*[1]

Reading this poem, I think about my mother and her family, interned at a camp in Poston, Arizona—how they must have lived through versions of this same, agonizing dilemma. The long-term consequences of my mother's internment for myself and my two sisters have been hard to predict, and even harder to identify as such when they have suddenly made their appearance decades after the event.

My grandmother died years ago, before I ever got the chance to ask her what life in the camp was like. My mother has kept a few photographs, letters, and newspaper clippings. The scattered, fragmented memories she has related to me about her childhood have been few, but very powerful: running away from a rattlesnake that threatened her on the way to an all-white school;

seeing her father, a gardener, behind bars before leaving for the camp in Poston; and wondering, once she had left the camp for good, whether she should be sitting at the front or the back of the bus.

Having written this book, I can better understand my mother's and grand-mother's predicaments. The transformation of mainstream American values undertaken by African-American philosophers has taught me something about all ethnic Americans: we are all inheritors of Emerson's legacy. In the rich, living tradition of Japanese-American literature, my grandmother's rediscovery of Emersonian and Du Boisian double-consciousness is still within the reach of cultural memory. As a result of the diversity and inclusiveness of the Amer-ican literary canon, the web of loyalties that constitutes my social and political world—the doubling and multiplying of consciousness—will be cause for cel-ebration, and never self-doubt.

How can double *possibly* mean nothing?

Notes

Introduction

1. Patricia Williams, *The Alchemy of Race and Rights: Diary of a Law Professor* (Cambridge: Harvard University Press, 1991), 153.

2. Although many political theorists have made a distinction between "liberal" and "democratic," I am using these terms interchangeably to designate the constellation of ideals set forth in the philosophy of John Locke, as well as popularly held cultural values (such as individualism, freedom, and voluntarism) that were central to politics and economic development in nineteenth-century America.

3. Derrick Bell enlists both literary models and legal precedents to discuss the failures of civil rights laws and policies in *And We Are Not Saved: The Elusive Quest for Racial Justice* (New York: Basic Books, 1979) and *Faces at the Bottom of the Well: The Permanence of Racism* (New York: Basic Books, 1992).

4. For an account of the way American expansion was regarded as evidence of the innate superiority of the Anglo-Saxon race during the mid- to late-nineteenth century, see Reginald Horsman, *Race and Manifest Destiny: The Origins of American Racial Anglo-Saxonism* (Cambridge: Harvard University Press, 1981); Thomas R. Hietala, *Manifest Design: Anxious Aggrandizement in Late Jacksonian America* (Ithaca: Cornell University Press, 1985); Alexander Saxton, *The Rise and Fall of the White Republic: Class Politics and Mass Culture in Nineteenth-Century America* (London: Verso, 1990); and David Roediger, *The Wages of Whiteness: Race and the Making of the American Working Class* (London: Verso, 1991).

5. Four collections of essays which exhibit a wide variety of critical approaches to the subject are Henry Louis Gates, ed., *"Race," Writing, and Difference* (Chicago: University of Chicago Press, 1986); Cornel West, *Race Matters* (Boston: Beacon Press, 1993); David Theo Goldberg, ed., *Anatomy of Racism* (Minneapolis: University of Min-

nesota Press, 1990); and Dominick LaCapra, ed., *The Bounds of Race: Perspectives on Hegemony and Resistance* (Ithaca: Cornell University Press, 1991). Recent sociological perspectives may be found in William Julius Wilson, "The Limited Visions of Race Relations and the War on Poverty," *The Truly Disadvantaged: The Inner City, the Underclass, and Public Policy* (Chicago: University of Chicago Press, 1987), chap. 6; Michael Omi and Howard Winant, *Racial Formation in the United States: From the 1960s to the 1980s* (New York: Routledge & Kegan Paul, 1986); Philip Cohen, " 'It's Racism What Dunnit': Hidden Narratives in Theories of Racism," *"Race," Culture and Difference*, eds. J. Donald and A. Rattansi (London: Sage, 1992), 62–103; and Yehudi Webster, *The Racialization of America* (New York: St. Martin's Press, 1992).

6. In The *Interpretation of Cultures*, published in 1973, the anthropologist Clifford Geertz argued for the viability of a *semiotic*, rather than a *scientific*, culture concept (New York: Basic Books, 1973), 3–30. Geertz's reconceptualization of "culture" as "thick description" and interpretation of cultural specifics led Aram Yangoyan to announce, in 1986, the demise of the concept of culture within anthropology. Yangoyan argued that "the move from culture to cultural specifics has created a situation in which traditional anthropological categories of explanation might have minimum importance or validity for analysis or construction of theory" ("Theory in Anthropology: On the Demise of the Concept of Culture," *Comparative Studies in Society and History* 28 [1986], 371). As a result of Geertz's work, many anthropologists (including James Clifford, George Marcus, and Renato Rosaldo) have placed increasing emphasis on the general significance of *ethnography* as a form of cultural practice. In stark contrast to this emphasis placed by anthropologists on the phenomenology, politics, and poetics of writing, many sociologists have, at least since the late 1970s, evinced a sustained, growing interest in developing a viably scientific culture concept. For an excellent summary of existing sociological literature on the culture concept, see Chris Jenks, *Culture* (London: Routledge Press, 1993). Other sociological sources may be found in Mike Featherstone, ed., *Cultural Theory and Cultural Change* (London: SAGE Publications, 1992) and Robert Wuthnow, *Meaning and Moral Order: Explorations in Cultural Analysis* (Berkeley: University of California Press, 1987). See also Robert Wuthnow and Marsha Witten, "New Directions in the Study of Culture," *Annual Review of Sociology* 14 (1988), 49-67.

American sociologists of culture whose work has the most obvious applicability to "cultural studies" (including black studies) as a distinct but related discipline have focused primarily on the way production processes determine the shape, content, and impact of literary forms. I am thinking here of studies done in the late 1970s and early 1980s by Robert Peterson ("The Production of Culture: A Prolegomen" in Peterson, ed., *The Production of Culture* [1976]; "Revitalizing the Culture Concept," *Annual Review of Sociology* 5 [1979]; and "Five Constraints on the Production of Culture: Law, Technology, Market, Organizational Structure and Occupational Careers," *Journal of Popular Culture* 16 [1982]), and by Paul Dimaggio ("Market Structure, the Creative Process, and Popular Culture: Toward an Organizational Reinterpretation of Mass Culture Theory," *Journal of Popular Culture* 11 [1977]). More recently, Wendy Griswold has studied the problem of literary production and interpretation in the United States, Great Britain, and the West Indies ("American Character and the American Novel," *American Journal of Sociology* 86 [1981]), and proposes an interesting heuristic model in *Cultures and Societies in a Changing World* (London: Pine Forge Press, 1994).

British sociologists whose writings are foundational to the emergence of black cultural studies in the United States are Richard Hoggart (*The Uses of Literacy* [Harmondsworth: Penguin, 1958]); Raymond Williams (*Culture and Society, 1780–1950* [New York: Harper & Row, 1966]); E. P. Thomson (*The Making of the English Working Class* [Harmondsworth: Penguin, 1968]); and more recently Stuart Hall (see, for example, "Cultural Studies: Two Paradigms," in *Culture, Ideology, and Social Process*, eds. T. Bennett, G. Martin, C. Mercer and J. Woolacott [London: Open University/Batsford, 1981]), and Paul Gilroy (*The Black Atlantic: Modernity and Double-Consciousness* [Cambridge: Harvard University Press, 1993]).

7. In *The Rise and Fall of the White Republic: Class Politics and Mass Culture in Nineteenth-Century America* (London: Verso, 1990), Alexander Saxton offers a set of plausible, economical, causal explanations of racism in America. Saxton argues that as an ideological construction, the theory of white supremacy that prevailed during the nineteenth century originated from justifications of the slave trade and was continuously modified and readjusted over the years because it met the justificatory needs of dominant groups interested in maintaining their status within changing class coalitions. For example, racialist dogma was used to neutralize the potential opposition of the white working class because it offered white indentured labor an identity that was distinct from that of black slaves—equal partnership in a *herrenvolk* democracy.

Although Saxton's study is rich in historical detail and insight, his argument about the role of literature in the development of American nationalism amounts to nothing more than a series of politically correct commonplaces: namely, that "the ideas of Manifest Destiny could also be expressed in the language of transcendental philosophy," and that nationalism "could justify territorial conquest as readily as inspire the search for . . . a distinctively American voice in art and poetry" (*The Rise and Fall of the White Republic*, 147). Emerson's name is briefly mentioned twice in the course of the entire volume, and Saxton makes no attempt to interpret or present any of Emerson's writings.

In contrast to Saxton, I am interrogating the reductive assumption that Emerson's philosophy and poetics simply reflect prevailing supremacist values and ideals. My study not only demonstrates how Emerson's writings performed the cultural work of reconciling racialism with the premises of American democracy. It also shows how, despite or even because of his racialism, Emerson proved to be an important cultural resource for subsequent critiques of racialism and the flourishing of protest literature written by African Americans.

8. Compare Orlando Patterson's claims regarding the sociohistorical necessity and consequences of the central contradiction between articulate defenses of freedom and the fact of slavery in America. Observing that "Americans have never been able to explain how it came to pass that the most articulate defender[s] of their freedoms . . . were large-scale, largely unrepentant slaveholders," Patterson finds that "[s]lavery is associated not only with the development of advanced economies, but also with the emergence of several of the most profoundly cherished ideals and beliefs in the Western tradition. The idea of freedom and the concept of property were both intimately bound up with the rise of slavery, their very antithesis. The great innovators not only took slavery for granted, they insisted on its necessity to their way of life. . . . The joint rise of slavery and cultivation of freedom was no accident. It was . . . a sociohistorical necessity" (*Slavery and Social Death: A Comparative Study* [Cambridge: Harvard University Press, 1982], viii–ix).

9. This book emphasizes the radical potential and historical influence of Emerson's rhetoric as a mode of protest that uses the master's tools to reform the master's house, so to speak, drawing on mainstream values and ideals in articulating the need for social change. Sacvan Bercovitch is right when he observes that "[t]he appeal of Emersonian dissent lies in . . . its capacity to absorb the radical communitarian visions it renounces, and its capacity to be nourished by the liberal structures it resists. It demonstrates the capacities of culture to shape the subversive in its own image, and thereby, *within limits*, to be shaped in turn by the radicalism it seeks to contain" (*The Rites of Assent: Transformations in the Symbolic Construction of America* [New York: Routledge, 1993], 348. Subsequent references are to *Rites of Assent* and will be cited parenthetically).

But whereas Bercovitch, in his chapter on Emerson and liberalism, focuses on the symbology of dissent associated with Emerson's effort to come terms with the word "individualism," I explore a range of contractarian concepts and cultural values that underlie Emerson's understanding of the self and are subject to scrutiny in his critique of American democracy. Moreover, whereas Bercovitch largely avoids the question of Emerson's racialism, I emphasize Emerson's contribution to our national debate on race and to the historical development of African-American literature and philosophies of protest.

10. Of all the recent writing done by political philosophers who have taken a serious interest in Emerson, George Kateb's *The Inner Ocean: Individualism and Democratic Culture* (Ithaca: Cornell University Press, 1992) and *Emerson and Self-Reliance* (Thousand Oaks, Ca.: SAGE Publications, 1995) come readily to mind as vividly demonstrating the importance of Emerson's writings as a rich conceptual resource for contemporary debates about liberalism. In his claim that "[t]he renovation of liberalism should not be undertaken, as it usually is, in complete disregard of Emerson, Thoreau, and Whitman" "Democratic Individuality and the Claims of Politics," *Political Theory* 12.3. [August 1984], 334), Kateb's work contributes to the larger philosophical recuperation of Emerson initiated by Stanley Cavell. Premising his claims on the belief that "democracy is a distinctive culture[;] . . . that there is such as thing as a distinctively democratic way of being," Kateb argues that Emerson (and, after Emerson, Thoreau and Whitman) created a concept of "democratic individuality" that represents the "completion and ultimate greatness" of liberal, rights-based individualism ("Thinking about Human Extinction (I)," *Raritan*, 6.2 [Fall, 1986], 3. Subsequent references are to "Human Extinction" and will be cited parenthetically).

Like Kateb, I am offering an account of Emerson's critique of liberal premises regarding the nature of ownership, personhood, and the bonds of civil society. And like Kateb, I am interested in the way Emerson's conception of the self necessarily complicates prospects for participation in the sphere of politics. But unlike Kateb, I explore Emerson's attempt to draw on a tradition in Protestant poetics and show how it shapes his conception of political identity. Whereas Kateb considers the religious foundations of Emerson's thought to be his greatest weakness as a philosopher—even going so far as to insist that "[r]eligious pressure continues to confine and distort [Emerson's] greatest thoughts" ("Thinking about Human Extinction (II): Emerson and Whitman," *Raritan* 6.3 [Winter, 1987], 22)—I regard Emerson's immersion in religious language and ideals not only as contributing to what is most inventive about his political thought, but also as forming the basis for Emerson's availability to subsequent critiques undertaken by King and West. For a useful discussion of Emerson's relationship to American Puritanism, as well as the cultural work of Puritan rhetoric more generally, see Sacvan Bercovitch, *The American Jeremiad* (Madison: University of Wisconsin Press, 1978); Bercovitch, "Emerson the Prophet: Romanticism, Puritanism, and Auto-American-Biography," in David Levin, ed., *Emerson: Prophecy, Metamorphosis, and Influence* (New York: Columbia University Press, 1975), 1–27; and Bercovitch, *The Puritan Origins of the American Self* (New Haven: Yale University Press, 1975).

11. In *The American Evasion of Philosophy: A Genealogy of Pragmatism* (Madison: University of Wisconsin Press, 1989), Cornel West has argued that "Emerson's conception of the worth and dignity of human personality is racially circumscribed" and that "race is central to his understanding of the historical circumstances which shape human personality" (34). As we shall see, this centrality of race is comprehensible only in the context of Emerson's dissatisfaction with the liberal-democratic model of the state and his attempt to imagine America as a nation. For Emerson, "the nation" is described *both* in terms of a liberal or contractual model of political relations, *and* in terms of a model in which national boundaries are delineated as distinctive racial boundaries. The critique of liberal democracy—Emerson's radical disavowal of the liberal and, for him, limited concept of democratic statehood expressed as the bonds of citizenship—leads him *also* to embrace a position of racial nationalism and a concept of "the nation" characterized by racial unity and uniqueness.

Whereas I, like West, regard Emerson's racialism as central to his thought, many of West's critics have tended to deny the importance of "race." For example, see *Emerson and Power: Creative Antagonism in the Ninetenth Century* (DeKalb: Northern Illinois University Press, 1996), in which Michael Lopez responds to West's claims regarding Emerson's and Nietzsche's accounts of the human struggle for power, but largely ignores the question of race; and *Emerson's Pragmatic Vision: The Dance of the Eye* (University Park: Pennsylvania State University Press, 1993), in which David Jacobson elaborates on West's argument concerning Emerson's role in the development of pragmatism, but argues against West's claim that "fate" in Emerson's writings involves the notion of biological determinism. A different approach to the recent debate over Emerson and the development of American pragmatism, which focuses on the larger ethical issues of conduct and purpose in the later writings, may be found in David Robinson, *Emerson and the Conduct of Life: Pragmatism and Ethical Purpose in the Later Work* (New York: Cambridge University Press, 1993).

12. Ralph Waldo Emerson, *Essays and Lectures*, ed. Joel Porte (New York: Library of America, 1983), 45.

13. Whereas my work focuses on the contradiction between *owning* and *not owning* expressed in Protestant poetry that examines the relationship between the self and God, Orlando Patterson has previously identified an analogous dialectical approach in the rhetorical mode exhibited in the writings of Paul. Consider, for example, Patterson's treatment of Paul's elaboration on the contradiction between *freedom* and *nonfreedom* (or slavery) entailed in visualizing the relationship between the self and God: "The free gift of freedom places the believer under a strong obligation to God, his righteous master. . . . Paul goes so far as to take over the Hellenistic-cum-Roman idea that true freedom exists only in enslavement to God. This, surely, is what Paul had in mind when he argued that Christians, 'having been set free from sin, have become slaves of righteousness' " (*Freedom in the Making of Western Culture* [New York: Basic Books, 1991], 341).

14. A recent examination of Emerson's "Friendship" that does not address his critique of contractarianism may be found in George Kateb, *Emerson and Self-Reliance*, 96–114. In a groundbreaking analysis of some romantic responses to liberalism, the political philosopher Nancy Rosenblum devotes a chapter to Thoreau's theory of civil disobedience as a critique of liberal consent theory, but she neglects Thoreau's writings on friendship and makes no mention whatsoever of Emerson's thinking on the subject of friendship as a concept of political obligation. This omission is particularly striking insofar as Rosenblum dwells at length on the significance of friendship for what she identifies as "romantic" communitarian critiques of liberalism (Michael Sandel's, among others), as well as the dangers friendship presents viewed from the standpoint of romanticism.

> From the point of view of liberalism which values imparitality, the danger of friendship as a criterion for social relations is evident. More interesting is how it poses a threat to romanticism. . . . Communitarians look to respirit arid relations, but judging from romanticism, there is no guarantee that intimacy will be edifying or constant. Indeed, affection may not be under our control at all, as romantics of the heart confess.
>
> This ought to discourage those who want friendship to serve community building, but communitarians tend to ignore or deny the pains of private affections and the difficulties that arise when private affections are injected into public life. (*Another Liberalism: Romanticism and Reconstruction of Liberal Thought*. [Cambridge: Harvard University Press, 1987], 182–183)

15. In *The Preacher King: Martin Luther King, Jr. and the Word that Moved America* (New York: Oxford University Press, 1995), Richard Lischer explores King's formation in the African-Baptist church and traces the passage of King's sermonic material in his mass-meeting speeches and civil addresses. Although Lischer does briefly mention the fact that King sought to align the aims of the Movement with the values of moderate-to-liberal white America—and, at one point in his study, observes that "[King's] profuse quotations from the standard white poets and philosophers . . . reinforced the commonality of culture that allows an educated American Christian Negro to address the AFL-CIO or B'nai B'rith with the pronoun *we*" (153)—the work does not address the question of King's engagement with the mainstream tradition in American philosophy and literature.

16. In *Dark Voices: W. E. B. Du Bois and American Thought, 1888–1903* (Chicago: University of Chicago Press, 1995), Zamir argues that "both James and Emerson conceive of consciousness as passive perception and of action as unreflective activity, and so fail to give an adequate account of the location of the subject in the world" (12). This dismissive claim regarding the "failure" of Emerson's thought is based on Zamir's interpretation of only two passages taken from Emerson's entire corpus. First, in Zamir's account, the famous transparent eyeball passage in *Nature* shows Emerson's transcendence of the material world—specifically, his withdrawal into consiousness conceived of as passive seeing—as a "strategy for overcoming the divided state of the self," a strategy that proves "Emerson had no usable or satisfying concept of society" because he "abolished" otherness and the self (163–164, 166; cf. 197, 15, 167, 196). Second, Zamir argues that in Emerson's rendering of "The American Scholar," "the scholar does not work from a social location" (197). As we shall see, read in the context of Emerson's other writings and nineteenth-century American culture more generally, the

innovative political critique put forward by Emerson deserves far more careful scrutiny than Zamir's summary judgment would lead us to believe.

17. In *The Black Atlantic: Modernity and Double Consciousness* (Cambridge: Harvard University Press, 1993), Paul Gilroy calls attention to the uses of African-American culture as an intellectual resource that casts new light on the double-consciousness, political activity, scholarship, and experience of black Britons in contemporary Europe. Like Gilroy, I am interested in developing a framework that will allow for more comparative, intercultural, and transnational work on the historical development of African-American philosophy and literature. And like Gilroy, I am interested in resisting the lure of "cultural insiderism" and ethnic absolutism in cultural criticism. But whereas Gilroy simply attacks nationalist perspectives as being inadequate to account for modern black political culture, and argues for the flat-out rejection of the "ontologically essentialist," morally charged language of ethnic absolutism, I am interested in exploring Emerson's contribution to the historical development of American nationalist rhetorics—a development that I regard as critical to understanding African-American political culture and the emergence of Du Boisian double-consciousness. As we shall see, Emerson's sole means of coming to terms with the premises of democracy is by also maintaining the importance of race in the expression of his nationalist vision.

18. Unlike Michael Gilmore's documentation of the contradiction in Emerson's attitude toward property and the market regime, in which Gilmore concludes that Emerson is "unwittingly indebted" (*American Romanticism and the Marketplace* [Chicago: University of Chicago Press, 1985], 29) to the marketplace, my discussion is designed to underscore the significance of contradiction as a gesture of critique. And in contrast to Walter Benn Michaels—who, as a corrective to Gilmore, argues in *The Gold Standard and the Logic of Naturalism* (Berkeley: University of California Press, 1987) that the values of the marketplace produce and contain the values of art—I am claiming that Emerson systematically embraces *and* repudiates the vocabulary and values of the marketplace.

19. In "Scarcity, Objectivity, and Emerson," Wai-chee Dimock has argued that what we find in Emerson's writings is his "internalization of property: the reinscription of the will to own in a realm of privacy and inwardness" (*Boundary* 2 [Spring 1990], 92). According to Dimock, Emerson's model of selfhood is essentially property rights-based and Lockean—although in Emerson's case the content of ownership is "profoundly different" (92): "What this self lays claim to, after all, is nothing as crude or mundane as material goods, but something less tangible and more sublime. Its entitlements range over the world of sensations" (92). In contrast to Dimock, I am arguing that Emerson affirms the right to property in material goods such as the body *as well as* other aspects of the self.

20. In both *The Renewal of Literature: Emersonian Reflections* (New York: Random House, 1987) and *Poetry and Pragmatism* (Cambridge: Harvard University Press, 1992), Richard Poirier argues that Emerson's use of the term "action" registers, above all else, his belief that verbal action—the poetic action of troping—can never be performed in the public realm of politics. Poirier's insistence that Emerson advocates the fundamental privacy of all such action reflects a broader claim regarding Emerson's (and Poirier's own) skepticism about the referential capacities and effects of language. He writes, "The Emersonian insistence on the necessity for 'action' presupposes that there are not verbal solutions. Literature is not in itself an effective political form of

action, except under rather limited conditions. . . . At best, it can help us to deal more critically and effectively than we otherwise might with rhetorics outside literature, as a regular game of neighborhood softball might have the unintended effect of preparing someone to cope a little better with the rigors of the workplace" (*Renewal of Literature*, 48). Because we cannot predict the meaning or effect of literature on its readers, Poirier argues, reading can never be assumed to have culturally redemptive power; it can never be relied on to ameliorate social crises. "Reading is nothing if it is not personal. It ought to get down ultimately to a struggle between what you want to make of a text and what it wants to make of itself and of you. The stakes do not seem to me much higher than that, even when a reader wants to show how a text carries within itself the enabling and sometimes discrediting structures of a surrounding political and oppressively gendered culture" (*Renewal of Literature*, 167).

For many people during the 1960s, the public interpretation of Emerson performed in King's lectures, speeches, and sermons had the effect of authorizing and designating a means of crossing the threshold onto the freedoms of public life. In contrast to Poirier, I am emphasizing the fact that Emerson's philosophy was used during the struggle for black liberation to facilitate access to the public realm, and that this consequence of Emerson's conceptualization of "the public" represents a necessary qualification of Poirier's claims regarding the personal nature and political inconsequentiality of the reading process, raising the stakes of reading considerably. Other important studies of Emerson's rhetoric are Barbara Packer, *Emerson's Fall* (New York: Continuum, 1982); Julie Ellison, *Emerson's Romantic Style* (Princeton: Princeton University Press, 1984); and Harold Bloom, *Poetry and Repression: Revisionism from Blake to Stevens* (New Haven: Yale University Press, 1976).

21. To take just one example, a recent *PMLA* essay titled "Ellison's *Invisible man* Emersonianism Revised" exhibits this type of politically correct, reductive generalization. In this article Kun Jong Lee argues that "Emerson's transcentalism . . . [is] steeped in the question of race"; that "Emerson's egalitarianism . . . is basically idealistic and abstract"; and that "True to his elitism, [Emerson's] social organicism is thus hierarchical" ("Ellison's *Invisible Man*: Emersonianism Revised," *PMLA* [March 1992], 332, 332, 333). Even worse is the fact that this purportedly historical analysis of the significance of Emerson's racism hinges, in the end, on the following tautology:

> Yet, Emerson's failure to recognize blacks as independent subjects having the dignity of human personality is not merely an echo of the racism of his time. As I have argued, it is an integral element of Emersonianism. In other words, Emersonianism includes and perhaps implicitly demands a racist dimension. . . . Given the centrality of race in Emersonianism, it is inevitable that Emerson's principles are racially circumscribed and that the black, whose race is "of appalling importance" (*Essays* 792), cannot draw more than Emerson's condescending attention. ("Emersonianism Revised," 335)

Such tautologies demonstrate the extent to which scholars have increasingly allowed themselves to neglect logic and substance in their discussions of racism, relying instead on a simple statement and restatement of their realization that such racism exists; that it is evil.

22. Toni Morrison, *Playing in the Dark: Whiteness and the American Literary Imagination* (Cambridge: Harvard University Press, 1992), 13.

23. This book thus represents a contribution to the growing body of works that explore the function of "race" and "ethnicity" in American literature, including Eric

Sundquist, *To Wake the Nations: Race in the Making of American Literature* (Cambridge: Harvard University Press, 1993); Kenneth Warren, *Black and White Strangers: Race and American Literary Realism* (Chicago: University of Chicago Press, 1993); Toni Morrison, *Playing in the Dark: Whiteness and the American Literary Imagination* (Cambridge: Harvard University Press, 1992); Shelly Fisher Fishkin, *Was Huck Black?: Mark Twain and African American Voices* (New York: Oxford University Press, 1993); Claudia Tate, *Domestic Allegories of Political Desire: The Black Heroine's Text at the Turn of the Century* (New York: Oxford University Press, 1993); Susan Gillman, *Dark Twins: Imposture and Identity in Mark Twain's America* (Chicago: University of Chicago Press, 1989); and Werner Sollors, *Beyond Ethnicity: Consent and Descent in American Culture* (New York: Oxford University Press, 1986).

Chapter One

1. Two treatises on "the public" that form much of the conceptual basis for the literature in this debate are Jurgen Habermas, *The Structural Transformation of the Public Sphere: An Inquiry into a Category of Bourgeois Society*, trans. Thomas Burger (Cambridge: MIT Press, 1993) and Hannah Arendt, *The Human Condition* (Chicago: University of Chicago Press, 1958).

2. Two collections of essays that exhibit a full range of strategies for critique are Bruce Robbins, ed., *The Phantom Public Sphere* (Minneapolis: University of Minneapolis Press, 1993) and Craig Calhoun, ed., *Habermas and the Public Sphere* (Cambridge: MIT Press, 1993).

3. Hannah Pitkin, *The Concept of Representation* (Berkeley: University of California Press, 1967), 7. In particular, Pitkin cites Emerson's *Representative Men* to support her claims regarding "descriptive representation," noting that "Emerson was concerned neither with the average man-in-the-street nor with the typical, but with what he himself called 'great men.' "

4. Judith Shklar, "Emerson and the Inhibitions of Democracy," *Political Theory*, 18.4 (November 1990), 609. All future citations are to "Inhibitions of Democracy" and will be cited parenthetically.

5. James Madison, *The Federalist Papers* (New York: New American Library, 1961), No. 52, 327. Subsequent references are to *FP* and will be cited parenthetically by number. For Madison, representative democracy has advantages over a pure or direct democracy in that "each representative will be chosen by a greater number of citizens in the large than in the small republic, [and] it will be more difficult for unworthy candidates to practise with success the vicious arts by which elections are too often carried; and the suffrages of the people being more free, will be more likely to center on men who possess the most attractive merit and the most diffusive and established characters" (*FP*, No. 10, 82–83).

6. Madison suggests that representation is what marks the distinction between a democracy and a republic, arguing that "in a democracy the people meet and exercise the government in person; in a republic they assemble and administer it by their representatives and agents."

7. Some useful critiques of this notion of consent have also been put forward. For example, in *Obligations: Essays on Disobedience, War, and Citizenship* (Cambridge: Harvard University Press, 1970), Michael Walzer argues that "it would be a great mistake to define consent or consenting acts too narrowly" (xiii), and in *The Problem of Political Obligation: A Critique of Liberal Theory* (Berkeley: University of California

Press, 1979), Carole Pateman suggests that liberal democratic voting does not necessarily give actual expression to the act of self-assumed political obligation. For a detailed analysis of the structural elements recurring in concepts of consent used in medicine, political philosophy, and marriage law, see Elaine Scarry, "Consent and the Body," *New Literary History* 21.4 (Autumn 1990), 867–896.

8. In *The Human Condition*, Arendt writes, "The distinctive trait of the household sphere was that in it men lived together because they were driven by their wants and needs. . . . The realm of the *polis*, on the contrary, was the sphere of freedom, and if there was a relationship between these two spheres, it was a matter of course that the mastering of the necessities of life in the household was the condition for freedom of the *polis*" (31). Compare Seyla Benhabib's critique of Hannah Arendt's account of the Greek polis:

> What disturbs the contemporary reader is perhaps less the high-minded and highly idealized picture of Greek political life that Arendt draws than her neglect of the following question: If the agonistic political space of the *polis* was only possible because large groups of human beings—like women, slaves, children, laborers, noncitizen residents, and all non-Greeks—were excluded from it while they made possible through their labor for the daily necessities of life that "leisure for politics" that the few enjoyed, then is the critique of the rise of the social, which was accompanied by the emancipation of these groups from the "shadowy interior of the household" and by their entry into public life, also a critique of political universalism as such? ("Models of Public Space: Hannah Arendt, the Liberal Tradition, and Jurgen Habermas," *Habermas and the Public Sphere*, 75)

9. *Records of the Federal Convention of 1787*, vol. 1, ed. Max Farrand (New Haven: Yale University Press, 1937), 561. Subsequent citations are to *Records* and will be cited parenthetically by volume number.

10. A few of the delegates expressed distaste for the use of euphemisms over the matter of slavery: for example, Paterson disapprovingly observed that Congress "had been ashamed to use the term 'slaves' and had substituted a description" in the eighth Article of Confederation (*Records*, I, 561); and Morris roundly criticized the vagueness of the term "wealth," arguing that "[i]f slaves were to be considered as inhabitants, not as wealth, then the said Resolution would not be pursued: If as wealth, then why is no other wealth but slaves included?" (*Records*, I, 581–882). In the end, on the motion of Edmund Randolph of Virginia, the word "wealth" was omitted:

> [T]he vote of Saturday last authorizing the Legislature to adjust from time to time, the representation upon the principles of *wealth* & numbers of inhabitants was reconsidered by common consent in order to strike out "Wealth" and adjust the resolution to that requiring periodical revisions according to the number of whites and three-fifths of the blacks: the motion was in the words following—"But as the present situation of the States may probably alter in the number of their inhabitants, that the Legislature of the U.S. be authorized from time to time to apportion the number of representatives: and in case any of the States shall hereafter be divided or any two or more States united or new States created within the limits of the U.S. the Legislature of U.S. shall possess authority to regulate the number of Rep-

resentatives in any of the foregoing cases, upon the principle of their number
of inhabitants; according to the provisions hereafter mentioned. (*Records*, I,
603)

11. See Kenneth M. Stampp's discussion in "Chattels Personal," *American Law
and the Constitutional Order*, eds. Lawrence M. Friedman and Harry N. Scheiber (Cambridge: Harvard University Press, 1988), 203–218.

12. In addition to this "three-fifths" clause of the Constitution, delegates to the
Convention also adopted a fugitive slave clause borrowed from the Northwest Ordinance of 1787, and provided that the United States could not interfere with the slave
trade before 1800, but rather could only within limits tax the importation of slaves.

13. For an example of the way compromise worked both to maintain and divide
union in nineteenth-century culture, see Sacvan Bercovitch, *The Office of the Scarlet
Letter* (Baltimore: Johns Hopkins University Press, 1991).

14. In *The Human Condition*, Arendt defines the public realm of politics as the
space of appearances (50–78).

15. Edmund Morgan, *Inventing the People: The Rise of Popular Sovereignty in England and America* (New York: W. W. Norton, 1988), 237.

16. John Stuart Mill, *Considerations on Representative Government* (Buffalo, N.Y.:
Prometheus Books, 1991), 308. Subsequent references are to CRG and will be cited
parenthetically. The implications of this unacknowledged contradiction in Mill's thinking about representative government, a contradiction that discloses the powerful, conflicting claims of of democracy and racialism in nineteenth-century liberal discourses
on political identity, will be more fully examined in chapter 6.

17. In chapter 8, I will have more to say about this visibility of the "representative" body and how it necessarily complicates or otherwise limits prospects for entry
into the public realm. Exploring this reliance on the body in the writings of Henry
Thoreau and Martin Luther King Jr., I will argue that whereas the whiteness and
maleness of Thoreau's "representative" body granted him access to formidable powers
of publicity in his expression of dissatisfaction with the state, for King, the aspiration
to a representative status as civil disobedience involves a dangerous, life-threatening
situation of racial visibility that has, historically speaking, denied black Americans
access to citizenship and resulted in a pernicious condition of political invisibility in
the public realm.

18. *Representative Men*, in *Emerson: Essays and Lectures*, ed. Joel Porte (New York:
Library of America, 1983), 628. Subsequent references are to *RM* and will be cited
parenthetically.

19. Shklar suggests that, rather than showing his repudiation of the democratic
ethos, Emerson's expression of such "democratic discontents"—for example, his concern with the threat posed to individuality by democracy—marks his inheritance of
the Anglo-American liberal philosophical tradition. She writes, "[T]o fret about equality is an enduring act of democratic American self-criticism as well as to lament that
democratic class society is more hostile to individuality than a society of castes. It was
certainly part of Emerson's democratic inheritance to accept these democratic discontents" ("Inhibitions of Democracy," 602).

20. Arendt's critique of Thoreau is discussed in chapter 8.

21. Arendt offers a useful analysis of these distinctions in *The Human Condition*.
She writes, "The distinction between a private and a public sphere of life corresponds

to the household and the political realms, which have existed as distinct, separate entities at least since the rise of the city-state; but the emergence of the social realm, which is neither private nor public, strictly speaking, is a relatively new phenomenon whose origin coincided with the emergence of the modern age and which found its political form in the nation-state" (28).

22. John Dewey, *The Public and Its Problems* (New York: Henry Holt, 1927), 75–77. All subsequent references are to *TPP* and will be cited parenthetically.

23. Only Napoleon, by Emerson's description, effectively bridges private and public, the spheres of thought and politics. But what is striking to note is that this entry into and constitution of "the public" precludes any possibility for debate: "Indeed, a man of Napoleon's stamp almost cease to have a private speech and opinion. He is so largely receptive, and is so placed, that he comes to be a bureau for all the intelligence, wit, and power, of the age and country. . . . Every sentence spoken by Napoleon, and every line of his writing, deserves reading, as it is the sense of France" (*RM*, 729).

Chapter Two

1. John Locke, *Two Treatises of Government*, ed. Peter Laslett (Cambridge: Cambridge University Press, 1960), 287–288. Subsequent references are to *ST* and will be cited parenthetically. The complex contradictions in Locke's thought have given support to various interpretations. To take just one isolated example: in *A Discourse on Property: John Locke and his Adversaries* (Cambridge: Cambridge University Press, 1980), James Tully has suggested that Locke's theory is not a justification of private property, whereas in *The Political Theory of Possessive Individualism: Hobbes to Locke* (Oxford: Oxford University Press, 1962), C. B. Macpherson has argued for a "possessive" quality that forms the basis for Locke's individualism.

2. In *The Body in Pain: The Making and Unmaking of the World* (New York: Oxford University Press, 1985), Elaine Scarry elaborates on this connection between embodiment and citizenship.

It might even be argued that the attributes of a particular political philosophy, its generosities and its failures, are most apparent in those places where it intersects with, touches or agrees not to touch, the human body—in the medical system it formally or informally sponsors that determines whose body will and whose body will not be repaired; in the guarantees it provides or refuses to provide about the quality and consistency of foods and drugs that will enter the body; in the system of laws that identify the personal acts toward another's body that the state will designate "unpolitical" (unsocial, uncivil, illegal, criminal) and that will thus occasion the direct imposition of the state on the offender's body and the separation of that unpolitical or uncivil presence from contact with the citizens." (111)

3. Ralph Waldo Emerson, *The Journals and Miscellaneous Notebooks of Ralph Waldo Emerson*, vol. 7, eds. William H. Gilman, Alfred Ferguson, Harrison Hayford, Ralph Orth, J. E. Parsons, and A. W. Plumstead (Cambridge: Harvard University Press, 1960–1982), 397. Subsequent references are to *JMN* and will be cited parenthetically by volume number.

4. Ralph Waldo Emerson, *The Early Lectures of Ralph Waldo Emerson*, vol. 3, eds. Stephen E. Whicher, Robert E. Spellers, and Wallace E. Williams (Cambridge:

Harvard University Press, 1972), 32. Subsequent references are to *EL* and will be cited parenthetically by volume number.

5. Although here I am not primarily interested in discussing Emerson's systematic representation of grief in his later writings, my claims regarding his highly abstract, theoretical, unsentimentalized rendering of grief and domestic life in "Home" do have obvious relevance to Sharon Cameron's findings in her recent study, "Representing Grief: Emerson's 'Experience' " (*The New American Studies: Essays from Representations*, ed. Philip Fisher [Berkeley: University of California Press, 1991], 201–227). Cameron's justification for using psychoanalytic terms in this analysis leads her to contest and ultimately dismiss previous critical categories, including the term "contradiction":

> I propose another set of terms, for "synthesis" and "contradiction" are not useful to describe Emerson's "Experience." These terms are inadequate partly because "Experience" is different from Emerson's other essays. . . . But they are also inadequate in a deeper sense. Specifically, to speak of the split between experience and idealism . . . is to appropriate the essay by a logic it resists. My discussion will suggest that what is at stake in the essay is not a question of logic but rather a question of the elegiac. In "Experience" . . . the elegiac has a logic of its own—not one of working through (not one of synthesis) and not one of explicit conflict. (203)

Like Cameron, I am arguing against previous critical commentaries that have traditionally regarded Emerson's contradictions as his failure to consciously account for or exert rhetorical control over his own internal ambivalences and textual discrepancies. However, in contrast to Cameron, I am arguing, first, that "contradiction" is a useful and indeed essential term in comprehending the political logic and cultural work of Emerson's writings on property and political community. Second, this logic of contradiction is not confined to the "elegiac" or to "Experience" alone but rather determines the shape of Emerson's imaginative work over the course of his entire career. Finally, I want to suggest that a full, subtle understanding of how Emerson deploys the rhetoric of contradiction does not, as Cameron suggests, lead us to appropriate Emerson's political thought by means of a logic it resists, but rather that it underscores the significance of his representation of grief as an innovative critique of democratic norms and rendering of political community that, taken together, serve as an alternative to the language and representational strategies of sentimental writers. For an interesting account of the relationship between sentimentality and ownership in nineteenth-century literature and culture, see Gillian Brown, *Domestic Individualism: Imagining Self in Nineteenth-Century America* (Berkeley: University of California Press, 1990).

6. See John L. Thomas, "Romantic Reform in America," *American Quarterly* 27.44 (Winter 1965).

7. Emerson's critique of Locke's contractarianism will be taken up in Part II, which looks at his thinking on political obligation.

8. Ralph Waldo Emerson, *Essays and Lectures*, ed. Joel Porte (New York: Library of America, 1983), 138. Subsequent references are to *Essays* and will be cited parenthetically.

9. Ralph Waldo Emerson, *Emerson in His Journals*, ed. Joel Porte (Cambridge: Harvard University Press, 1982), 416. Subsequent references are to this edition and will be cited parenthetically. Another, later version of the same passage occurs in the 1860 essay "Culture": "We must have an intellectual quality in all property and in all action, or they are nought. I must have children, I must have events, I must have a

social state and history, or my thinking and speaking want body or basis. But to give these accessories any value, I must know them as contingent and rather showy possessions, which pass for more to the people than to me" (*Essays*, 1029).

10. The contradiction expressed in Emerson's attitude toward property and the market regime has been duly noted by his critics, most compellingly by Michael Gilmore. In *American Romanticism and the Marketplace* (Chicago: University of Chicago Press, 1985), Gilmore suggests that contradiction situates Emerson within history, rendering him truly and representatively Jacksonian (19). Describing Emerson as profoundly and unwittingly indebted to the marketplace, Gilmore observes that Emerson's writings are marked by this ambivalence, both by his "enthusiastic assessment" of the market economy and by a radically opposed "revulsion from commodity" (26, 29). In contrast to Gilmore, I am arguing that Emerson's rhetoric of contradiction represents a deliberate, meaningful gesture of critique. Subsequent references are to *ARM* and will be cited parenthetically.

11. See, for example, Cameron Thomson's article titled "John Locke and New England Transcendentalism," *New England Quarterly* (December 1962), 435–457.

12. My emphasis on the various ways property rights discourse was used in popular nineteenth-century debates over the meaning of slavery points up what is most problematic about the deployment of modern, legalistic ownership concepts in many theoretical accounts of slavery. The referential ambiguities of rights discourse—the proliferation of contradictory claims put forward to define the nature of slaves and slavery in these debates—support Orlando Patterson's finding that the idiom of power, and not property, represents a constituent element of slavery. See *Slavery and Social Death: A Comparative Study* (Cambridge: Harvard University Press, 1982), 17–34. In *Without Consent or Contract: The Rise and Fall of American Slavery* (New York: W. W. Norton, 1989), Robert William Fogel shows that in order to address the moral issues associated with American slavery, we need first to review all the major results of previous research undertaken by historians of the ideological struggle to end slavery. During the course of his analysis, which offers an account of changing interpretations of slave culture, Fogel criticizes Patterson's prior claim that no slave ever internalized the conception of degradation held by their masters. Fogel writes, "Why then were reformist activities rather than revolutionary ones the predominant form of resistance by slaves, especially in the South? The short answer is that 'revolution grows out of the barrel of a gun,' and slaves rarely had the necessary firepower" (197). In the concluding chapter of this book, I offer a thoroughgoing analysis of the moral and political complications associated with both violent acts of rebellion and nonviolent acts of civil disobedience that is designed to work against such reductive formulations of black experience on the part of historians of slave culture.

13. For example, see Kenneth Stampp's "Chattels Personal" in *American Law and the Constitutional Order: Historical Perspectives*, 203–218.

14. Thomas Roderick Dew, "Abolition of Negro Slavery," *The Ideology of Slavery: Proslavery Thought in the Antebellum South, 1830–1860*, ed. Drew Gilpin Faust (Baton Rouge: Louisiana State University Press, 1981), 29, 34.

15. Dew, "Abolition of Negro Slavery," 87.

16. *The South Vindicated from the Treason and Fanaticism of the Northern Abolitionists* (New York, 1839), 200, 211, 310.

17. *An Essay in Defence of Slave Holding as Existing in the Southern States of Our Union. By a Citizen of New York* (New York, 1837), 5, 141.

18. As Drew Gilpin Faust argues in *The Ideology of Slavery*, "Slavery became a vehicle for the discussion of fundamental social issues—the relationship between tradition and progress, the respective roles of liberty and equality, dependence and autonomy" (2).

19. Iveson Brookes, *A Defence of the South Against the Reproaches and Incroachments of the North* (Hamburg, S.C. 1850), 10, 16, 37, 43.

20. *A Defence of Southern Slavery Against the Attacks of Henry Clay and Alex'r. Campbell* (Hamburg, S.C.: Robinson and Carlyle, 1851), 12, 17.

21. Samuel How, *Slaveholding Not Sinful* (New Bruswick, N.Y.: J. Terhune's Press, 1856), 92.

22. E. N. Elliott, ed., *Cotton Is King, and Proslavery Arguments* (Augusta, Ga.: Pritchard, Abbott and Loomis, 1860). That same year, in *The Right of American Slavery* (St. Louis, Mo.: L. Bushnell, 1860), T. W. Holt argued that "the injustice of that partial legislation which would discriminate against the property of one class of citizens, to destroy its value, by proposing the confiscation of its increase, or excluding it from the State,—this is oppression" (17).

23. Alexis de Tocqueville, *Democracy in America*, trans. George Lawrence, ed. J. P. Mayer (Garden City, N.Y.: Doubleday, 1969), 638–639.

24. William Ellery Channing, *Slavery* (Boston: J. Munroe and Co., 1835), 14.

25. Chapter 4 examines Emerson's thinking and writings about slavery, and about social reform more generally, in light of the concept of obligation put forward in the essay "Self-Reliance."

26. This moment will be discussed more fully in chapter 3.

27. In *The Body in Pain*, Scarry looks at nineteenth-century paintings as registering Marx's recognition that the land and the tool are prolongations of the laborer's body:

> In paintings by Millet, for example, the laborer's physical presence stops not at what would be conventionally understood as the boundaries of his or her own body, but at the boundaries of the canvas. In the *Winnower*, the dark mergence of man and world creates a uniform blue and brown surface on which there float luminous white pools of grain, hands, ankles, back—the shared radiance of the materials of work and those parts of the human body most acutely engaged in the activity. In the *Peasant Women Carrying Firewood*, a rhythm is established by the two human figures, each merging with the other and with the wood they carry: the foremost carrier is still distinguishable from the wood she carries; the second is much less so, and behind her looms up the forest itself which merges with her load and becomes the snowfilled thing she (and by extension, her comrade) carries on her back. (248)

28. Eric Foner, *Free Soil, Free Labor, Free Men: The Ideology of the Republican Party before the Civil War* (Oxford: Oxford University Press, 1970), 15.

29. Ronald Walters, *American Reformers, 1815–1860* (New York: Farrar, Straus and Giroux, 1978), 183.

30. Orestes Brownson, "The Laboring Classes," *Boston Quarterly Review* 3 (July 1840), 367.

31. Albert Brisbane, *Social Destiny of Man; or, Association and Re-organization of*

Industry, in *United States Magazine and Democratic Review* 8 (November-December 1840), 434.

32. Henry Charles Carey, *Principles of Political Economy. Part the First: Of the Laws of the Production and Distribution of Wealth* (Philadelphia: Carey, Lea and Blanchard, 1837), 19.

33. Theodore Sedgwick, *Public and Private Economy* (New York: Harper, 1836), 76.

34. Ibid., 22.

35. Ibid., 26.

36. William Paley, *Works* (Philadelphia, 1850), 46.

37. Ibid., 47.

38. Ibid., 112.

39. On this point, see MacPherson, *The Political Theory of Possessive Individualism: Hobbes to Locke*, (New York: Oxford University Press, 1967), 218.

40. Whereas I am claiming that Emerson's theory of labor accounts for moods such as doubtfulness and grief, Stanley Cavell has argued, in his groundbreaking essay titled "An Emerson Mood," that Emerson is a philosopher, an epistemologist of moods: "Emerson may be said to be a philosopher of moods and it is one wise with moods who observes that 'Our moods do not believe in each other' ('Circles'). Neither do our philosophies, or visions, which is why the idea of a pluralism in philosophy, however well meant, is so often an empty hope; and neither do our nonphilosophical and our philosophical moods believe in each other" (*The Senses of Walden* [San Francisco: North Point Press, 1981], 151).

41. Perhaps Emerson's use of Locke's name, albeit in a generic sense, to refer to one of the landowners, is not entirely accidental.

42. By Emerson's account, art is produced only after the laborious act of filling the self with nature's first works has already been accomplished; thus both nature and the artist are agents of creative making.

43. As I stated in my introduction, recent commentators on Emerson's writings on commodity (most notably Michael Gilmore and Walter Benn Michaels) have argued that Emersonian property is indistinguishable from Lockean property; that, as Gilmore puts it, "the poet's song is a mimicry of the capitalist spirit it otherwise condemns" (*ARM*, 29)—an inference, from what we have seen here, that clearly does not follow.

44. In the 1837 lecture titled "Politics," Emerson deploys the idea of a "common nature" to mediate between the theoretical "idea of a State" and the practice of living within a particular system of government. "In actual society certainly the purity of the idea suffers some deduction," he observes. "As friction permits no machine to coincide with its results with theory so the willfulness of individual men suffers never a purely ideal government to exist. But as it is only on the supposition of a common nature, of an identical mind that any government is possible, so always the bases of politics must be explored and all corrections of political errors derived out of the ideal Commonwealth" (*EL*, II, 69–70). Even though his critique of Jacksonian society derives from the idea of a more perfect Commonwealth and a nature held by men in common, we see here that Emerson also persistently returns to the bases of politics and the errors he seeks to correct. At the same time that the supposition of his ideal is a necessary first step to its realization, the energies of such supposition are also directed, in Emerson's view, toward acts of social reform. The question of whether, and how, Emerson relates writing to public, political action will be approached again in chapter 8.

45. George Kateb, "Democratic Individuality and the Claims of Politics," *Political Theory* 12.3 (August 1984), 343.

46. Ibid., 344.

47. Ibid., 345.

48. Compare Barbara Lewalski's description of Traherne's use of the emblematic disembodied eye in *Protestant Poetics and the Seventeenth-Century Religious Lyric* (Princeton: Princeton University Press), 209.

49. In *Seeing and Being: The Plight of the Participant Observer in Emerson, James, Adams, and Faulkner* (Middletown, Conn.: Wesleyan University Press, 1981), Carolyn Porter explores the function of contradiction in Emerson's *Nature*, in particular the self-contradictory formulation "I am nothing, I see all." For Porter the contradiction between observer and participant is disruptive and one that Emerson avoids by positing "a dynamic fluid reality," and that "[t]hus the 'transparent eyeball' had to float on 'currents of Universal Being.'" My reading suggests that Emerson not only acknowledges such contradiction, but that he embraces it. We have seen that for Emerson, vision is associated with possession. The statement "I am nothing, I see all" may thus be construed as the assertion that "I have no self, I have everything."

50. Ralph Ellison's critique and inheritance of the philosophy of personhood put forward by Emerson in these early writings is evident in the model of subjectivity Ellison constructs in *Invisible Man*. In this novel, Ellison, like Emerson, works to substantiate and thereby justify his claims to property in himself by claiming a right to his own state of invisibility or transparency. He writes, "Well, I was, and yet I was invisible, that was the fundamental contradiction. I was and yet I was unseen. It was frightening and as I sat there I sensed another frightening world of possibilities" (507). For Emerson, as for the Invisible Man, expressive possibilities are created only when he accepts and explores the contradiction inherent in his condition as a representative American Self. But unlike Emerson, Ellison is careful to point out that the transparency of the eyeball membrane itself obscures the fact of its embodiment and thus the fundamental raciality of the self. Ellison's depiction of the membrane's transparency thus calls our attention to the particularity of whiteness—the fact that (as the philosopher Cornel West also observes) Emerson's conception of the self in all its aspects is racially circumscribed.

51. As Sacvan Bercovitch has observed, Emerson's "model of spiritual growth reflected a teleology that eliminated the tension between process and fulfillment" (*The Puritan Origins of the American Self* [New Haven: Yale University Press, 1975], 161). Subsequent references are to *Puritan Origins* and will be cited parenthetically.

52. In many respects, the central contradiction concerning self-ownership that characterizes Emersonian conversion in *Nature* anticipates his rendering of conversion in "Experience." In chapter 6, it will be argued that in "Experience" conversion is depicted as a single moment in which the Emersonian self both makes (and thus owns) and does not make (or own) itself.

53. *The Human Condition* (Chicago: University of Chicago Press, 1958), 99–100.

54. In this sense, Emersonian self-ownership is the result of both "work" and "labor," as Arendt defines these terms in *The Human Condition*: "The common characteristic of . . . the biological process in man and the process of growth and decay in the natural world, is that they are part of the cyclical movement of nature and therefore endlessly repetitive; all human activities which arise out of the necessity to cope with them are bound to the recurring cycles of nature and have in themselves no beginning and no end, properly speaking; unlike *working*, whose end has come when the object

is finished, ready to be added to the common world of things, *laboring* always moves in the same circle, which is prescribed by the biological process of the living organism and the end of its 'toil and trouble' comes only with the death of this organism" (98).

Whereas Arendt's claims against mass production devolve upon her main point that modern society breaks down the distinction between objects of consumption and objects of use—and that Marx's distinction between productive and unproductive labor contains "in a prejudicial manner" what she regards as a "more fundamental distinction" between work and labor (87)—in *Making and Effacing Art: Modern American Art in a Culture of Museums* (New York: Oxford University Press, 1991), Philip Fisher puts forward a model of origin for modern works of art that points out what is fundamentally wrong about Arendt's view of the artist as the sole, exceptional worker left in a society of laborers. Pointing out the falsity of the central, Arendtian distinction between objects of use, objects of consumption, and works of art, Fisher calls our attention to the medieval and artisanal force of the term "masterpiece" (a term that also designates the time-bearing features of objects) and gives as a compelling illustration the masterpieces required by aspiring cooks in Calais:

> Unlike many of the objects that we consider works of art, this elaborate feast is not designed to outlast the maker, to survive him and become part of what we know as the past. These are precisely the traits that Hannah Arendt would list in her chapter on the work of art in her book *The Human Condition*. The Calais chef is not contributing to what Arendt calls the durability of the world, one feature of which is made up of just that set of things that outlast the maker. To make a table is different from making a loaf of bread because the very premise of the second is that it will be used up and destroyed so as to prolong the life of the man or woman who baked it. The table, if well built, and lucky in its history, can become part of the durability of the world for tens of generations that are born, draw their chairs up to the table to eat, and then pass away and are replaced by others in the same seats at the same table. The loaf of bread is Arendt's example of human labor; the table, of human work. As an even more exalted category she keeps the work of art as an object as far above the table as the table is above the loaf of bread. (176)

See also *The Body in Pain*, the note in which Scarry suggests that Arendt's analysis of the distinction between work and labor actually derives from the "much more elaborated account of the distinction between objectless and objectified work in Marx, whose entire political critique depends on it" (357 n. 11).

55. The image of the wilderness calls our attention to the Puritan origins of Emersonian identity, because it conjoins Emerson's personal experience of self-recovery, the founding of America as a particular, historical venture, and the figuring of this event in sacred history. Bercovitch indirectly raises the question of self-ownership in this connection when he notes that "[c]haracteristically, the self [Emerson] sought was not only his but America's, or rather his *as* America's, and therefore America's as his" (*Puritan Origins of the American Self* [New Haven: Yale University Press], 165).

56. "Will" is closely related to "labor," and appears to have been habitually used by Emerson in place of labor. In the lecture series "Human Culture," delivered in 1837, he wrote that "[man] is so related to the elements that they are his stock, flexible

in his hands; he takes the obedient mountain and puts his own will into it and it becomes a city, temples and towers" (*EL*, II, 221).

57. Compare Sacvan Bercovitch's description of this passage as "an *ultimum* of the rhetoric of transcendence—an interpretation of the origins and ends that appropriates the mysteries of gender, nature, and the Oversoul to the culturally transparent "I" (*Rites of Assent*, 26).

58. Compare Stanley Cavell's contention in "Aversive Thinking: Emersonian Representations in Heidegger and Nietzsche" that "[Emerson's] aversion provides for the democratic aspiration the only internal measure of its truth to itself—a voice only this aspiration could have inspired, and, if it is lucky, must inspire. Since his aversion is a *continual turning away* from society, it is thereby a continual turning *toward* it" (*Conditions Handsome and Unhandsome* [Chicago: University of Chicago Press, 1990], 59).

59. The same aversion that characterizes Emerson's critique of Lockean liberalism is expressed as an aversion to history in *Nature*. The similarity between Emerson's aversion to property in history and to democratic aspirations regarding property in the body is evident in the section titled "Idealism." Emerson figures historical narrative first as property acquired from a painful process of accumulation and then as an aging human body. "Idealism . . . beholds the whole circle of persons and things, of actions and events, of country and religion, not as painfully accumulated, atom after atom, act after act, in an aged creeping Past, but as one vast picture, which God paints on the instant eternity, for the contemplation of the soul," he writes (*Essays*, 39). The private confines of the body and the creeping past it represents are discarded by Emerson in favor of the universal and vast picture that God paints and owns. But even the limits of Idealism as "a hypothesis to account for nature" are ultimately exposed in Emerson's text. The contempt for nature (or history, or the body), which the ideal theory represents and which "makes nature foreign," does not account, in Emerson's view, "for that consanguinity which we acknowledge to [nature]" (*Essays*, 41).

60. Louis Hartz, *The Liberal Tradition in America* (New York: Harcourt Brace Jovanovich, 1955), 11. Subsequent references are to *LTA* and will be cited parenthetically.

61. Hartz's starting place is the assumption that "[i]t is not accidental that America which has uniquely lacked a feudal tradition has uniquely lacked also a socialist tradition" (*LTA*, 6). He makes no reference at all to the rhetoric of racialism in his analysis and effectively dismisses the pervasive uses of the symbology of feudalism inherent in nineteenth-century racialist discourse when he writes, "I do not mean to imply that no trace of the feudal urge, no shadow whatsoever of Sir Walter Scott, has been found on the hills and plains of the New World. One can get into a lot of useless argument if he affirms the liberalness of a liberal society in absolute mathematical fashion" (*LTA*, 7–8).

62. The critical role of Emerson's racialism in his construction of a nationalist rhetoric that represents both a revolutionary threat to and affirmation of political order will be elaborated in chapter 6.

Chapter Three

1. Karl Marx, *Capital*, vol. 1, ed. Frederick Engels, trans. Samuel Moore (New York: International Publishers, 1967), 352.

2. In *Prophesy Deliverance: An Afro-American Revolutionary Christianity* (Phila-

delphia: The Westminster Press, 1982), West argues for the importance of Christian thought as an intellectual resource and outlines the main differences between Christian and Marxian dialectics. Whereas Christian gospel exhibits a dialectic between, on the one hand, a natural, human condition of dignity or depravity that is born into or found, and, on the other, human history conceived of as "the realm of the pitiful and the tragic" (17), West observes that Marxism posits a dialectic between human practice and human history that unveils the historical conditions and determinants of human nature:

> This *collapse* of human nature into human practice and into human history— as opposed to a dialectical relation of human nature to human practice and to human history—is the distinctive difference between Christianity and Marxism. The Christian espouses a dialectical historicism which stresses the dignity and the depravity of persons, whereas the Marxist puts forward a full-blown historicism in which the eventual perfectibility of persons within history is inevitable. The Christian world view is a clandestine complaint against history, the Marxist an avowed apotheosis of it. (19)

3. For a discussion of nineteenth-century American writings on reform in which communitarianism is presented as the ultimate expression of perfectionist and millennialist logic, see Ronald Walters, *American Reformers, 1850–1860* (New York: Farrar, Straus and Giroux, 1978), 21–60.

4. A useful analysis of the development of Protestant emblematics may be found in Barbara Lewalsi, *Protestant Poetics and the Seventeenth-Century Religious Lyric* (Princeton, N.J.: Princeton University Press, 1979), 179-212. Subsequent references are to *Protestant Poetics*. See also Rosalie Colie, *The Resources of Kind: Genre Theory in the Renaissance*, ed. B. Lewalski (Berkeley, Ca.: University of California Press, 1973), 36–75.

5. Francis Quarles, *Quarles' Emblems* (London: James Nisbet and Co., 1861).

6. *George Herbert and Henry Vaughan*, ed. Louis Martz (Oxford: Oxford University Press, 1986), 22. Subsequent references are to this edition and will be cited parenthetically.

7. For a discussion of Herbert's practices as an emblematist, see Lewalski's *Protestant Poetics*, 283–316.

8. For an account of the transmission of the emblem iconography on material objects such as porringer handles and colonial silverwork see Sylvester Crosby, *The Early Coins of America* (Boston, 1875), 41–42, and Anthony Garvan, "The New England Porringer, An Index of Custom," Smithsonian Institution Annual Report 1958 (Washington, D.C., 1959). On the use of emblems in stonecarving and memorial mason work, see Harriet M. Forbes, *Gravestones of New England and the Men Who Made Them, 1653–1800* (Boston: Houghton Mifflin Co., 1927); Allan I. Ludwig, *Graven Images: New England Stonecarving and Symbols, 1650–1815* (Middletown, Conn.: Wesleyan University Press, 1966); Francis Duval, *Early American Gravestone Art in Photographs* (New York: Dover Publications, 1978); and David Watters, *"With Bodilie Eyes": Eschatological Themes in Puritan Literature and Gravestone Art* (Ann Arbor: UMI Research Press, 1981). For a study of the iconological influence of emblems in early American architecture and cabinetmaking see Anthony Garvan, "The New England Plain Style," *Comparative Studies in Society and History* 3 (Oct., 1960), 106–122; and Wallace Nutting, *Furniture Treasury*, vol. 1 (Farmingham, Mass.: Old American, 1928), figures 444, 446, 448, 451.

9. For a discussion of Edward Taylor as an early American emblematist, see Barbara Lewalski, *Protestant Poetics*, 209–212; Alan Howard, "The World as Emblem: Language and Vision in the Poetry of Edward Taylor," *American Literature* 44.3 (November, 1972), 359–384; and Thomas Johnston, "Edward Taylor: An American Emblematist," *Early American Literature* 3.3 (Winter 1968–69), 186–198. For a description of the uses of emblems in the poetry of Emily Dickinson and the presence of this emblematic, popular religious tradition, see George Monteiro and Barton Levi St. Armand, "The Experienced Emblem: A Study of the Poetry of Emily Dickenson," *Prospects* 6 (1981), 186–280. For a discussion of Poe as an emblematist, see St. Armand, "Poe's Emblematic Raven: A Pictorial Approach" *ESQ: A Journal of the American Renaissance*, Vol. 22, 4th quarter (1976), 193.

10. Ralph Waldo Emerson, *Essays and Lectures*, ed. Joel Porte (New York: Library of America, 1983), 275, 272, 282. Subsequent references are to *Essays* and will be cited parenthetically.

11. In "Circles," an essay published five years after *Nature*, Emerson insists that "[t]he eye is the first circle. . . . It is the highest emblem in the cipher of the world" (*Essays*, 403).

12. In *The American Renaissance* (New York: Oxford University Press, 1941), F. O. Matthiessen briefly mentions Emerson's "kinship" with Traherne and the practices of other seventeeth-century meditational poets in *Nature* (67). The emblematic eye was frequently used in poems such as Traherne's "An Infant-Eye": "A simple Light from all Contagion free,/a Beam that's purely Spiritual, an Eye/That's altogether Virgin, Things doeth see/Ev'n like unto the Deity."

13. On this point, see David Watters, *"With Bodilie Eyes": Eschatological Themes in Puritan Literature and Gravestone Art* (Ann Arbor: UMI Research Press, 1981).

14. In *Liberalism and the Limits of Justice* (Cambridge: Cambridge University Press, 1982), Michael Sandel looks at the relation between persons and endowments. Including guardianship as one possible sense of possession, he argues that "[t]his is a notion of possession reminiscent of the early Christian notion of property . . . and . . . fits with various communitarian notions of property" (97). My claim is that although Emerson self-consciously derives his idea of property from seventeenth-century Protestant constructions, his political critique is not, strictly speaking, communitarian in Sandel's terms. As I showed in the previous chapter, Emersonian property is as much a measure of his belief in the conceptual necessity of property and the free market as it is a marker of his insistence on the insufficiency of the concept of privacy and personhood that determines free-market practice.

15. Barbara Franco, "Masonic Imagery," *Aspects of American Printmaking, 1800–1950*, ed. James O'Gorman (Syracuse: Syracuse University Press, 1988), 14. Subsequent references are to "Masonic Imagery" and will be cited parenthetically.

16. On this point, see Elinor Horowitz, *The Bird, the Banner, and Uncle Sam: Images of America in Folk and Popular Art* (Philadelphia: J. B. Lippincott, 1976).

17. In her study of Masonic imagery, Barbara Franco takes note of the fact that Cross's book "included one new symbol, a broken column, that Cross apparently designed" ("Masonic Imagery," 24), but fails to locate this symbol within the moral or religious emblem tradition.

18. In their study of Dickinson's emblematics, Montiero and St. Armand have identified the conventional emblem of Prudence as a visual referent to the well-known epigram " 'Faith' is a fine invention/When Gentlemen can *see*—/But Microscopes are prudent/In an Emergency." Raising the question of why Dickinson changed the em-

blematic image of the telescope for that of a microscope, they suggest that perhaps Dickinson could not remember the emblem accurately, or that she felt "the need to update the image" ("The Experienced Emblem: A Study of the Poetry of Emily Dickinson," *Prospects* 6 [1981], 214). My discussion of Emerson's practices as an emblematist suggests a context for Emerson's influence upon Dickinson's emblematics, even in the deliberate substitution of a microscope for a telescope.

19. In a letter to Lidian Emerson written in October 1843, Thoreau wrote that in "reading what of Quarles's poetry [he] could get," he believed that "[i]t is rare to find one who was so much a poet and so little an artist." Recommending that Lidian read Quarles, Thoreau added that "[h]e uses language as greatly as Shakespeare, and though there is not much straight grain in him, there is plenty of rough crooked timber." See *The Correspondence of Henry David Thoreau*, eds. Walter Harding and Carl Bode (New York: New York University Press, 1958), 143–144.

20. Francis Quarles, *Emblems Divine and Moral* (1635), eds. A. Toplady and J. Ryland (London: Milton Press, 1839), 59.

21. John Locke, *Two Treatises of Government*, ed. Peter Laslett (Cambridge: Cambridge University Press, 1960), Second Treatise, 288.

22. Compare Orlando Patterson's claim, put forward in his forthcoming analysis of Locke's conception of God as divine slave master, that Locke's dialectical approach to the problem of freedom derives from that found in the biblical writings of Paul. "More than any secular philosopher in the history of the West, Locke knew the writings of St. Paul; indeed, given his method of reading and coming to understand Paul, the texts would have been imprinted on his consciousness, if not known by heart. . . . No reading of Locke's theory of freedom is credible without a thorough understanding of Locke's reading of Paul. Locke's theory of freedom is easily shown to be only a partially secularized adaptation of the Pauline conception of freedom" ("Agrarian Capitalism and Personal Freedom: The Lockian Synthesis," forthcoming, 16).

23. This imperialist dimension of Emerson's critique of property is also visible in his invention of another emblematic body position—the embrace—which, like comprehension, represents a critique of Lockean property. The model of political association entailed by the innovative mode of possession symbolized by the embrace is one that accounts for a powerful, intimate, monarchical identification of the individual with the public realm. "It is one of those fables, which, out of an unknown antiquity, convey an unlooked-for wisdom, that the gods, in the beginning, divided Man into men, that he might be more helpful to himself," he observes. "The fable implies, that the individual, to possess himself, must sometimes return from his own labor to embrace all other laborers" (*Essays*, 53, 54). Elsewhere, the emblematic embrace is used to facilitate the scholar's experience of "low," "familiar" aspects of nature. Just as he describes Swedenborg's use of emblems that allow him to explore nature's "lower parts," so Emerson himself deploys an emblem of appropriative, affectionate enclosure to make nature his own. The gesture is one that strategically claims the ordinary domestic world as the fit domain of the poetic:

I embrace the common, I explore and sit at the feet of the familiar, the low. Give me insight to-day, and you may have antique and future worlds. What would we really know the meaning of? The meal in the firkin; the milk in the pan; the ballad in the street; the news of the boat; the glance of the eye;

the form and gait of the body;—show me the ultimate reason of these matters; show me the ultimate presence of the highest spiritual cause lurking, as
always it does lurk, in these suburbs and extremities of nature; let me see
every trifle bristling with the polarity that ranges it instantly on an eternal
law; and the shop, the plough, and the leger, referred to the like cause by
which light undulates and poets sing,—and the world lies no longer a dull
miscellany and lumber room, but has form and order; there is no trifle; there
is no puzzle; but one design unites and animates the farthest pinnacle and
the lowest trench. (*Essays*, 69).

24. See for example Eric Hobsbawm's "Mass-Producing Traditions: Europe, 1870–
1914" in *The Invention of Tradition* (Cambridge: Cambridge University Press, 1983)
and Lynn Hunt's "Symbolic Forms of Political Practice" in *Politics, Culture, and Class
in the French Revolution* (Berkeley: University of California Press, 1984).

25. Hannah Arendt, *The Human Condition* (Chicago: University of Chicago Press,
1958), 3.

26. Ralph Waldo Emerson, *The Early Lectures of Ralph Waldo Emerson*, vol. 2, ed.
Stephen Whicher, Robert E. Spiller, and Wallace E. Williams. (Cambridge: Harvard
University Press, 1964), 230. Subsequent references are to *EL* and will be cited par-
tenthetically by volume number.

27. Ibid., vol. 3, 92.

28. In "The Match," Vaughan responds to the opening words of Herbert's earlier
poem, "Love Unknown," by addressing Herbert as a "Dear friend" whose "holy, ever-
living lines . . . have checked my blood" (*George Herbert and Henry Vaughan* [Oxford:
Oxford University Press, 1986], 290, ll. 1–3). Vaughan deploys the central emblem of
"joining" hands—as opposed to Emerson's more appropriative image of "grasping"
hands—to align his poetic project and ambitions with Herbert's. In this connection,
Vaughan also explicitly invokes the central metaphor of the "Deed" used by Herbert
in the poem *Obedience*: "Here I join hands, and thrust my stubborn heart/Into thy
Deed." (ll. 7–8). Taken as whole, Vaughan's poem is a response to Herbert's wish,
expressed in the last two stanzas of "Obedience", that "He that will pass his land,/As
I have mine, may set his hand/And heart unto this Deed, when he hath read;/ . . .
How happy were my part,/If some kind man would thrust his heart/Into these lines"
(ll. 36–38, 41–43).

29. Elsewhere Emerson writes, "If it were only for a vocabulary, the scholar would
be covetous of action. Life is our dictionary. Years are well spent in country labors; in
town,—in the insight into trades and manufactures; in frank intercourse with many
men and women; in science; in art; to the one end of mastering in all their facts a
language by which to illustrate and embody our perceptions" (*Essays*, 61–62).

30. Smith argues that "[o]nly by an extreme irony or a thoroughly artistic failure
to distinguish the actual from the imagined can Emerson . . . exclaim, 'I run eagerly
into this resounding tumult [of the world]. I grasp the hands of those next to me, and
take my place in the ring to suffer and to work. . . . ' And the proposed end is still
merely literary: the Scholar enters the world not in order to reform it, but in order
that the dumb abyss of his inarticulate thought may become 'vocal with speech.'" See
Henry Nash Smith, "Emerson's Problem of Vocation," *Emerson, A Collection of Critical
Essays*, eds. Milton Konvitz and Stephen Whicher (Westport, Conn.: Greenwood Press,
1962), 68.

Chapter Four

1. For a lively account of Emerson's life which suggests that the urbanization of his native New England may have contributed to the development of a philosophy of self-reliance, see Mary Cayton, *Emerson's Emergence: Self and Society in the Transformation of New England* (Chapel Hill: University of North Carolina Press, 1989), 221–231. A useful history of the Transcendentalists' involvement in reform activities may be found in Anne C. Rose, *Transcendentalism as a Social Movement, 1830–1850* (New Haven, Conn.: Yale University Press, 1979).

2. For a useful history of Emerson's involvement in the abolitionist movement, see Len Gougeon, *Virtue's Hero: Emerson, Antislavery, and Reform* (Athens: University of Georgia Press, 1990).

3. James Elliot Cabot, *A Memoir of Ralph Waldo Emerson* (Boston: Houghton Mifflin, 1887), 426.

4. In a note in his journal Emerson observed that "[t]his stirring in the philanthropic mud, gives me no peace. I will let the republic alone until the republic comes to me.... It is not my impulse to say it & therefore my genius deserts me, no muse befriends, no music of thought or of word accompanies. Bah!" (*JMN*, V, 479).

5. In *Democracy in America* (vol. 1, ed. J. P. Mayer, trans. George Lawrence [Garden City, New York: Doubleday, 1969]), Alexis de Tocqueville identified the need for such a framework when he observed that "[a] new political science is needed for a world itself quite new" (12). Subsequent references are to this edition and will be cited parenthetically.

6. Emerson's insistence on the reciprocity of philosophy, poetry, and political culture is evident in this 1846 journal entry: "The metre of poetic genius is the power to fuse the circumstance of today. Thus it is boyish in Swedenborg to cumber himself with the dead scoriae & exuviae of the Hebrew and Canaanitish antiquity when the questions that were then alive & fraught with good & evil to men have vanished before the questions of property, of politics, of democratic life" (*JMN*, IX, 418).

7. To take just one, isolated example of Emerson's criticisms of existing reform movements: in contrast to the prevailing, moralistic view of temperance promoted by contemporary philanthropists, Emerson viewed the whole problem of temperance as deriving from the fact that we eat with shame, because our diet is not "agreeable to our imagination": "I conceive that the whole movement in England and America which has made so loud a din in all ears proceeds from the simple fact that the diet of men in these countries is not agreeable to the imagination. Other creatures eat without shame. We paint the bird pecking at the fruit, the browsing ox, the lion leaping on his prey, but no painter ever ventured to draw a man eating.... We have made eating a science and an end not a means" (*EL*, III, 260–261).

8. In *The Human Condition* (Chicago: University of Chicago Press, 1958), Hannah Arendt writes that "[w]ith word and deed we insert ourselves into the human world, and this insertion is like a second birth, in which we confirm and take upon ourselves the naked fact of our original physical appearance" (176).

9. We know that Emerson specifically mentions Locke in "Self-Reliance," and that a reference to Locke's name in an 1839 journal entry ("You do not say 'I think,' 'I am,' but quote St. Paul or Jesus or Bacon or Locke" [*JMN*, VII, 221]) was deliberately effaced when the entry was incorporated into Emerson's essay.

10. William Ellery Channing, *Self-Culture* (Boston: James Munroe and Co., 1838). Subsequent references are to this edition and will be cited parenthetically.

11. Channing argues:

> Not a few persons desire to improve themselves only to get property and rise in the world; but such do not properly choose improvement, but something outward and foreign to themselves; and so low an impulse can produce only a stinted, partial, uncertain growth. A man . . . is to cultivate himself because he is a man. He is to start with the conviction, that there is something greater within him than in the whole material creation, than in all the worlds which press on the eye and ear; and that inward improvements have a worth and dignity in themselves, quite distinct from the power they give over outward things. Undoubtedly a man is to labor to better his condition, but first to better himself. If he knows no higher use of his mind than to invent and drudge for his body, his case is desperate as far as culture is concerned." (*Self-Culture*, 34)

12. Later in the same lecture Channing makes a similar point, observing that "[t]he laborer is not a mere laborer. He has close, tender, responsible connections with God and his fellow creatures. He is a son, husband, father, friend, and Christian. He belongs to a home, a country, a church, a race; and is such a man to be cultivated only for a trade? . . . A higher culture, than that has yet been dreamt of, is needed by our whole race" (*Self-Culture*, 30–31).

13. For Emerson, the physical experience of belief—the relation of a person to his or her own embodied personhood—is thus one primary ground of any obligation to obey the law. Compare Elaine Scarry's description of the material anchoring of consent in the body in "Consent and the Body: Injury, Departure, and Desire" (*New Literary History* 21.4 [Autumn 1990], 867–896).

14. Rosenblum makes no mention of Emerson's writings in connection with her analysis of romanticism and legal formalism.

15. Nancy Rosenblum, *Another Liberalism: Romanticism and the Reconstruction of Liberal Thought* (Cambridge: Harvard University Press, 1987), 45. Subsequent references are to *Another Liberalism* and will be cited parenthetically.

16. At the opening of her study, Rosenblum claims that "[t]his book describes *the* romantic response to liberalism" (*Another Liberalism*, 1; emphasis added).

17. This correspondence of private and public meanings within "ordinary" language is visible in Cavell's description of Wittgenstein's philosophical undertaking in *The Claim of Reason: Wittgenstein, Skepticism, Morality, and Tragedy* (Oxford: Oxford University Press, 1979). Cast in Cavell's terms, what distinguishes Wittgenstein's practice of proceeding from ordinary language is that he at times seems to accomplish an Emersonian voicing of our secret presentiments, making them most public and universally true.

> Wittgenstein, in sampling what we say, goes beyond the mere occurrence of the words, in ways that make him unlike other philosophers who proceed from ordinary language; unlike Austin, say. He proposes words that he says force themselves upon us in a certain context, or words that we wish or would like or are tempted to say, and he cites words he says we do not mean or only have the illusion of meaning. How does he know such things? I mean, apart from any philosophical claim into whose service he would press

such findings, how can he so much as have the idea that these fleets of his own consciousness, which is obviously all he's got to go on, are accurate wakes of our own? But the fact is, he does have the idea; and he is not the only one who does. And the fact is, so much of what he shows to be true of his consciousness is true of ours (of mine). (20)

18. Lawrence Friedman, *A History of American Law* (New York: Simon & Schuster, 1973), 278.

19. In "Compensation," an essay published in the same volume as "Self-Reliance," Emerson argues that a mob is not a true society, but only a "society of bodies voluntarily bereaving themselves of reason" (*Essays*, 299).

20. In "Compensation," Emerson writes, "He is base . . . to receive favors and render none. . . . In the order of nature we cannot render benefits to those from whom we receive them, or only seldom. But the benefit we receive must be rendered again, line for line, deed for deed, cent for cent, to somebody" (*Essays*, 295–296). For a discussion of the rise of consensualism and the decline of "reliance" and "benefit" as sources of liability in nineteenth-century England, see P. S. Atiyah, *The Rise and Fall of Freedom of Contract* (Oxford: Clarendon Press, 1979), 455–505.

21. The passage from Barclay cited by Locke runs as follows:

Self defence is a part of the Law of Nature; nor can it be denied the Community, even against the King himself. . . . Wherefore if the King shall shew an hatred, not only to some particular Persons, but sets himself against the Body of the Commonwealth, whereof he is the Head, and shall, with intolerable ill usage, cruelly tyrannize over the whole, or a considerable part of the People; in this case the People have a right to resist and defend themselves from injury: But it must be with this Caution, that they only defend themselves, but do not attack their Prince: They may repair the Damages received, but must not for any provocation exceed the bounds of Reverence and Respect." (*ST*, 420)

22. "Self-reverence" (1835) and "self-respect" (1840) are two variants of "self-reliance" that appear throughout Emerson's sermons, early journals, and letters.

23. Stanley Cavell, *The Senses of Walden* (San Francisco: North Point Press, 1981), 154.

24. The perversity of the questions left unanswered by Emerson in this passage would prompt a famous critical response from Thoreau. Eight years later, in his essay "On the Duty of Civil Disobedience" (originally published under the title "Resistance to Civil Government"), Thoreau emphasizes the necessity of public action, and thus the inadequacy of Emersonian reform as "cheerful self-reliance." By pointing out the uses of visible, public action—not paying his tax and going to jail—as an expressive vehicle for protesting against slavery, Thoreau offered an interpretation of Emerson's ambiguous rhetorical mode that underscored Thoreau's own awareness of the social and moral consequences of Emerson's refusal to speak clearly about slavery.

25. The connection between Emerson's theory of political obligation, disobedience, and the racialist formulation of his nationalism will be fully developed in chapter 6.

26. Compare Emerson's imagining of his own consent to what is presumably an inactive, thoughtful association of true reformers with Thoreau's imagining of an as-

sociation of disobedients whose revolutionary act of withdrawal is in fact compatible with the existence of the state. "I please myself with imagining a State at last," he finds, "which can afford to be just to all men, and to treat the individual with respect as a neighbor; which even would not think it inconsistent with its own repose, if a few were to live aloof from it, not meddling with it, nor embraced by it, who fulfilled all the duties of neighbors and fellow-men" ("Civil Disobedience," *Reform Papers*, ed. Wendell Glick [Princeton: Princeton University Press, 1987], 89–90). The significance of Emerson's early writings on reform and public action—both for Thoreau's subsequent conceptualization of civil disobedience as visible, symbolic action, and for King's philosophy of protest—will be taken up in the concluding pages of this book.

27. The connection established in this passage between the prudence, inaction, and self-reliance as social reform is more fully developed in a later version occurring in Emerson's "Lecture on the Times," read in the subsequent year at the Masonic Temple in Boston:

> I must act with truth, though I should never come to act, as you call it, with effect. I must consent to inaction. A patience which is grand; a brave and cold neglect of the offices which prudence exacts, so it be done in a deep, upper piety; a consent to solitude and inaction, which proceeds out of an unwillingness to violate character, is the century which makes the gem. Whilst therefore I desire to express the respect and joy I feel before this sublime connection of reforms, now in their infancy around us, I urge the more earnestly the paramount duties of self-reliance. (*Essays*, 163)

28. Viewed in these terms, the significance of Emerson's recourse to sentimental values bears interesting comparison to Thoreau's appeal to conscience in "Civil Disobedience." In "Harriet Jacobs, Henry Thoreau, and the Character of Disobedience," (*Harriet Jacobs and Incidents in the Life of a Slave Girl: New Critical Essays* [New York: Cambridge University Press, 1996]) I show that Thoreau's appeal to conscience is coercive, because this appeal entails an assumption of political obligations—obligations that bind him to a nation of disobedients—that cannot be regarded as a purely voluntary act:

> For Thoreau, political obligations and the ties of nationhood are not only voluntarily assumed; they are also, like the bonds of race, born into or found. The language of conversion through which Thoreau describes his experience inside the prison is also used to discover a self-evidently natural and already existing bond, between the white, male disobedient, on the one hand, and the slave or the Mexican or the Indian on the other. . . . Indeed, once again outside the prison, Thoreau goes so far as to insist that he views the white people among whom he lives as "a distinct race from me by their prejudices and superstitions, as the Chinamen and Malays are" (CD, 83). The claim to a status within a race which is "distinct" from the white people among whom he lives is an essential gesture in Thoreau's strategy which has never, to my knowledge, been commented on. Thoreau's recourse to the discourse of race in this brief passage not only allows him to speak on behalf of the oppressed and justify his act of disobedience by the fact of their enslavement, but also allows him to represent and rhetorically ensure the coherence of an exceed-

ingly diverse nation of disobedients in racialist and deceptively unproblematic terms. (245)

Chapter Five

1. In *The Human Condition* (Chicago: University of Chicago Press, 1958), Arendt writes that "[a]ll human activities are conditioned by the fact that men live together, but it is only action that cannot even be imagined outside the society of men," and that "[a]ction alone is the exclusive prerogative of man; neither a beast nor a god is capable of it, and only action is entirely dependent upon the constant presence of others" (22, 23). In *Men in Dark Times* (New York: Harcourt Brace Jovanovich, 1955), she observes that "[w]hen men are deprived of the public space—which is constituted by acting together and then fills of its own accord with the events and stories that develop into history—they retreat into their freedom of thought" (9).

2. For example, Arendt writes of the housebound activity of labor that "[n]othing, to be sure, is more private than the bodily functions of the life process, its fertility not excluded, and it is quite noteworthy that few instances where even a 'socialized mankind' respects and imposes strict privacy concern precisely such 'activities' as are imposed by the life process itself" (*The Human Condition*, 111).

3. Arendt's unwavering adherence to the agonistic political model of the Greek *polis* and her relative lack of emphasis on historical fact seriously limit the usefulness of her model of the public in thinking about contemporary political life. For a thoroughgoing critique of Arendt's model of public space and adherence to Greek thought, see Seyla Benhabib, "Models of Public Space: Hannah Arendt, the Liberal Tradition, and Jurgen Habermas," *Habermas and the Public Sphere*, ed. Craig Calhoun (Cambridge: MIT Press, 1993), 73–98.

4. As a corrective to Arendt's theory of action, which hinges on the relegation of all biologically driven activities to the domestic realm, in *The Body in Pain* Elaine Scarry analyzes some major difficulties that presently exist in publicly speaking about the bodily experience of pain. Elaborating on the political and perceptual complications that arise as a result of those difficulties, Scarry demonstrates the necessary, deep involvement of the body in political life—such as the body's role in certifying and making real political and other socially abstract facts and its importance in transferring reality between the domestic (i.e., privately physical) and political realms. Whereas Arendt fails to prescribe precisely what the modern public ought to look like, Scarry imagines a political world in which people are free to speak meaningfully about their private experience of pain and thus to act upon a shared, unabashedly biological need to keep one another alive. The discovery of essential attributes of expressibility or "making" that follow from Scarry's analysis contribute, in the end, to bridging the gap between imagining a better world and making that world real.

5. In *The Human Condition*, Arendt broaches and then quickly retreats from the subject of friendship when she observes that love is confined to a "narrowly circumscribed sphere." In the public domain of human affairs, Arendt argues, love is replaced by respect, which she defines as "a kind of 'friendship' without intimacy and closeness; it is a regard for the person from the distance which the space of the world puts between us, and this regard is independent of qualities which we may admire or of achievements which we highly esteem" (243).

6. Ralph Waldo Emerson, *The Sermons of Ralph Waldo Emerson*, vol. 3, ed. Ron-

ald Bosco (Columbia: University of Missouri Press, 1991), 77. Subsequent references
are to *Sermons* and will be cited parenthetically by sermon number. There have been
some very interesting studies that deal with Emerson's ministry and sermonic rhetoric.
See Susan Roberson, "The Private Voice behind the Public Text: Two Emerson Ser-
mons," *ESQ: A Journal of the American Renaissance* 32, 3rd quarter (1986), 173–82;
Yukio Irie, *Emerson and Quakerism* (Tokyo: Kenkyusha, 1967); Sue Kelsey Tester,
"Ralph Waldo Emerson's Sermons: A Critical Introduction" (Ph.D. dissertation, Boston University, 1978); David Robinson, *Apostle of Culture: Emerson as Preacher and
Lecturer* (Philadelphia: University of Pennsylvania Press, 1982); and Wesley Mott, *The
Strains of Eloquence: Emerson and His Sermons* (University Park: Pennsylvania State
University Press, 1989). For a more general discussion of how Unitarian moral and
aesthetic values helped to shape the American Renaissance, see Lawrence Buell, *Literary Transcendentalism: Style and Vision in the American Renaissance* (Ithaca, NY: Cornell University Press, 1973).

7. It is possible that Emerson was creating a double standard for girls when he
insisted that it is the aim of education to make children wise, not learned: "And it
may be the effect of a too exclusive attention to the outer faculties of one of your
pupils, that when she is grown up, she shall be a fairfaced enemy, an ingenious liar, a
very dextrous cheat, or elegantly licentious,—which God forbid" (*Sermons*, CXXVIII,
227).

8. Emerson's effort to imagine a model of obligation and Christian community
was driven by a need to ensure his own strictest obedience to God's law as the necessary
precondition to discovering the full extent of his creative powers.

9. Plato, *Lysis*, trans. W. Lamb (Cambridge: Harvard University Press, 1925).
Subsequent references are to this edition and will be cited parenthetically.

10. For example, see *Plato's Dialogue on Friendship: An Interpretation of the Lysis,
with a New Translation* (Ithaca: Cornell University Press, 1979), in which David Bol-
otin concludes, "We are left to wonder about a perfect friendship, independent of
wants and needs, which seems not to exist, and an imperfect one, admittedly depending
on need, which fails to account for the whole phenomenon of friendship. . . . The
dialogue seems to offer no resolution of this perplexity. . . . Instead, it encourages us to
seek clarity on our own" (12).

11. The drama of seduction begins when Socrates first sees Lysis "with a garland
on his head . . . , deserving not merely the name of well-favored, but also of well-made
and well bred." Socrates observes that Lysis was "obviously eager to join us," but "too
shy to approach us alone; till Mexenus stepped in for a moment . . . and . . . came to
take a seat beside us" (*Lysis*, 19). Once Socrates has had the opportunity to speak
privately with Lysis, the bonds of intimacy between teacher and student become visible
to the reader: "Then Lysis, in a most playful, affectionate manner, unobserved by
Menexenus, said softly to me: Socrates, tell Menexenus what you have been saying to
me" (*Lysis*, 31).

12. Aristotle, *Nicomachean Ethics*, trans. Terence Irwin (Indianapolis: Hackett
Publishers, 1985). Subsequent references are to this edition and will be cited parenthetically.

13. Although Stoic philosophers generally dismissed friendship as a form of egoism, Epicurus and his followers emphasized the value and significance of friendship as
being intimately associated with human freedom. As Orlando Patterson observes in
his recent study of freedom (*Freedom in the Making of Western Culture* [New York: Basic
Books, 1991]),

Epicurus felt strongly that a crucial part of the return to our real, spontaneous, and humanly free selves involved a return with others of like mind. Hence his strong emphasis on friendship with kindred free spirits. Friendship is an intrinsically good value and is critically linked to human freedom; like all such values, it is ultimately based on pleasure. This does not exclude altruism, for, as Plutarch pointed out, Epicurus felt that it was "more pleasurable to confer a benefit than to receive one." The emphasis on friendship is tied to the central role of freedom in their ethics. (190)

14. Cicero, *De Amicitia*, trans. William A. Falconer (Cambridge: Harvard University Press, 1923). Subsequent references are to this edition and will be cited parenthically.

15. In 1597, Francis Bacon's "Of Friendship" first appeared in his *Essays*, offering insight into friendship as the promoter of peace in the affections, as a valuable support to judgment, as a form of immortality, and especially as a threat to the safety and greatness of kings. But the Renaissance essayist who represents the profoundest influence upon Emerson's thinking about friendship is Montaigne.

16. Michel de Montaigne, "Of Friendship," *The Complete Essaays of Montaigne*, trans. Donald M. Frame (Stanford: Stanford University Press, 1965), 135–144. Subsequent references are to OF and will be cited parenthetically.

17. For a largely biographical discussion of Emerson's interest in Montaigne, see Charles Lowell Young, *Emerson's Montaigne* (New York: Macmillan, 1941).

18. Carole Pateman presents a clear and illuminating discussion of these two conceptually distinct stages of the liberal social contract in *The Problem of Political Obligation: A Critique of Liberal Theory* (Berkeley: Unviersity of California Press, 1979), 68–72.

19. John Locke, *Two Treatises of Government*, ed. Peter Laslett (Cambridge: Cambridge University Press), 347–348.

20. The notion that political obligations are tacitly assumed by the voluntary or willed movement of the body along a public highway has been used as an effective means of retaining a powerful voluntarist justification for the relationship of obligation—a justification that, viewed in historical terms, has proved to be a necessary conceptual barrier to social injustice. In a recent study of free movement, Elaine Scarry explores the importance of willed bodily movement in social contract theory and, in particular, in Locke's description of the citizen's tacit consent as "consent . . . [that] is detached from property rights and attached to the voluntary motion of 'travelling freely on the highway'" ("The Railway Emergency Brake: the Use of Analogy in Legal and Political Argument," chapter 4 in *The Matter of Consent*. Paper delivered at Law and Literature Seminar, Center for Literary and Cultural Studies, Harvard University, March 1991). For Scarry, the importance of consent defined as willed movement extends well beyond her examination of the technological example or materialization of consent—"the train with its quiet but conspicuous emergency brake"—that she selects. Tacit as voluntary consent is conceptually necessary for Scarry's larger project, the examination of the "radical building-out of consent from the interior structure of nuclear weapons, and the restructuring of political life that results," because, as she points out, this is a situation in which members of the population have lost authority over their ability to tacitly consent and hence their authority over the willed movement of their bodies.

21. The incapacity for movement (and for action) as described by Arendt is thus closely associated with dishonor, which Orlando Patterson has more recently identified as a constituent element of slavery. See Orlando Patterson, *Slavery and Social Death: A Comparative Study* (Cambridge: Harvard University Press, 1982), 11. For a sociohistorical account of freedom as a cultural value that shows the inaccuracy of Arendt's account of free movement as the oldest and most elementary of liberties, see *Freedom in the Making of Western Culture*.

22. This contradiction between voluntarily and involuntarily assumed obligations that structures Emerson's thinking about friendship—and, in particular, his insistence on the tenacity and validity of involuntarily assumed obligations owed to one's "natural" friends or family—calls our attention back to Emerson's critical response to Montaigne's earlier essay on the subject. In "Of Friendship," Montaigne contends that the ancient type of natural friendship that exists between family members should not be considered true friendship. According to Montaigne, children should feel respect and not friendship toward their fathers because of their natural, existing condition of inequality. Montaigne writes, "For neither can all the secret thoughts of fathers be communicated to children lest this beget an unbecoming intimacy, nor could the admonitions and corrections, which are one of the chief duties of friendship, be administered by children to fathers" (OF, 136). Similarly, with respect to natural friendship that develops between brothers, Montaigne argues that the confusion of ownership and the fact that "the richness of one is the poverty of the other, wonderfully softens and loosens the solder of brotherhood. Father and son may be of entirely different dispositions, and brothers also. He is my son, he is my kinsman, but he is an unsociable man, a knave, or a fool" (OF, 136–137).

In his flat-out rejection of this ancient type of natural, familial friendship, Montaigne moves instead to a wholly voluntaristic definition of friendship between kin. "Why should the harmony and kinship which begets these true and perfect friendships be found in them?" he demands. "And then, the more they are friendships which law and natural obligation impose on us, the less of our choice and free will is there in them. And our free will has no product more properly its own than affection and friendship" (OF, 136–137). Although he insists that obligations associated with what he identifies as a "more equitable and more equable kind of friendship" may be assumed by an involuntary, "inexplicable and fateful force" (OF, 139), Montaigne ultimately concludes that, in general, the obligations associated with friendship must be freely and voluntarily assumed.

23. In *Literary Transcendentalism: Style and Vision in the American Renaissance* (Ithaca, N.Y.: Cornell University Press, 1973), Lawrence Buell observes that there is a "certain tension or rivalry at the heart of friendship" in Thoreau's writings. Although Thoreau is wary of strangers, Buell suggests that his "disdain . . . seems to mask a greater longing for friendship than that of Emerson. . . . [Thoreau] has known the pain of loss, and the pain of misunderstanding . . . , but still he clings to the vision of an ideal human relationship" (*Literary Transcendentalism*, 228). For a useful discussion of Emerson's "Friendship," which examines the uses of friendship as a means of establishing a "reciprocity" between society and solitude, see George Kateb, *Emerson and Self-Reliance* (Thousand Oaks, Calif.: SAGE Publications, 1995), 96–114.

24. Henry David Thoreau, *A Week on the Concord and Merrimack Rivers*, ed. Robert F. Sayre (New York: Library of America, 1985). Subsequent references are to *A Week* and will be cited parenthetically.

25. Henry David Thoreau, "Civil Disobedience," *Reform Papers*, ed. Wendell Glick (Princeton: Princeton University Press, 1973), 89–90. Subsequent references are to CD and will be cited parenthetically.

Chapter Six

1. Compare Elaine Scarry's analysis of John Donne's poetry in *Literature and the Body: Essays on Populations and Persons* (Baltimore: Johns Hopkins University Press, 1988), in which she argues, "This, finally, is Donne's most characteristic reflex, to bring forward the human hand at moments of both desire and repulsion; to say, but yet he is my friend" (97).

2. Precise definition and analysis of the significance of "nationhood," "nationality," and "nationalism" have proved to be notoriously difficult tasks. Only the difficulty and necessity of the effort to define these terms seem beyond dispute. As Benedict Anderson has observed, "nation-ness is the most universally legitimate value in the political life of our time." See *Imagined Communities: Reflections on the Origin and Spread of Nationalism* (London: Verso Press, 1983), 12.

3. In *Freedom and Fate: An Inner Life of Ralph Waldo Emerson* Philadelphia: University of Pennsylvania Press, (1953) Stephen Whicher argues that Emerson's belief in "a radical recovery of natural freedom" (50), which he expresses in his early writings, shifts later in his career toward a new, increasingly organic, evolutionary point of view. "Emerson's submission to a sublime and friendly Destiny grew up in his mind in close association with a changed attitude toward nature, one which went hand in hand with his whole shift away from egoism," Whicher writes. "The cause of this shift was . . . the entrance into his thought of a new way of conceiving nature, the general idea of evolution" (141). What Whicher describes as an evolutionary point of view represents, more specifically, a concern with race. As we shall see, this concern is central to the theory of self and society offered throughout Emerson's career, even in his earliest writings.

4. Orlando Patterson has more recently raised a similar argument to critique this concept of property as a "bundle of powers"—a concept that was first developed by the Romans and that persists within present day legal and socioeconomic structures. Insisting that this notion of property is in no way required by modern capitalism and that there can be no direct relationship between the growing complexity of property and the growing complexity of socioeconomic systems, Patterson writes, "The whole weight of Anglo-American jurisprudence, as well as the sociology and economics of property, comes down heavily against the validity of such a concept. Why is this? Because, first, in sociological and economic terms (as in the view of common law) there can be no relation between a person and a thing. Relations only exist between persons. Second, relations between persons with respect to some object are always relative, never absolute." See *Slavery and Social Death*, 20–21.

5. Theophilus Parsons, *The Political, Personal, and Property Rights of a Citizen of the U.S.* (Cincinnati, Ohio: National Publishing Co., 1876), 3.

6. John Hopkins, *The American Citizen: His Rights and Duties, According to the Spirit of the Constitution of the United States* (New York: Pudney and Russell, 1857), 457, 459.

7. George Smith, *The Law of Private Right* (New York: Humbolt Publishing Co., 1890); A. Jenkins Williard, *An Examination of the Law of Personal Rights* (New York: D. Appleton and Co., 1882); Oliver Barbour, *A Treatise of the Rights of Persons and the*

Rights of Property (Rochester, N.Y.: Williamson Law Book Co., 1890); Francis Lieber, *Manual of Political Ethics* (Boston: C.C. Little and J. Brown, 1838).

8. Benjamin Oliver, *The Rights of An American Citizen* (Boston: Marsh, Capen and Lyon, 1832); David McConaugy, *The Nature and Origin of Civil Liberty* (Gettysburg, Penn.: J. Lefever, 1823); James Stewart, *The Rights of Persons* (London: E. Spettigue, 1839).

9. *Writings of John Quincy Adams*, ed. W. Ford (New York: Macmillan, 1913), 359–360.

10. "The Texas Question," *Democratic Review*, 14 (April, 1844), 427, 429.

11. "Our Indian Policy," *Democratic Review*, 14 (February, 1844), 174.

12. "Mexico," *Democratic Review* 18 (June, 1846), 434.

13. "Thayendanegea," *Democratic Review* 3 (October, 1838), 129.

14. "Our Indian Policy," 171.

15. "Thayendanegea," 114.

16. In "Self-Reliance," published five years after *Nature*, Emerson's disruptive call to revolution requires his explicit reference to the body in his efforts to imagine a racially cohesive and circumscribed nation: "[L]et us enter the state of war," he writes, "and wake Thor and Woden, courage and constancy, in our Saxon breasts" (*Essays*, 273). In "Self-Reliance," Emerson performs a call to the disruptive act of casting off ties to the state. In so doing, he is faced with the problem of constructing a position from which to articulate this call. If, for Emerson, the very act of exhorting his readers to enter the state of war is one that marks the sundering of all social ties, this exhortation also calls into question the nature and existence of the community that he addresses and his own position in relation to that community. What Emerson's reference to the Anglo-Saxon body in "Self-Reliance" suggests is that in the rhetorical act of casting off ties to the state, only the ties of race remain as a means of imagining the political community he addresses. The brief but crucial allusion to "our Saxon breasts" in "Self-Reliance" simultaneously describes a coherent, racialist concept of nationhood and expresses the act of withdrawal from Britain as a state.

17. Ralph Waldo Emerson, "Anglo Saxon" (Manuscript bMS Am 1280.202 [1], Houghton Library, Harvard University, 1853). Publication by permission of the Ralph Waldo Emerson Memorial Association and of Houghton Library, Harvard University.

18. Ralph Waldo Emerson, *English Traits*, in *Essays and Lectures*, ed. J. Porte (New York: Library of America, 1983), 806. Subsequent references are to *ET* and will be cited parenthetically.

19. For a discussion of how the belief in the superiority of early Anglo-Saxon political institutions held during the revolutionary era evolved into a belief in the innate superiority of the Anglo-Saxon race, see Reginald Horsman's *Race and Manifest Destiny: The Origins of American Racial Anglo-Saxonism* (Cambridge: Harvard University Press, 1981). Subsequent references are to *RMD* and will be cited parenthetically.

20. Thomas Jefferson, *Summary View of the Rights of British America* (Delmar, N.Y.: Scholars' Facsimiles and Reprints, 1976).

21. As Gordon Wood has observed in *The Creation of the American Republic, 1776–1787* (New York: Norton, 1969), "in the minds of most Whigs in 1776 individual rights, even the basic civil liberties that we consider so crucial, possessed little of their modern theoretical relevance when set against the will of the people. This is why, for example, throughout the eighteenth century the Americans could contend for the broadest freedom of speech against the magistracy, while at the same time

punishing with a severe strictness any seditious libels against the representatives of the people in the colonial assemblies" (63).

22. Thomas Paine, *Rights of Man*, ed. H. Collins (New York: Penguin, 1984), 40.

23. Elisha Mulford, *The Nation: The Foundations of Civil Order and Political Life in the United States* (New York: Hurd and Houghton, 1870). Subsequent references are to *Nation* and will be cited parenthetically.

24. In *Nations and Nationalism Since 1780* (New York: Cambridge University Press, 1990), E. J. Hobsbawm argues that nineteenth-century liberals who accepted the arguments of classical political economy would recognize the economic significance of nations far more readily in practice than they could in theory. Because classical economic theories such as Adam Smith's were "elaborated uniquely on the basis of individual units of enterprise," Hobsbawm suggests that the markets such theories described had no clear spatial limits. "At the limit was, and could not but be, the world market" (26). In part, Emerson's dissatisfaction with the liberal theory of nations stems from the fact that the nation it describes is not clearly defined in spatial terms.

25. Ralph Waldo Emerson, "Permanent Traits of English National Genius" (Manuscript bMS Am 1280.195 [3], Houghton Library, Harvard University, 1835), 42. Subsequent references are to "Permanent Traits" and will be cited parenthetically. Published by permission of the Ralph Waldo Emerson Memorial Association and of Houghton Library, Harvard University.

26. Robert Chambers, *Vestiges of Creation* (New York, 1845); Johann Friedrich Blumenbach, *On the Natural Variety of Races* (London: Longman, 1865).

27. Charles Pickering, *Races of Man* (Boston: C.C. Little and J. Brown, 1848); Robert Knox, *The Races of Men: A Philosophical Enquiry into the Influence of Race over the Destinies of Nations* (London: H. Renshaw, 1850).

28. Ralph Waldo Emerson, *Conduct of Life*, in *Essays and Lectures*, ed. J. Porte (New York: Library of America, 1983), 937–1124. Subsequent references are to *CL* and will be cited parenthetically.

29. Ralph Waldo Emerson, "American Nationality" (Manuscript bMS Am 1280.206 [12], Houghton Library, Harvard University, 1861), 58, 41. Published by permission of the Ralph Waldo Emerson Memorial Association and of Houghton Library, Harvard University.

30. As in *English Traits*, in *Conduct of Life* Emerson refers to the racial theory of Robert Knox, although his selection of quotations from Knox's treatise indicates that Emerson seems to have reversed his position on the subject of racial hybridization: "Nature respects race, and not hybrids." "Every race has its own *habitat*." "Detach a colony from the race, and it deteriorates to the crab" (*CL*, 950). In *Emerson on Race and History: An Examination of English Traits* (New York: Columbia University Press, 1961), Philip Nicoloff speculates that Emerson had studied the work of theorists such as Henri Lecoq, Dominique-Alexandre Godron, and Charles-Victor Naudin in France, or of Josiah Nott and Samuel Morton in America, who had observed that hybrid varieties were inherently unstable and over successive generations tended to revert to parental types. "While hybridization was an immense initial asset in the founding of a nation," Nicoloff writes, "it was no final protection against nature's irresistible decree that all cultivated life must experience a lapse from power" (129).

31. In *Conduct of Life* the contradictory gesture of repudiation and affirmation that characterizes Emerson's early meditations on the subject of property reemerges, and some passages reveal his careful scrutiny and revision of early journal notes. In 1839, Emerson noted that "[i]t is a noble fact that Heeven refers in his 'Greece,' that

in that country every statue & painting was public, it being considered as absurd & profane to pretend property in a Work of Art,—which belonged to whosoever could see it" (*JMN*, VII, 310), and in the essay "Wealth," he writes, "In the Greek cities, it was reckoned profane, that any person should pretend a property in a work of art, which belonged to all who could behold it. . . . If properties of this kind were owned by states, towns, and lyceums, they would draw the bonds of neighborhood closer" (996). In the essay "Culture," written in 1860, Emerson recasts an 1850 journal entry that, as we have seen, sets forth the contradiction "I must have an intellectual property in all property and in all action. . . . But . . . , I must also have them not (so to speak)," a decade later arguing that "[w]e must have an intellectual quality in all property and in all action, or they are nought. I must have children, I must have events, I must have social state and history, or my thinking and speaking want body or basis. But to give these accessories any value, I must know them as contingent and rather showy possessions, which pass for more to the people than to me" (*CL*, 1029).

32. Emerson's shift in emphasis from property to freedom is a response to what I have already identified in chapter 2 as the referential ambiguities of nineteenth-century rights discourse—the habitual slip from Locke's concept of self-ownership to popular justifications of ownership of slaves in proslavery argument. More recently, in an attempt to come to a definitive statement of the fundamental processes of slavery, the sociologist Orlando Patterson has developed a dialectical model that describes a "ghost" concept of freedom, a concept that is roughly analogous to the concept of liberty Emerson discovers in "Fate." See *Slavery and Social Death: A Comparative Study* (Cambridge: Harvard University Press, 1982), 341–342.

33. In this connection, we should note that in his later writings Emerson's confrontation with racial science and his recognition of the conceptual necessity of race lead him to propound an antislavery argument in racist terms. In an 1844 journal entry, he argues that "[i]f the black man is feeble & not important to existing races, not on a par with the best race, the black man must serve & be sold & exterminated. But if the black man carries in his bosom an undispensible element of a new & coming civilization, for the sake of that element no wrong nor strength nor circumstance can hurt him, he will survive & play his part. So now it seems to me that the arrival of such men as Toussaint if he is pure blood, or of Douglass, if he is pure blood, outweighs all the English & American humanity" (*JMN*, IX, 123–5).

34. In an effort to demonstrate that Emerson's writings underwrite the defense of proceeding in philosophy from ordinary language, Stanley Cavell points out a relationship between the process of finding a self in Emerson's "Experience" and the act of founding a nation: "The endlessly repeated idea that Emerson was only interested in finding the individual should give way or make way for the idea that this quest was his way of founding a nation" (*This New yet Unapproachable America: Lectures after Emerson After Wittgenstein* [Albuquerque: Living Batch Press, 1989], 93). Subsequent references are to *New yet* and will be cited parenthetically.). Whereas Cavell emphasizes the *finding* or birth of a self and a nation in Emerson's "Experience," in *The American Evasion of Philosophy*, Cornel West suggests that Emerson shares the future-oriented instrumentalism of American pragmatists such as William James and John Dewey—the assumption that identity is *made* or socially constructed. The fact of Emerson's availability to philosophical positions as diverse as those represented by Cavell and West demonstrates the extent to which the contradiction between the invented and the organic structures Emerson's thinking about identity. For a critical discussion of the way in which West's own rhetoric and analysis of the genealogy of

American pragmatism exhibits this characteristically Emersonian mode of contradiction between organicism and rupture, see Robert Gooding-Williams, "Evading Narrative Myth, Evading Prophetic Pragmatism: Cornel West's *The American Evasion of Philosophy*," *The Massachusetts Review* 35 (Winter 1991), 517–542.

35. Stanley Cavell's insight into this passage—his claim, put forward in *This New yet Unapproachable America*, that Emerson's finding of a self in "Experience" directly relates to the cultural process of nation-building—thus fits well with the connection I am making here between Emerson's nationalism and his development of a full-blown philosophy of obligation. But whereas Cavell emphasizes Emerson's inheritance of ordinary language philosophies by Austin and Wittgenstein, I am interested in the way in which Emerson's writings represent a cultural critique of Lockean contractarianism as the mainstay of Anglo-American political philosophy.

Chapter Seven

1. For a variety of useful literary, historical, and sociological approaches to the subject, see Henry Louis Gates, Jr., ed., *"Race," Writing, and Difference* (Chicago: University of Chicago Press, 1986); David Theo Goldberg, ed., *Anatomy of Racism* (Minneapolis: University of Minnesota Press, 1990); Dominick LaCapra, ed., *The Bounds of Race: Perspectives on Hegemony and Resistance* (Ithaca, N.Y.: Cornell University Press, 1991); William Julius Wilson, *The Declining Significance of Race: Blacks and Changing American Institutions* (Chicago: University of Chicago Press, 1978); and Gerald Jaynes and Robin Williams, eds., *A Common Destiny: Blacks and American Society* (Washington, D.C.: National Academy Press, 1989).

2. W. E. B. Du Bois, *Dusk of Dawn: An Essay toward an Autobiography of a Race Concept* (New York: Schocken Books, 1940), 116. Subsequent references are to *DD* and will be cited parenthetically.

3. Anthony Appiah, *In My Father's House: Africa and the Philosophy of Culture* (New York: Oxford University Press, 1992), 30. Subsequent references are to *In My Father's House* and will be cited parenthetically.

4. In an earlier essay, Appiah argues for the limited applicability of Du Bois's theoretical framework and concludes by "adumbrating the argument he never quite managed to complete. . . . The truth is that there are no races: there is nothing in the world that can do all we ask 'race' to do for us. . . . What we miss through our obsession with the structure of relations of concepts is, simply, reality" ("The Uncompleted Argument: Du Bois and the Illusion of Race," *"Race," Writing, and Difference*, ed. Henry Louis Gates, Jr. [Chicago: University of Chicago Press, 1986], 35).

5. Kimberly Benston, "I Yam What I Am: The Topos of (Un)Naming in Afro-American Literature," *black Literature and Literary Theory*, ed. Henry Louis Gates, Jr. (New York: Routledge, 1990), 170. For a discussion of William James's influence on Du Bois's theory of double-consciousness, see Arnold Rampersad, *The Art and Imagination of W. E. B. Du Bois* (New York: Schocken Books, 1976), 74. Like James, Du Bois believes that identity has many facets, and that consciousness of self is in some respects socially constructed because it involves being recognized by others. But as I show in the course of this book, Du Bois's theory of double-consciousness is also a radical departure from James's psychology, insofar as Du Bois, like Emerson, uses nationalist, democratic, and racialist discourses to describe what he regards as fundamental aspects of identity.

6. Cornel West, *The American Evasion of Philosophy: A Genealogy of Pragmatism*

(Madison, Wisc.: University of Wisconsin Press, 1989), 142. I agree with West, who emphasizes the important differences between Emersonian and Du Boisian double-consciousness and insists that whereas, for Emerson, "being an American was not a problem but rather a unique occasion to exercise human powers to solve problems[,] Du Bois's 'double-consciousness' views this unique occasion as the *cause* of a problem." I would also add that Du Bois's articulation of the contradictory claims of rights and race in *The Conservation of Races* is an act that rhetorically transforms a state of potential disempowerment into a powerful and unifying construct: "The American Negro." Du Bois's invention of a name for this contradiction as "double-consciousness," a name that like "The American Negro," reaches an area of experience that was previously inaccessible to language, is an act that rhetorically realizes the national unity Du Bois imagines in his writings. Compare Thomas Holt's contention that "the logic of Du Bois's formulation suggests a radical proposition: that African-Americans should celebrate their alienation, for it is a source of 'second-sight in this American world.' Although Du Bois implies in the 1903 version of the paradox the eventual resolution of the divided self in historical time . . . , much of what he writes later suggests that African-Americans accept, even embrace, the contradiction and paradox arising from dual identities and consciousness" ("The Political Uses of Alienation: W. E. B. Du Bois on Politics, Race, and Culture, 1903–1940," *American Quarterly* 42 [June 1990], 306).

7. See W. E. B. Du Bois, *Against Racism: Unpublished Essays, Papers, Addresses, 1887-1961*, ed. H. Aptheker (Amherst, Mass.: University of Massachusetts Press, 1985), 320; and Du Bois *Selections from the Horizon*, ed. H. Aptheker (White Plains, N.Y.: Kraus-Thomson Organization Limited, 1985), 44, 52.

8. W. E. B. Du Bois, "The Contribution of the Negro to American Life and Culture," *Pacific Review* 2 (June 1921), 127–132; Du Bois, "The Negro as a National Asset," *Homiletic Review* 86 (July 1923), 52–58

9. *The Correspondence of W. E. B. Du Bois*, ed. H. Aptheker (Amherst: University of Massachusetts Press, 1973), 149.

10. W. E. B. Du Bois, "Does Education Pay?" *Writings of W. E. B. Du Bois in Periodicals Edited by Others*, vol. 1, 1891–1909, ed. Herbert Aptheker (Millwood N.Y.: Kraus-Thomson, 1981) 3–4. Subsequent references are to DEP and will be cited parenthetically.

11. W. E. B. Du Bois, "Postgraduate Work in Sociology at Atlanta University," *Against Racism: Unpublished Essays, Papers, Addresses, 1887–1961*, ed. Herbert Aptheker (Amherst: University of Massachusetts Press, 1985), 66–67.

12. As both John Hope Franklin and Wilson Jeremiah Moses have shown, the Compromise of 1850—and, in particular, the Fugitive Slave Law—was central to the development of American black nationalisms, insofar as it stimulated the proliferation of emigration schemes. See Wilson Jeremiah Moses, *The Golden Age of Black Nationalism, 1850–1925* (New York: Oxford University Press, 1978), and John Hope Franklin, *Reconstruction: After the Civil War* (Chicago: University of Chicago Press, 1961).

13. For example, in "Hope for Africa," a sermon preached in England on behalf of the Ladies' Negro Education society in 1852, Crummell's racialism is obviously distinguishable from that of his white contemporaries insofar as he attributes a divine destiny to the Negro as well as to the Anglo-Saxon race. "First of all, the Negro race possesses strong vital power . . . ," he insists; "in the second place, . . . God has given this race a *strong moral character* . . . [and], in the last place, . . . in His gifts of nature and in His preserving favor upon my race, we may see the training hand of God upon them, in all their scattered homes, for high ends and purposes, in the future." (*Future*

of Africa [New York: Negro Universities Press, 1962], 319, 230, 321. Subsequent citations are to FOA and will be cited parenthetically). For a thoroughgoing discussion of Crummell's views on race, see Appiah's *In My Father's House*, 3–27.

14. Crummell writes, "For you will remember that the first anniversaries of this Republic have passed away, and the warm exhuberence of new-born nationality has given place to care, to thought, to the consciousness of burdened duty, the weight of national responsibility, and the heavy cares of citizenship and government" (FOA, 58).

15. Adam Smith, *Inquiry into the Nature and Causes of the Wealth of Nations* (Chicago: University of Chicago Press, 1976), 477

16. As E. J. Hobsbawm has argued, theoretical frameworks such as Adam Smith's, which emphasize the significance of free trade and a market that has no specific spatial extension, preclude the conceptual possibility of clear and distinct boundaries between nations. What Hobsbawm suggests is that classical economic theory, which was "elaborated uniquely on the basis of individual units of enterprise . . . in a market which had no specific spatial extension" had no place for the nation: "At the limit was, and could not but be, the world market" (*Nations and Nationalism Since 1780: Programme, Myth, Reality* [New York: Cambridge University Press, 1990], 26).

17. Crummell thus participates in a philosophical tradition that, as I show in the final chapter of this book, extends to Thoreau's (and ultimately King's) deliberations on the role of conscience in "Civil Disobedience." In this connection, it is striking to note that whereas in "Civil Disobedience" Thoreau argues for the existence of a conscience that is both personal and corporate, Crummell writes in "The Duty of a Rising Christian State" that "[w]e cannot, indeed, speak of the conscience of a nation; for conscience is so personal a quality, that it is only by a strong figure of speech that we can apply it to nations. But all those moral qualities which are subsidiary to conscience are so manifestly brought out and recognized in all, even the minutest, acts and offices of government, that is but a bare, distinct verity, and no metaphor, to speak of the moral duties and obligations of nations" (FOA, 65).

18. W. E. B. Du Bois, "The Conservation of Races," *W. E. B. Du Bois Speaks: Speeches and Addresses, 1890–1919*, ed. P. Foner (New York: Pathfinder Press, 1970), 74. Subsequent references are to CR and will be cited parenthetically.

19. Paradoxically, Du Bois's repudiation of Emerson's call for cultural as national unity—a call that, as we have seen in "The American Scholar," promotes the idea of an original, monolithic, and homogenous American culture of letters—results in an equally monolithic concept of a "Negro nation" possessed of "Negro literature and art." "Negroes . . . are a nation, stored with wonderful possibilities of culture, [and] their destiny is not a servile imitation of Anglo-Saxon culture, but a stalwart originality which shall unswervingly follow Negro ideals," Du Bois writes. "For the development of Negro genius, of Negro literature and art, of Negro spirit, only Negroes bound and welded together, Negroes inspired by one vast ideal, can work out in its fulness the great message we have for humanity" (CR, 79). In this respect, Du Bois's "Conservation of Races" reproduces Emerson's nationalist rhetoric in "The American Scholar," in which Emerson calls for a symbolic break from Britain.

20. The rhetorical, typological significance Du Bois assigns to women in "The Conservation of Races" recurs throughout his writings. For example, in "The Damnation of Women" (*Darkwater: Voices from within the Veil* [Millwood, N.Y.: Kraus-Thomson Organization Limited, 1975], 185), Du Bois calls attention to the central role of women, "who had freedom thrust upon them," in the shaping of national identity:

With that freedom they are buying an untrammeled independence and dear as is the price they pay for it, it will in the end be worth every taunt and groan. We have still our poverty and degradation, our lewdness and cruel toil; but we have, too, a vast group of women of Negro blood who for strength of character, cleanness of soul, and unselfish devotion of purpose, is today easily the peer of any group of women in the civilized world. . . . No other women on earth could have emerged from the hell of force and temptation which once engulfed and still surrounds black women in America with half the modesty and womanliness they retain. (185)

Viewed in the context of his nationalist writing as a whole, Du Bois's relatively limited rendering of black women's subjectivity—the narrow, typological significance he assigns to them throughout his writings—is a gesture which in turn opens the possibility for critique and the production of models of African-American identity in which *both* gender *and* race play a central role. I am thinking in particular of Nella Larsen's novels, *Quicksand* and *Passing*, which explore difficulties that both race and gender present for the formation of identity as double-consciousness. For Larsen, double-consciousness is experienced as a painful moment of hesitating between contradictory poles or aspects of the self; as a destructive process in which identity is achieved only as the habitual negation of social ties.

21. It is not until *Dusk of Dawn* that Du Bois records a sea change in the function and formal expression of his nationalism, and reveals a markedly increased interest in an internationally expansive model of Pan-Africanism that largely eclipses the concern with African-American identity registered in his earlier writings. Compare Thomas Holt's suggestion that in *Dusk of Dawn* Du Bois recognizes "the international dimensions of the racial conflict, indeed, that African-Americans could be the vanguard of an international assault on class privilege" ("The Political Uses of Alienation: W. E. B. Du Bois on Politics, Race, and Culture, 1903–1940," *American Quarterly* 42 [June 1990], 310). Subsequent references are to "The Political Uses of Alienation" and will be cited parenthetically.

22. W. E. B. Du Bois, *The Souls of Black Folk*, in *Three Negro Classics* (New York: Avon Books, 1965), 215. Subsequent references are to *Souls* and will be cited parenthetically. This description of Du Boisian double-consciousness shows the influence of William James's writings on consciousness of self. As James once observed, "A man's *Social Self* is the recognition which he get from his mates. . . . Properly speaking, *a man has as many social selves as there are individuals who recognize him and carry an image of him* in their mind" (*Principles of Psychology*, vol. 1 [New York: Dover Publications, 1918], 293, 294).

23. As in Du Bois's nationalist nonfiction prose writings, in his novel *The Quest of the Silver Fleece* (Millwood, N.Y.: Kraus-Thomson Organization, 1974) Du Bois also makes a simultaneous, contradictory appeal to raciality and rights. The novel depicts the cultivation of swampland by Blessed Alwyn and Zora, two lovers who eventually become man and wife, and their symbolic quest toward economic uplift: the establishment of a right to property in the land which they till with their own hands. The white Veil woven from the cotton they raise, and which Zora wears on her wedding day, is not only a Christian symbol of purity; it is also emblematic of a collective right to property. What Du Bois's description of the Veil suggests is that his model of African-American identity is both inextricable from racial identity and also transcends it: we are told that as Zora drapes the shimmering white cloth around her body, she is awed by her experience of "a living new born self" (231).

24. Booker T. Washington, *Up from Slavery*, in *Three Negro Classics* (New York: Avon Books, 1965), 25–205. Subsequent references are to this edition and will be cited parenthetically. Published in 1901, this self-told account of Washington's life is essentially the compilation of a series of articles he wrote for the *Outlook* and ended up being a much more successful work than his first attempt at autobiography published the previous year.

25. Accounts of the disagreement between Washington and Du Bois may be found in Louis Harlan, *Booker T. Washington: The Wizard of Tuskegee* (New York: Oxford University Press, 1983), and August Meier, *Negro Thought in America, 1880–1915: Racial Ideologies in the Age of Booker T. Washington* (Ann Arbor: University of Michigan Press, 1990). See also *Long Black Song* (Charlottesville: University Press of Virginia, 1972), in which Houston Baker addresses the conceptual and rhetorical complexities of Du Bois's "cultured contempt for Washington" (102).

26. A recent discussion of Washington's *Up from Slavery* that shows the applicability of his philosophy for present debates over civil rights policy and racial progress in America may be found in Glenn Loury, *One by One from the Inside Out: Essays and Reviews on Race and Responsibility in America* (New York: Free Press, 1995), 63–82. For an account of how Martin Luther King rejected Washington's strategy of "passive acceptance," see John Ansbro, *Martin Luther King, Jr.: The Making of a Mind* (Maryknoll, N.Y.: Orbis Books, 1982), 198–204.

27. For example, in his 1891 Tuskegee commencement address, Washington observed:

> It is said of Ralph Waldo Emerson, the great philosopher, that at one time one of his friends noticed him standing near a window seemingly intently gazing at something in the distance. When the question was asked, "What are you looking for, Mr. Emerson?" the answer came, "I am trying to find Ralph Waldo Emerson." Ladies and gentlemen ... I would remind you to remember Emerson's reply. Find yourselves as often as possible. (*The Booker T. Washington Papers*, vol. 3, ed. Louis Harlan [Urbana: University of Illinois Press, 1972], 487)

28. On this point, see Harlan's *Booker T. Washington*, 275–276. Years later, Ralph Ellison would describe Washington as an ardent devotee of Emerson in his fictionalized account of Tuskegee in *Invisible Man*.

29. In this connection, it is interesting to note that, like Emerson, in *Up from Slavery* Washington engages in a critique of Lockean property. But in stark contrast to Emerson, who questions ownership by juxtaposing religious (and later racialist) ideas with Locke's definition of property, Washington's recasting of Lockean property involves the question of what property and ownership could properly mean under conditions of enslavement. Early in his narrative, Washington writes:

> There was a wooden floor in our cabin, the naked earth being used as a floor. In the centre of the earthen floor there was a large, deep opening covered with boards, which was used as a place in which to store sweet potatoes during the winter. An impression of this potato-hole is very distinctly engraved upon my memory, because I recall that during the process of putting the potatoes in or taking them out I would often come into possession of one or two, which I roasted and thoroughly enjoyed. (*Up from Slavery*, 30–31)

30. Martin Luther King, Jr., *Where Do We Go from Here: Chaos or Community?* (Boston: Beacon Press, 1968), 111. Subsequent references are to *Where Do We Go from Here* and will be cited parenthetically.

31. It is very interesting to note that King relates this strategy of juxtaposing the dialectical (or Du Boisian) and processual (or Washingtonian) models of double-consciousness to Thoreau's critique of modernity in his essay on civil disobedience. King writes:

> Every man lives in two realms, the internal and the external. The internal is that realm of spiritual ends expressed in art, literature, morals and religion. The external is that complex of devices, techniques, mechanisms and instrumentalities by means of which we live. Our problem today is that we have allowed the internal to become lost in the external. We have allowed the means by which we live to outdistance the ends for which we live. So much of modern life can be summarized in that suggestive phrase of Thoreau: "Improved means to an unimproved end." This is the serious predicament, the deep and haunting problem, confronting modern man.

The above quotation comes from *A Testament of Hope: The Essential Writings and Speeches of Martin Luther King, Jr.*, ed. J. Washington (New York: Harper Collins, 1986), 620. Subsequent references are to *TH* and will be cited parenthetically.

Chapter Eight

1. According to Herbert Cobb, owner of Erbo's Printing and Copy Services, the mural was done on his storefront by graffiti artist Gregory R. Penrice on February 17, 1993. (The aphorism is actually Oliver Goldsmith's.)

2. Martin Luther King Jr., "Antidotes for Fear," *Strength to Love* (New York: Harper & Row, 1963), 109. Subsequent references are to this edition and will be cited parenthetically.

3. Hannah Arendt, *The Human Condition* (Chicago: University of Chicago Press, 1958), 49.

4. Seyla Benhabib, "Models of Public Space: Hannah Arendt, the Liberal Tradition, and Jurgen Habermas," *Habermas and the Public Sphere*, ed. Craig Calhoun (Cambridge: MIT Press, 1992), 79.

5. *Emerson in His Journals*, ed. Joel Porte (Cambridge: Harvard University Press, 1982), 458–459.

6. Stanley Cavell, *Must We Mean What We Say?* (Cambridge: Cambridge University Press, 1969), xxviii-xxix.

7. As Philip Fisher has argued, "On a plane beyond Dickens or Twain, Emerson had, in the previous generation, created American philosophy in public as the performance of philosophy and thought before the lecture hall crowd" ("Appearing and Disappearing in Public: Social Space in Late-Nineteenth-Century Literature and Culture," *Reconstructing American Literary History*, ed. Sacvan Bercovitch [Cambridge: Harvard University Press, 1986], 157).

8. For example, King mentions Thoreau's work on civil disobedience in "The Time for Freedom Has Come" to explain the actions and subsequent arrests of a new generation of black youth committed to the freedom struggle (*TH*, 164), and in a sermon titled "Antidotes for Fear" he refers to Thoreau's journal entry, "Nothing is so much feared as fear" (*TH*, 512). In "The American Dream," a 1961 commencement

address delivered at Lincoln University, King quotes Thoreau's aphorism "Improved means to an unimproved end" and glosses it by saying, "If we are to survive today and realize the dream of our mission and the dream of the world, we must bridge the gulf and somehow keep the means by which we live abreast with the ends for which we live" (*TH*, 211). Another gloss of the same aphorism appears in *Where Do We Go from Here: Chaos or Community*, published in 1967:

> Every man lives in two realms, the internal and the external. The internal is that realm of spiritual ends expressed in art, literature, morals and religion. The external is that complex of devices, techniques, mechanisms and instrumentalities by means of which we live. Our problem today is that we have allowed the internal to become lost in the external. We have allowed the means by which we live to outdistance the ends for which we live. So much of modern life can be summarized in that suggestive phrase of Thoreau: "Improved means to an unimproved end." This is the serious predicament, the deep and haunting problem, confronting modern man. Enlarged material powers spell enlarged peril if there is not proportionate growth of the soul. (*TH*, 620)

9. For an account of how King "became a luminous media personality whose fame spread to the nation and the world" (29) and the symbology of cover treatment by news magazines such as *Time*, *Newsweek*, and *U.S. News and World Report* , see Richard Lentz, *Symbols, the News Magazines, and Martin Luther King* (Baton Rouge: Louisiana State University Press, 1990). For a clear, useful analysis of visibility, public performance, and their implications for social forces at work in shaping personality in late-nineteenth-century literature and culture, see Fisher's "Appearing and Disappearing in Public: Social Space in Late-Nineteenth-Century Literature and Culture," in *Reconstructing American Literary History*, ed. Sacvan Bercovitch (Cambridge: Harvard University Press, 1986), 155–188, and Fisher, *Hard Facts: Setting and Form in the American Novel* (New York: Oxford University Press, 1987), 128–178.

10. In *The Structural Transformation of the Public Sphere* (trans. Thomas Burger [Cambridge: MIT Press, 1991]), published in 1962, the sociologist Jurgen Habermas sharply criticized the role of the mass media in creating a sentimentalized, depoliticized, impoverished, and "faked" public sphere that curtailed the capacity for rational criticism of public authority. King's contribution to the proliferation of revitalized publics during the sixties—a contribution that enlisted the same media strategies deplored by Habermas—suggests important, effective uses for this "degenerated" bourgeois public sphere that Habermas himself failed to anticipate in his analysis.

11. There are a few existing studies that discuss Martin Luther King's relationship to the mainstream tradition in American philosophy and political thought. In *Builders of the Dream: Abraham Lincoln and Martin Luther King* (Fort Wayne, Ind.: Louis A. Warren Lincoln Library, 1982), Stephen Oates offers a general comparison of the nationalist rhetoric and vision developed by Lincoln and King. An interesting analysis of King's rhetoric that shows how he deliberately draws on democratic values such as individualism and the dignity of civil rights heroes may be found in Haig Bosmijian, "The Rhetoric of Martin Luther King's 'Letter from the Birmingham Jail,' " *Midwest Quarterly* 21 (June 1979), 46–62. In *Martin Luther King, Jr.: The Making of a Mind* (Maryknoll, N.Y.: Orbis Books, 1982), John Ansbro explores the influences of Socrates, Nietzsche, Kant, Gandhi, Thoreau, and others on the formation of King's ideas about

agape, the sacredness of human personality, resistance to collective evil, and the church's social mission. Ansbro's study is an invaluable resource insofar as it documents how widely King drew on Western and Eastern philosophies. But much of what Ansbro has to say about Thoreau's philosophy is reductive and largely incorrect: for example, he writes that Thoreau "wanted noncooperation to develop into an attempt to destroy the political system" (112) and that Thoreau "approved of violence" (113).

Two studies of King's philosophy of nonviolence that discuss his sources but do not emphasize the contribution of American philosophers such as Emerson and Thoreau are Ernest Lyght, *Religious and Philosophical Foundations in the Thought of Martin Luther King* (New York: Vintage Press, 1972) and James Hanigan, *Martin Luther King, Jr., and the Foundations of Nonviolence* (Lanham, Md.: University Press of America, 1984). For a cursory look at King's attempt to align black aspirations with mainstream American values, see Richard Lischer, *The Preacher King: Martin Luther King, Jr. and the Word that Moved America* (New York: Oxford University Press, 1995), 142–160.

Many recent studies of King have emphasized how Black American culture more generally—and, in particular, the African Baptist, sermonic, and liberal theological traditions—were formative influences on King's rhetoric and development as an American religious advocate. See Preston Williams, "Contextualizing the Faith: The African-American Tradition and Martin Luther King, Jr.," in *One Faith, Many Cultures: Inculturation, Indegenization, and Contextualization*, ed. R. Costa (Cambridge, Mass.: Boston Theological Institute, 1988), 129–135; Williams, "The Problem of a Black Ethic," in *The Black Experience in Religion*, ed. C. Eric Lincoln (Garden City, N.Y.: Anchor Press, 1974), 180–186; Williams, "Black Perspectives in Utopia," in *Utopia/Dystopia?*, ed. P. Richter (Cambridge, Mass.: Schenkman, 1975), 43–56; Richard Lischer, *The Preacher King: Martin Luther King, Jr., and the Word that Moved America* (New York: Oxford University Press, 1995); Lewis Baldwin, *There is a Balm in Gilead: The Cultural Roots of Martin Luther King, Jr.* (Minneapolis: Fortress Press, 1991); Baldwin, *To Make the Wounded Whole: The Cultural Legacy of Martin Luther King, Jr.* (Minneapolis: Fortress Press, 1991); Baldwin, "Martin Luther King, Jr., the Black Church, and the Black Messianic Vision," *Journal of the Interdenominational Theological Center* 12 (June 1984), 93–108; James Cone, *Martin and Malcolm and America: A Dream or a Nightmare?* (Maryknoll, N.Y.: Orbis Books, 1991); Thomas Mikelson, "The Negro's God in the Theology of Martin Luther King, Jr.: Social Commentary and Theological Discourse" (Th.D. dissertation, Harvard University, 1988); and Keith Miller, *Voice of Deliverance: The Language of Martin Luther King, Jr. and Its Sources* (New York: The Free Press, 1992).

The two best biographies to date are David L. Lewis, *King: A Critical Biography* (New York: Praeger Publishers, 1970) and David Garrow, *Bearing the Cross: Martin Luther King and the Southern Leadership Conference* (New York: William Morrow, 1986).

12. Stanley Cavell, *This New yet Unapproachable America: Lectures after Emerson after Wittgenstein* (Albuquerque: Living Batch Press, 1989). Subsequent references are to *New Yet* and will be cited parenthetically.

13. Cornel West, *The American Evasion of Philosophy: A Genealogy of Pragmatism* (Madison: University of Wisconsin Press, 1989). Subsequent references are to *American Evasion* and will be cited parenthetically.

14. Stanley Cavell, *Conditions Handsome and Unhandsome: The Constitution of Emersonian Perfectionism* (Chicago: University of Chicago Press, 1990), 21.

15. Compare Cavell's discussion of Dewey and Wittgenstein in *Conditions Hand-*

some and Unhandsome: "If what Wittgenstein means by 'bringing words back' represents thinking, it bears a relation to words and the world different from that in, say, Dewey's application of intelligence to the world; it may seem its opposite. I have emphasized its opposite sound." (21). Even more recently, in *A Pitch of Philosophy: Autobiographical Exercises* (Cambridge: Harvard University Press, 1994), Cavell reiterates this argument. He observes that although Dewey, in a 1911 review of Maurice Maeterlinck, speaks of the present barrenness of philosophy, "the figure Dewey is more significantly confessing his inability to paraphrase is Emerson, the one whose writing he misses in his own, whose words he cannot bury in his own. This matters to me in being at odds with the common view—perhaps it is the price—of the recent revival of interest in Emerson, I believe not just in North America, which takes Emerson as, let's say, a proto-pragmatist" (168).

16. In *Race Matters* (Boston: Beacon Press, 1993), West argues for the necessity of present-day black scholars engaging in public life by invoking the concept of a vital "public square": "We must focus our attention on the public square—the common good that undergirds our national and global destinies. The vitality of any public square ultimately depends on how much we *care* about the quality of our lives together. The neglect of our public infrastructure . . . reflects not only our myopic economic policies, which impede productivity, but also the low priority we place on our common life" (7).

17. In *The Public and Its Problems* (Athens: Ohio University Press, 1927), Dewey writes, "[T]he essence of the consequences which call a public into being is the fact that they expand beyond those directly engaged in producing them. Consequently special agencies and measures must be formed if they are to be attended to. . . . The obvious external mark of the organization of a public or of a state is thus the existence of officials" (27).

18. For example, in "The Postmodern Crisis of the Black Intellectual," West argues, "It behooves us to think about the degree to which the waning of public spheres in this society tends to displace politics into the few spheres where there is in fact some public discussion—spheres like the academy. Hence so much of academic politics is a displacement of the relative absence of serious politics within the larger 'public' spheres where serious resources are being produced, distributed, and consumed. And so much of academic politics—in terms of the level of what's at stake—seems to be exorbitant in a country in which our actual politics are comical. No real public sphere: we know about the theatricalization of our politics and the packaged character of our candidates and so forth" (*Cultural Studies*, ed. Lawrence Grossberg, Cary Nelson, and Paula Treichler [New York: Routledge Press, 1992], 692). In "Learning to Talk of Race," West writes, "The tragic plight of our children clearly reveals our deep disregard for public well-being. . . . One essential step is some form of large-scale public inter-vention to ensure access to basic social goods—housing, food, health care, education, child care, and jobs. . . . After a period in which the private sphere has been sacrilized and the public square gutted, the temptation is to make a fetish of the public square. We need to resist such dogmatic swings" (*Reading Rodney King, Reading Urban Uprising*, ed. Robert Gooding-Williams [New York: Routledge Press, 1993], 259). And in "The New Cultural Politics of Difference," West calls for a "new cultural criticism" that will expose the exclusions that have in the recent past been built into a public sphere, a sphere constituted and regulated by "immoral patriarchal, imperial, jingoistic and xen-ophobic constraints" (*Out There: Marginalization and Contemporary Cultures*, ed. Russell

Ferguson, Martha Gever, Trinh T. Minh-ha, and Cornel West [Cambridge: MIT Press, 1990], 35).

19. On this point see Mary P. Ryan, *Women in Public: Between Banners and Ballots, 1825–1880* (Baltimore, Md.: John Hopkins University Press, 1990).

20. John Stuart Mill, *On Liberty*, ed. Elizabeth Rapaport (Indianapolis: Hackett Publishing Co., 1978), 8. Subsequent references are to this edition and will be cited parenthetically.

21. Alexis de Tocqueville, *Democracy in America*, trans. George Lawrence, ed. J. P. Mayer (Garden City, N.Y.: Doubleday, 1969), 435. Subsequent references are to this edition and will be cited parenthetically.

22. In *Democracy in America*, Tocqueville insists that public opinion in the United States, as in any democracy, derives much of its influence from the fact of equality between citizens. Although equality is a source of pride and independence it is also, according to Tocqueville, a primary cause for feeling insignificant and weak: when a citizen compares himself with all his fellow citizens put together as one vast entity, he is bound to feel isolated and defenseless in the face of the majority. Thus it is that in democracies, by Tocqueville's account, public opinion exerts its strange, powerful appeal: "It uses no persuasion to forward its beliefs, but by some mighty pressure of the mind of all upon the intelligence of each it imposes its ideas and makes them penetrate men's very souls. The majority in the United States takes over the business of supplying the individual with a quantity of ready-made opinions and so relieves him of the necessity of forming his own. So there are many theories of philosophy, morality, and politics which everyone adopts unexamined on the faith of public opinion" (*Democracy in America*, 435–436).

23. As Habermas points out, the demotion of the existing public by liberal theorists resulted in the constitution of a new, elite public: "Against a public opinion that, as it seemed, had been perverted from an instrument of liberation into an agent of repression, liberalism, faithful to its own *ratio*, could only summon public opinion once again" (137).

24. Ralph Waldo Emerson, *Essays and Lectures*, ed. Joel Porte (New York: Library of America, 1983), 264.

25. Mill observes:

> At present individuals are lost in the crowd. In politics it is almost a triviality to say that public opinion now rules the world. The only power deserving the name is that of masses, and of governments while they make themselves the organ of the tendencies and instincts of masses. . . . [The] mass do not now take their opinions from dignitaries in Church or State, from ostensible leaders, or from books. Their thinking is done for them by men much like themselves, addressing them or speaking in their name, on the spur of the moment, through the newspapers. (*On Liberty*, 63)

Mill's stated concern at this point in his argument is less what he calls "the present low state of the human mind" per se than it is the obstacles such a low state would present for a government attempting to rise above mediocrity.

26. Although he notes that, sociologically speaking, distinct public and private realms did not exist in the feudal society of the High Middle Ages, Habermas argues that lordship was something publicly represented: "This *publicness* (or *publicity*) *of representation* was not constituted as a social realm, that is, as a public sphere; rather, it

was something like a status attribute. . . . [The manorial lord] presented himself as an embodiment of some sort of 'higher' power. The concept of representation in this sense has been preserved down to the most recent constitutional doctrine. . . . For representation pretended to make something invisible visible through the public presence of the person of the lord" (*Structural Transformation*, 7).

27. Compare Habermas's observation that the transformed and degenerated bourgeois public sphere "becomes privatized in the consciousness of the consuming public" (*Structural Transformation*, 171).

28. The same point applies to Cavell's use of the Emersonian term "constitution" when he describes Emerson's inheritance of philosophy as a conversion and rebirth into America: "Emerson's writing is (an image or promise of, the constitution for) this new yet unapproachable America: his aversion is a rebirth of himself into it (there will be other rebirths) . . . The identification this writer proposes between his individual constitution and the constitution of his nation is a subject on its own" (*New yet Unapproachable*, 92–93). This claim, taken with Cavell's observation that Emerson's "quest was his way of founding a nation, writing its constitution, constituting its citizens," invites us to consider how Emerson's notion of constitution (which conjoins senses that are both personally physical and legal or public) relates to the actual process and consequences of forming political community.

29. In *The American Evasion of Philosophy*, West points out a connection between King and Emerson, arguing that although King contributed to the political project of building of an "Emersonian culture of creative democracy" (235), he himself was not a prophetic pragmatist:

> The social movement led by Martin Luther King, Jr., represents the best of what the political dimension of prophetic pragmatism is all about. Like Sojourner Truth, Walter Rauschenbusch, Elizabeth Cady Stanton, and Dorothy Day, King was not a prophetic pragmatist. Yet like them he was a prophet, in which role he contributed mightily to the political project of prophetic pragmatism. His all-embracing moral vision facilitated alliances and coalitions across racial, gender, class, and religious lines. His Gandhian method of nonviolent resistance highlighted forms of love, courage, and discipline worthy of a compassionate prophet. And his appropriation and interpretation of American civil religion extended the tradition of American jeremiads, a tradition of public exhortation that joins social criticisms of America to moral renewal and admonishes the country to be true to its founding ideals of freedom, equality, and democracy. (235)

30. In *Civil Rights and the Idea of Freedom*, Richard King explores a concept of "self-respect" that, he argues, was central to the political experience of participants in the civil rights movement: "Self-respect is not just a state of mind; it implies some form of action which transforms self-respect from a subjective or private certainty into a public truth" ([New York: Oxford University Press, 1992], 72). Martin Luther King's interpretation of Emersonian "self-reliance" bears a striking resemblance to this concept of "self-respect" and, as I argue throughout this discussion, represented a rich resource for the revitalization of political culture and experience for participants in the civil rights movement.

31. Henry David Thoreau, "Resistance to Civil Government," *Great Short Works*

of Henry David Thoreau, ed. Wendell Glick (New York: Harper & Row, 1982), 139. Subsequent citations are to "Resistance" and will be cited parenthetically.

32. Compare Cavell's reference to the significance of visibility for Thoreau's project in *Walden*: "[T]he writer's claims to privacy, secrecy, and isolation are as problematic, in the achievement and in the depiction of them, as any other of his claims. . . . This is one way I understand [his] placing himself 'one mile from any neighbor.' It was just far enough to be seen clearly. . . . The withdrawal he depicts in *Walden* creates a version of what the Puritan Congregationalists called a member of the church congregation: a visible saint" (*The Senses of Walden* [San Francisco: North Point Press, 1972], 10–11).

33. Hannah Arendt, *Crises of the Republic* (New York: Harcourt Brace Jovanovich, 1969), 60–61. Subsequent citations are to *Crises* and will be cited parenthetically.

34. Compare Elaine Scarry's claims regarding the objectification, denial, and falsification of pain in the torturer's use of the sufferer's body to confer reality onto the illusory but (to the torturers and represented regime) convincing spectacle of power: "As a perceptual fact, [a weapon] lifts the pain out of the body and makes it visible or, more precisely, it acts as a bridge or mechanism across which some of pain's attributes—its incontestable reality, its totality, its ability to eclipse all else, its power of dramatic alteration and world dissolution—can be lifted away from their source, can be separated from the sufferer and referred to power, broken off from the body and attached instead to the regime" (*The Body in Pain: The Making and Unmaking of the World* [New York: Oxford University Press, 1985], 56).

35. On the performative aspects of King's rhetoric and his interaction with the audience, see *Martin Luther King, Jr., and the Sermonic Power of Public Discourse*, ed. Carolyn Calloway-Thomas and John Louis Lucaites (Tuscaloosa: University of Alabama Press, 1993), 5–6.

36. E. Culpepper Clark, "The American Dilemma in King's 'Letter from Birmingham Jail,'" *Martin Luther King, Jr., and the Sermonic Power of Public Discourse*, 45.

37. For a discussion of Frantz Fanon's analysis of the look and his indebtedness to the phenomenological tradition of European philosophical thought, see Robert Gooding Williams, "Look, A Negro!", *Reading Rodney King, Reading Urban Uprising*, ed. Robert Gooding-Williams (New York: Routledge, 1993), 164–165, 173–174.

38. Richard King, *Civil Rights and the Idea of Freedom* (New York: Oxford University Press, 1992), 106–107.

39. Manning Marable's study of the historical relationship between religion and black protest thought and his observation that King's philosophy of disobedience "provided a theoretical framework for thousands of committed black men, women and children to lie down in the streets in protest, to be arrested and physically beaten by white policemen" supports my claim that King's success as an activist and political leader entailed his aspiration to a representative status (*Blackwater: Historical Studies in Race, Class Consciousness, and Revolution* [Niwot: University Press of Colorado, 1993], 45). An earlier discussion by Marable may be found in "Evaluating King's Journey," *Democratic Left* (September 1983), 12–21.

40. Ervin Smith, *The Ethics of Martin Luther King, Jr.* (New York: Edwin Mellen Press, 1981), 61.

41. For a discussion of King's devotion to the ideal of a beloved community and aspects of its theological and philosophical foundations (including Personalism, Evangelical Liberalism, and the influence of Niebuhr, Royce, and Rauschenbusch), see Ken-

neth L. Smith, *Search for the Beloved Community: The Thinking of Martin Luther King, Jr.* (Lanham, Md.: University Press of America, 1986), and Ira G. Zepp, *The Social Vision of Martin Luther King, Jr.* (Brooklyn: Carlson Publishing, 1989), 207–234.

42. Cornel West, "The Religious Foundations of the Thought of Martin Luther King, Jr.," *We Shall Overcome: Martin Luther King, Jr., and the Black Freedom Struggle*, ed. Peter J. Albert and Ronald Hoffman (New York: Pantheon Books, 1990), 127. The terms of this debate are much the same as they were in 1971 when Hanes Walton Jr. wrote the following criticisms of King's views on love: "King stressed that one is able to love a person while hating the deeds of that person. But how much of a person can actually be separated from his actions? And who, if not that person, is to be held responsible for those actions? . . . On these recurrent questions King's philosophy is silent. . . . To impose a pure love ethic in a realm where, at best, only relative justice can be attained is a utopian attempt" (*The Political Philosophy of Martin Luther King, Jr.* [Westport, Conn.: Greenwood 1971], 80).

43. In this novel, Bambara alludes to Ralph Ellison's analysis of invisibility and the complications it presents for entry into public life; the fact that, in the words of one character, "Your true nature invisible because you're in some incongruous getup or in some incongruous place or the looker's got incongruous eyes." Even more central to Bambara's project is her vivid detailing of the public appeal and inadequacies of what she describes as a derivative contemporary black leadership: "Some leader. He looked a bit like King, had a delivery similar to Malcom's, dressed like Stokely, had glasses like Rap, but she'd never heard him say anything useful or offensive. But what a voice. And what a good press agent. And the people had bought him. What a disaster. But what a voice" (*The Salt Eaters* [New York: Random House, 1980], 158, 35).

44. In *Race Matters*, West refers to Toni Morrison's *Beloved* in order to elaborate on the significance of love for the development of what he calls "a politics of conversion" that will work against the threat of nihilism in black America. "A love ethic has nothing to do with sentimental feelings or tribal connections," he writes. "Rather it is a last attempt at generating a sense of agency among a downtrodden people. . . . For my purposes here, *Beloved* can be construed as bringing together the loving yet critical affirmation of black humanity found in the best of black nationalist movements, the perennial hope against hope for trans-racial coalition in progressive movements, and the painful struggle for self-affirming sanity in a history in which the nihilistic threat *seems* insurmountable" (19).

45. Consider, for example, Baraka's "SOS" (in *The Black Poets*, ed. Dudley Randall [New York: Bantam Books], 181), in which he modulates from a revolutionary, public, "representative" call for cohesion and political action voiced over radio waves to the personal invitation to come on in extended in the poem's concluding lines:

Calling black people
Call all black people, man woman, child
Wherever you are, calling you, urgent, come in
Black People, come in, wherever you are, urgent, calling
you, calling all black people
calling all black people, come in, black people, come
on in

And in Nikki Giovanni's "The Funeral of Martin Luther King, Jr.," the tragedy of King's death and the writing of his words on a tombstone are transformed into a collective, articulate, motivated rage that works toward the imagining and construction of a better world:

His headstone said
FREE AT LAST, FREE AT LAST
But death is a slave's freedom
We seek the freedom of free men
And the construction of a world
Where Martin Luther King could have lived and preached non-violence
                                                        (*The Black Poets*, 323).

46. Alice Walker, *Meridian* (New York: Simon & Schuster, 1976). Subsequent references are to this edition and will be cited parenthetically.

47. Alice Walker, *In Search of Our Mothers' Gardens* (New York: Harcourt Brace Jovanovich, 1983), 124. Subsequent references are to this edition.

48. Walker, *In Search of Our Mothers' Gardens*, 144. Another, more recent commentary on the impact of King's media publicity may be found in Henry Louis Gates's memoir, *Colored People* (New York: Alfred A. Knopf, 1994). Gates recalls the torturous experience of watching television and then arguing about King and the Movement with his father: "Daddy was jaundiced about the civil rights movement, and especially about the Reverend Dr. Martin Luther King, Jr. . . . Sometimes he'd just mention King to get a rise from me, to make a sagging evening more interesting, to see if I had *learned* anything real yet, to see how long I could think up counter arguments before getting so mad that my face would turn purple. I think he just liked the color purple on my face, liked producing it there" (26). In contrast to Walker, Gates suggests that T.V. was not an enabling vehicle of identification with King but, rather, a terrifying reminder of Gates's own utter helplessness in the face of danger. The very presence of a T.V. in his parents' house forced Gates, even as a very young boy, to watch ritual acts of genocide against blacks and thus to know what the white world held in store for him:

> The TV was the ritual arena for the drama of race. We watched people getting hosed and cracked over their heads, people being spat upon and arrested, rednecks siccing fierce dogs on women and children, our people responding by singing and marching. . . . Whatever tumult our small screen revealed, though, the dawn of the civil rights era could be no more than a spectator sport in Piedmont. It was almost like a war being fought overseas. And all things considered, white and colored Piedmont got along pretty well in those years, the fifties and early sixties. At least as long as colored people didn't try to sit down in the Cut-Rate or at the Rendezvous Bar, or eat pizza at Eddies, or buy property, or move into the white neighborhoods, or dance with, date, or dilate upon white people. Not to mention try to get a job in the craft unions at the paper mill. Or have a drink at the white VFW, or join the white American Legion, or get loans at the bank, or just generally get out of line. (27)

Epilogue

1. Mitsuye Yamada, *Camp Notes and Other Poems* (Berkeley: Shameless Hussy Press, 1976), 39.

Index